Studies in Military and Strategic History

William Philpott (General editor), Professor of Diplomatic History, King's College London

Published titles include:

Martin Alexander and William Philpott (*editors*)
ANGLO-FRENCH DEFENCE RELATIONS BETWEEN THE WARS

Christopher M. Bell
THE ROYAL NAVY, SEAPOWER AND STRATEGY BETWEEN THE WARS

Peter Bell
CHAMBERLAIN, GERMANY AND JAPAN, 1933–34

Antony Best
BRITISH INTELLIGENCE AND THE JAPANESE CHALLENGE IN ASIA, 1914–41

Antoine Capet (*editor*)
BRITAIN, FRANCE AND THE ENTENTE CORDIALE SINCE 1904

Philippe Chassaigne and Michael Dockrill (*editors*)
ANGLO-FRENCH RELATIONS, 1898–1998
From Fashoda to Jospin

Michael Dockrill
BRITISH ESTABLISHMENT PERSPECTIVES IN FRANCE, 1936–40

Michael Dockrill and John Fisher
THE PARIS PEACE CONFERENCE, 1919
Peace without Victory?

John P. S. Gearson
HAROLD MACMILLAN AND THE BERLIN WALL CRISIS, 1958–62

John Gooch
ARMY, STATE AND SOCIETY IN ITALY, 1870–1915

G. A. H. Gordon
BRITISH SEA POWER AND PROCUREMENT BETWEEN THE WARS
A Reappraisal of Rearmament

Raffi Gregorian
THE BRITISH ARMY, THE GURKHAS AND COLD WAR STRATEGY IN THE FAR EAST, 1947–1954

Stephen Hartley
THE IRISH QUESTION AS A PROBLEM IN BRITISH FOREIGN POLICY, 1914–18

Ashley Jackson
WAR AND EMPIRE IN MAURITIUS AND THE INDIAN OCEAN

James Levy
THE ROYAL NAVY'S HOME FLEET IN WORLD WAR II

Stewart Lone
JAPAN'S FIRST MODERN WAR
Army and Society in the Conflict with China, 1894–95

Thomas R. Mockaitis
BRITISH COUNTERINSURGENCY, 1919–60

Bob Moore and Kent Fedorowich
THE BRITISH EMPIRE AND ITS ITALIAN PRISONERS OF WAR, 1940–47

T. R. Moreman
THE ARMY IN INDIA AND THE DEVELOPMENT OF FRONTIER WARFARE, 1849–1947

Kendrick Oliver
KENNEDY, MACMILLAN AND THE NUCLEAR TEST-BAN DEBATE, 1961–63

Paul Orders
BRITAIN, AUSTRALIA, NEW ZEALAND AND THE CHALLENGE OF THE UNITED STATES, 1934–46
A Study in International History

Elspeth Y. O'Riordan
BRITAIN AND THE RUHR CRISIS

G. D. Sheffield
LEADERSHIP IN THE TRENCHES
Officer–Man Relations, Morale and Discipline in the British Army in the Era of the First World War

Adrian Smith
MICK MANNOCK, FIGHTER PILOT
Myth, Life and Politics

Martin Thomas
THE FRENCH NORTH AFRICAN CRISIS
Colonial Breakdown and Anglo-French Relations, 1945–62

Simon Trew
BRITAIN, MIHAILOVIC AND THE CHETNIKS, 1941–42

Steven Weiss
ALLIES IN CONFLICT
Anglo-American Strategic Negotiations, 1938–44

Studies in Military and Strategic History
Series Standing Order ISBN 0-333-71046-0 Hardback 0-333-80349-3 Paperback
(*outside North America only*)

You can receive future titles in this series as they are published by placing a standing order. Please contact your bookseller or, in case of difficulty, write to us at the address below with your name and address, the title of the series and the ISBN quoted above.

Customer Services Department, Macmillan Distribution Ltd, Houndmills, Basingstoke, Hampshire RG21 6XS, England

---

Britain, France and the Entente Cordiale since 1904

Edited by

Antoine Capet

Professor of British Studies, University of Rouen, France

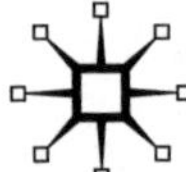

First published 2006 by
PALGRAVE MACMILLAN
Houndmills, Basingstoke, Hampshire RG21 6XS and
175 Fifth Avenue, New York, N.Y. 10010
Companies and representatives throughout the world

PALGRAVE MACMILLAN is the global academic imprint of the Palgrave Macmillan division of St. Martin's Press, LLC and of Palgrave Macmillan Ltd. Macmillan® is a registered trademark in the United States, United Kingdom and other countries. Palgrave is a registered trademark in the European Union and other countries.

ISBN-13: 978–0–230–00902–8 hardback
ISBN-10: 0–230–00902–6 hardback

This book is printed on paper suitable for recycling and made from fully managed and sustained forest sources.

A catalogue record for this book is available from the British Library.

Library of Congress Cataloging-in-Publication Data

Britain, France, and the Entente Cordiale since 1904/edited by Antoine Capet.
p.cm. -- (Studies in military and strategic history)
Includes bibliographical references and index.
ISBN 0-230-00902-6
1. Great Britain–foreign relations–France. 2. France–Foreign relations–Great Britain. 3. Great Britain–Foreign relations–20th century. 4. France–Foreign relations–20th century. I. Capet, Antoine. II. Series: Studies in military and strategic history (Palgrave Macmillan (Firm))

DA47.1.B75 2006
327.41044--dc22

2006043616

10 9 8 7 6 5 4 3 2 1
15 14 13 12 11 10 09 08 07 06

Printed and bound in Great Britain by
Antony Rowe Ltd, Chippenham and Eastbourne

Contents

Notes on Contributors

Robert Boyce teaches international history at the London School of Economics. He has published several books including *British Capitalism at the Crossroads, 1919–1932: A Study in Politics, Economics and International Relations* (1987), (editor and translator), *French Foreign and Defence Policy, 1918–1940: The Decline and Fall of a Great Power* (1998), (edited with Joseph Maiolo), *The Origins of World War Two: The Debate Continues* (2003), and some forty articles on aspects of twentieth-century international economic and political history. His new book, *The Dual Crisis: The Collapse of the International Economic and Political Systems between the Two World Wars, and the Origins of Our Time,* will be published soon.

John Campbell is a freelance political historian and biographer. His books include *Edward Heath,* which won the 1994 NCR Award for Non-Fiction, and two volumes on Margaret Thatcher, *The Grocer's Daughter* (2000) and *The Iron Lady* (2003). His latest, *If Love Were All ...: The Story of Frances Stevenson and David Lloyd George,* will be published in 2006.

Antoine Capet, FRHistS, is Professor of British Studies at the University of Rouen (France). His Doctorat d'État, on *Le poids des années de guerre: Les classes dirigeantes britanniques et la réforme sociale, 1931–1951*, was published in book form in 1991. He is currently 'Britain since 1914' Section Editor of the Royal Historical Society Bibliography and sits on the Editorial Committees of *Cultural and Social History* and *Twentieth Century British History*. As head of the CERCLA research group at Rouen, he has organised many conferences with invited British scholars, notably one on Anglo-French relations in 2004, from which this book is largely derived.

Peter Catterall teaches history and public policy both at the Hansard Society and at Queen Mary, University of London, and European Studies at Cass Business School. He has published extensively on twentieth-century British history, including the award-winning

British History 1945–1987: An Annotated Bibliography (Oxford: Blackwell, 1990). The founder editor of *National Identities*, he also edited *Contemporary British History* from 1991 to 2003. Currently he is editing for publication the diaries of Harold Macmillan, the first volume of which appeared in 2003.

James Ellison is Senior Lecturer in Modern and Contemporary History at Queen Mary, University of London. He is a specialist on Anglo-American and Anglo-European relations after 1945 and has a specific interest in the history of the Cold War and European integration. Anglo-French relations are a particular theme in his research as can be seen in his first book, *Threatening Europe: Britain and the Creation of the European Community, 1955–58* (London: Macmillan, 2000). They are also an important feature of his next book on Anglo-American relations and the Gaullist challenge of the 1960s.

Klaus Larres is Professor of History and International Affairs and Director of Research at the University of Ulster in Northern Ireland. He is also a Distinguished Scholar at the Library of Congress in Washington, DC, where he previously held the Henry A. Kissinger Chair in Foreign Policy and International Relations. He has published widely on transatlantic relations, including *Churchill's Cold War: The Politics of Personal Diplomacy* (Yale University Press, 2002). He currently works on a study of European-American relations from the Cold War to the post-Cold War world and is completing a book on Germany since World War II (Oxford University Press, 2008).

Kenneth O. Morgan was Fellow of The Queen's College, Oxford, 1966–89, Vice-Chancellor in the University of Wales, 1989–95, and since 2000 has been a Labour member of the House of Lords as Lord Morgan of Aberdyfi. He was elected a Fellow of the British Academy in 1983. His twenty-five books on British and Welsh history include six on Lloyd George. He has lectured widely in France and is attached to the University of Rouen research school. His new biography of Michael Foot for Harper Collins will be published shortly.

John Ramsden is Professor of Modern History at Queen Mary, University of London. He has contributed all three twentieth-century volumes to the Longman History of the British Conservative Party, and published in 2001 a single-volume history of the Party, *An Appetite for Power*. In 2003 he produced *Man of the Century: Winston Churchill and his Legend since 1945*, a book on *The Dam Busters* film of 1955, and (as General Editor) the *Oxford Companion to 20th-Century British Politics*. His study of British views of twentieth-century Germany, *Don't Mention the War*, appeared in May 2006.

David Reynolds is Professor of International History at Cambridge University and a Fellow of the British Academy. He is the author or editor of ten books including *Britannia Overruled: British Policy and World Power in the Twentieth Century* (1991), *The Origins of the Cold War in Europe* (editor, 1994), and *In Command of History: Churchill Fighting and Writing the Second World War* (2004), which was awarded the Wolfson History Prize.

Andrew Thorpe is Professor of Modern British History at the University of Exeter, UK. His publications include *The British General Election of 1931* (Clarendon Press, 1991), *Britain in the 1930s* (Blackwell, 1992), *A History of the British Labour Party* (1997; 2nd edn, Palgrave, 2001), and *The British Communist Party and Moscow, 1920–1943* (Manchester University Press, 2000). He is currently completing a monograph on party organisation in Second World War Britain for Oxford University Press.

Andrew Webster is the European Union Centre Lecturer in Modern European History at Murdoch University, Perth, Western Australia. His Ph.D. dissertation at Cambridge University was on 'Anglo-French relations and the problems of disarmament and security, 1929–1933' (2001). He has published several articles on Anglo-French relations and the disarmament process between the world wars, and is presently writing a history of international disarmament between 1899 and 1945.

John W. Young holds the Chair of International History at the University of Nottingham. He is the author of *Britain, France and the*

Unity of Europe (1984), *Winston Churchill's Last Campaign: Britain and the Cold War, 1951–55* (1996), *Britain and European Unity, 1945–99* (2000) and *The Labour Governments 1964–70*, Volume 2, *International Policy* (2003). He is currently researching on British diplomatic practice in the 1960s and 1970s.

Introduction: 'Britain's most enduring Special Relationship'

Antoine Capet

In the present collection, Lord Morgan concludes his contribution by referring to 'Britain's most enduring Special Relationship – the *Entente Cordiale*'. Most readers will disagree with this deliberately provocative distortion of the general acceptation of the phrase, 'Special Relationship'. This is because of what we might call 'the Churchill legacy': from Churchill to Blair, with perhaps the brief exception of Heath's premiership (see John Campbell's chapter), it is clear that the 'common sense' understanding of the 'Special Relationship' – in France as well as in Britain – refers to 'another country'. Whether Churchill actually said to de Gaulle two days before the Normandy landings 'Each time I must choose between you and Roosevelt, I shall always choose Roosevelt' is in fact almost irrelevant, because, as David Reynolds convincingly argues, this no doubt reflects Churchill's position.

Some, however, will agree that there has always been something 'special' in Anglo-French relations – going back far before the Americas were discovered. Biologists describe the simplest form of reproduction as 'scissiparity', when a cell separates into two distinct ones – and arguably it is such a process that Lord Macaulay described in the introductory chapter to his celebrated *History of England*, when 'the history of the English nation' really started under John Lackland/Jean sans Terre:

> But it is certain that, when John became King, the distinction between Saxons and Normans was strongly marked, and that before the end of the reign of his grandson it has almost disappeared. In

> the time of Richard the First, the ordinary imprecation of a Norman gentleman was, 'May I become an Englishman!' His ordinary form of indignant denial was, 'Do you take me for an Englishman?' The descendant of such a gentleman a hundred years later was proud of the English name.[1]

To pursue the biological analogy further: the Anglo-Norman (or Anglo-Saxon-Norman) cell and the Franco-Norman cell may have now become independent creatures, on opposite sides of the Channel (though the last foothold of the former Anglo-Normans on the French side only disappeared in the mid-sixteenth century, with the 'loss' of Calais by Mary Tudor) – but their common parentage has left traces to this day: how deep being precisely the question which this book addresses from the British side.

Being of the same stock of course does not preclude family quarrels – which can be among the most bitter ones, as everyone knows. The Hundred Years' War has long been recognised as forming a whole, which amalgamates recurring, though intermittent, conflicts to eliminate Anglo-Norman claimants from the French throne. Now there seems to be a tendency towards the recognition of a similar Anglo-French North Atlantic war, from Louis XIV to 1815, for the control of the seas and territories in that area of the globe.[2] The phrase quoted by Andrew Webster, 'The French are essentially feminine', which immediately suggests Gillray's caricatures, reminds us that it was also a ferocious war in the minds, which was bound to leave profound traces. It then took 89 years before the 'hereditary enemies' finally buried the hatchet in the form of official accords which were tantamount to a treaty of alliance – but how final the reconciliation was is another facet of this book, and as Klaus Larres argues, the recent events of Iraq have shown how precarious Anglo-French *entente* still is in the early twenty-first century.

The historiography of the *Entente Cordiale* is considerable: the Bibliography of the Royal Historical Society[3] has 65 entries with the actual expression in the title – and this leaves out other works on Anglo-French relations generally which contain at least some material on the subject. Interestingly, the first one chronologically (1916) is a French book whose title suggests that all the past conflicts were merely elements of the *Entente Cordiale* to be: *Histoire de l'Entente cordiale franco-anglaise: Les relations de la France et de l'Angleterre depuis le XVI*[e] *siècle jusqu'à nos jours.*[4] Though they admittedly cast a far wider net, Adrien Charbeau and Isabel Fernandez provide over 300 in the classified Bibliography which concludes the modish bilingual Anniversary volume published by the Ministère des Affaires étrangères.[5] On the other hand, in his magnificently illustrated book,[6] Maurice Vaïsse restricts the expression *Entente Cordiale* to its narrow sense – the accords of 1904 and their context – and selects his Bibliography accordingly, with just over two pages of references. This shows the difficulty for the historian today, as the phrase is now ambiguously – sometimes deliberately – used in both senses: the initial accords *and/or* subsequent developments in Anglo-French relations.

This was made clear in the field covered by the other publications which have appeared on the occasion of the centenary. In the two versions (in English and in French) of the same collection sponsored by the *Conseil franco-britannique* in France, *L'Entente cordiale dans le siècle*[7] and *Cross Channel Currents: 100 Years of the Entente Cordiale*,[8] the titles make it clear that the *Entente* is examined in the *longue durée*. The same holds good for *France-Angleterre: Un siècle d'Entente cordiale 1904–2004: Deux nations, un seul but?*[9] and the theme issue[10] of the respected journal, *Relations Internationales*, devoted to 'Cent ans d'Entente cordiale'. Though the title is not so explicit, *L'Entente cordiale: de l'événement au concept*, edited by the *Société d'histoire diplomatique*,[11] also covers the period 1904–2004. With the same time span, but more restrictive in its topic – defence – we also have the theme issue of the journal *Les Champs de Mars*: 'Cent ans d'Entente cordiale: La défense au Royaume-Uni'.[12] So, apart from Maurice Vaïsse's scholarly study, we are left with only one book dealing specifically with the original *Entente*, from the 'popular' author Antoine d'Arjuzon, with a 'bandwagon' title for a volume published in 2004: *Édouard VII, 1841–1910: Le prince de l'Entente cordiale*.[13]

When looking at all these centenary publications, one is struck by a phenomenon which commentators of the 'other' Special Relationship always point out, viz. the asymmetric nature of the involvement in the alliance, which this literary output seems to emphasise, with the enormous imbalance between British and French efforts at taking stock of the initial accords and their legacy. This used to be said of the Fashoda incident – hardly known outside specialist circles in Britain, standard *lycée* fare in France until recently. Does this British academic detachment denote indifference towards the 'peculiar facility for being misrepresented' of the French (to take up John Ramsden's quotation) and what sort of interest is revealed by French enthusiasm for the *Entente* – at least in the field of historical research?

Here we come to a far greater difficulty in this 'Special Relationship' – as in all human relations – namely what the French call *le non-dit*: what goes unsaid, and Robert Boyce reminds us that thirty years ago, James Joll already insisted on the motives that often 'go without saying'. How significant was it that Harold Wilson took his summer holidays in the Isles of Scilly? *Prima facie*, this had nothing to do with his approach to Anglo-French relations, and probably 'the General' had other, more important, reservations about his renewed application for membership of the EEC, as explained by James Ellison and John Young with complementary arguments. But the sub-text was undoubtedly one of diffidence, the subliminal message was that of a 'Little Englander' – a poor start for discussions with a man who always thought in geostrategical terms like de Gaulle, of course.

Conversely, Churchill easily holds the record for holidays spent in France – but is it iconoclastic to ask how many French people he met on equal terms – that of intelligent conversation – in his wealthy Canadian or American friends' secluded villas? From that point of view, it seems that he could equally well have stayed in the Isles of Scilly, too – and yet, he did not (for all sorts of reasons which are outside our subject), and we *sense* that he was playing in a different league as far as his understanding of the meaning of the *Entente* was concerned.

Another, paradoxical, obstacle to a full assessment of Anglo-French relations that includes not only the *longue durée* but also the *profondeur* is the wealth of statistics produced by all sorts of organisations – chief among them the respective Embassies and their commercial attachés. Thus we read that so many million French people visited the United Kingdom in the year 2000 – with a great increase on previous figures. Or that the British 'peaceful invasion' of the Dordogne (or Provence, or whatever) continues unabated – the best proof of succesful integration being that so many expatriates (figures duly provided – on the increase, of course) now try to cheat on French unemployment benefit, like the native population.[14] But if we keep to the definition suggested above of meeting people on equal terms – that of intelligent conversation – how many of these millions of French people (most of them *lycée* pupils spending two or three weeks in 'language schools', hosted in families who hardly speak English) derive any mental benefit from their visit to the United Kingdom (generally limited to South-East England, with the *de rigueur* cultural foray to Oxbridge and Stratford)? The clichés and prejudices with which they came are usually in fact reinforced, not dispelled, by such superficial acquaintance with the country and its inhabitants. It is always extremely unpleasant to hear French *lycéens* just back from their 'immersion' in the 'lives of real British families', as advertised by the industry, or for that matter adult tourists who go for a long weekend in London and only have contacts with public transport and museum staff and members of the hotel and catering trades (with the attendant language barrier), invariably recount their hackneyed lists of grievances – unpleasant because one feels that it was all a lamentable (and predictable) failure, that these French people are lost for ever for the cause of understanding, let alone appreciating, their neighbours across the Channel. The superior, patronising tone of books like the Provence series (and Andrew Thorpe's description of similar attitudes in the 'sister parties' rings an ironic bell here) also reflects on the fact that it is not only familarity that breeds contempt (as reflected in the Macmillan diary entries given by Peter Catterall) – superficiality can have the same result and generally does.

Once more, we *sense* that these Orwellian statistics have little to tell us on the real nature of Anglo-French relations. How is the historian, trained to rely on facts and figures, to make real sense of them? The history of mentalities is of some help – but it soon finds its limits. It is easy to explain that, from July 1940, the unsophisticated French population was submitted to extreme brainwashing, with the encouragement of Anglophobia perhaps the main component: we have surviving copies of the only authorised newspapers, we have recordings of the notorious Radio-Paris broadcasts, we have posters which remind the good French Catholic patriots of 'Saint Joan of Arc' and her fate 'at the hands of the English', we have booklets on 'the martyrs of Mers el-Kébir'. One does not have to be an expert in mass psychology to accept that this may have had at least some long-term effect on the French electorate – the unanswered question being how long. Another factor which is often forgotten is that because of the geographical division of labour between the

British (including Canadian and other Commonwealth troops) and American armies at the time of the Normandy landings, few areas of France were actually liberated by *les Anglais* as opposed to *les Américains*: after the break-out following the fierce fighting for Caen, Rouen was liberated by a Canadian force, Le Havre by a British one, like Amiens and Arras – and the Germans evacuated Lille before the British arrived. It is therefore easy to visualise the relatively narrow arc from Caen to Lille bordering the Channel: the vast majority of the country attributed its liberation to the Americans, and Hollywood did the rest. Again, how can the historian – even the historian of mentalities – measure the impact of that?

If there is one certainty, therefore, it is that it is impossible to pass hasty judgment on the men who initiated and pursued (or spurned) the *Entente Cordiale* according to their lights and in sometimes intractable situations. There is no room for all these 'popular' publications which confuse 'critical distance' with 'systematic criticism' – and it is to be hoped that the present collection will demonstrate that English-speaking scholars can adopt this critical distance towards Anglo-French relations without falling into the pitfall of denigration.

Notes

1. Macaulay, (Baron) Thomas Babington. *History of England* (London: 1849–1861). Popular Edition (London: Longman, 1895), p. 8.
2. See for instance Michel Depeyre, *Tactiques et stratégies de la France et du Royaume-Uni, de 1690 à 1815.* (Paris: Economica, 1998), derived from his *Thèse de doctorat d'histoire*, Université Paris IV, 1994.
3. Now with free on-line access: <www.rhs.ac.uk/>
4. Lanessan, Jean-Louis de. *Histoire de l'Entente cordiale franco-anglaise: Les relations de la France et de l'Angleterre depuis le XVI*[e] *siècle jusqu'à nos jours.* Bibliothèque d'histoire contemporaine. (Paris: F. Alcan, 1916). Leaving out the copyright libraries, Glasgow, Liverpool and Manchester University Libraries seem to have bought it.
5. Curiously in its series *Association pour la diffusion de la pensée française.* Boyd, William and Mougel, François-Charles. *France – Grande-Bretagne: l'Entente Cordiale: Great Britain – France.* (Paris: ADPF, 2004). Adrien Charbeau and Isabel Fernandez's Bibliography is on pp. 91–128.
6. Vaïsse, Maurice (ed.). *L'Entente cordiale de Fachoda à la Grande Guerre: dans les archives du Quai d'Orsay.* Avant-propos de Dominique de Villepin. (Bruxelles: Éditions Complexe/Paris: Ministère des Affaires étrangères, 2004). Thus the *Ministère des Affaires étrangères* sponsored the publication

of two volumes to celebrate the centenary, offering its invaluable iconographic documents for colour reproduction. What conclusions are we to draw from the fact that the Foreign & Commonwealth Office did not follow suit? Its only contribution in the publishing field seems to have been the 35-page pamphlet, Cecil, Hugh P., *Lord Lansdowne: From the Entente Cordiale of 1904 to the 'Peace Letter' of 1917: A European Statesman Assessed.* (London: Foreign & Commonwealth Office, 2004).

7. Sous la direction de Jacques Viot et Giles Radice; préfaces de Dominique de Villepin et Jack Straw (Paris: Odile Jacob, 2004).
8. Edited by Richard Mayne, Douglas Johnson and Robert Tombs; Forewords by Jack Straw and Dominique de Villepin (London: Routledge, 2004).
9. Sous la direction de Laurent Bonnaud (Paris: L'Harmattan, 2004).
10. No. 117, Spring 2004.
11. (Paris: Fondation Singer-Polignac, 2004).
12. Sous la direction de Frédéric Charillon; avant-propos de Pierre Lacoste. *Les Champs de Mars: Cahiers du Centre d'études en sciences sociales de la défense*, premier semestre 2004, No. 15 (Paris: la Documentation française).
13. (Paris: Perrin, 2004). Antoine d'Arjuzon has also written *Castlereagh (1761–1822) ou, Le défi à l'Europe de Napoléon* (Paris: Tallandier, 1995) and *Wellington* (Paris: Perrin, 1998).
14. A good example of this reliance on statistics to put forward a positive view of Anglo-French relations is provided by Sir Christopher Mallaby (H.M. Ambassador to France, 1993–96) in his chapter, 'Britain and France: some comments on a complex relationship', in Chassaigne, Philippe and Dockrill, Michael (eds). *Anglo-French Relations 1898–1998: From Fashoda to Jospin*, Studies in Military and Strategic History Series (Basingstoke: Palgrave, 2002) pp. 7–10.

1
'French people have a peculiar facility for being misrepresented': British Perceptions of France at War, 1914–18

John Ramsden
Queen Mary University of London

Britain and France fought alongside each other throughout the Great War, and in this sense the *Entente Cordiale* of 1904 was the bedrock of each country's war effort, the military alliance without which neither country could possibly have avoided defeat by Germany. On occasion, the *Entente* could be hymned as a natural and historic harmony, as when G.K. Chesterton celebrated Allied victory in the First Battle of the Marne: 'the empire of blood and iron rolled slowly back towards the darkness of the northern forests, and the great nations of the West went forwards; side by side as after a long lovers' quarrel, went the ensigns of St Denys and St George'. Several centuries of bruising Anglo-French warfare had been quite some 'lovers' quarrel'.[1] More often though, it was noted that Britain and France had been ancient enemies until 1815, and that fighting as allies during the Crimean War of the 1850s had been uncharacteristic of a nineteenth century mainly notable for continued rivalry and near-wars. There had almost been war over Fashoda as recently as 1898, and when British readers thrilled to flesh-creeping invasion tales in the 1890s it was invariably the French who were expected to invade. Only with the onset of Anglo-German naval rivalries after 1900 did the British see France as a lesser threat; only after the 1904 *Entente* did the British and French authorities begin to plan combined operations; only in 1911 did the British government envisage commitments to France from which ministers might be unable to escape during a Franco-German war. These cooperative developments in the last decade of peacetime were, though, largely confidential, hypothetical and conditional; even most cabinet ministers did not entirely grasp their significance until July 1914. So, although there was in Britain a widespread expectation of war with Germany, very little had been done to prepare British people for fighting alongside France. The British elite had long loved France (and especially Paris), its culture and its cooking; even the Prime Minister, Sir Henry Campbell-Bannerman, had enjoyed popping over to Boulogne for lunch. The lower classes on the other hand would never have been there, knew nothing of the country and remembered from schooldays little except that Johnny Crapaud was the historic enemy of liberty and Protestantism.

It was quickly recognised in August 1914 that a proper understanding of Britain's allies was as important for the maintenance of morale as the generation of hatred for the enemy, especially since France would mainly bear the burden of the land war in autumn 1914. British newspaper readers were therefore given enough material in battle reports from Lorraine and the Marne to ensure positive opinions of the French army. To an extent, this continued for the rest of the war, at least until British troops first appeared on the Western Front in comparable numbers, which was only in summer 1916. Newspapers enjoyed official support in presenting positive impressions of French heroism and would no doubt have been censored as defeatist if they had offered any other view, but they needed neither encouragement nor censorship, for in the early propaganda war voluntaristic patriotism in a pluralistic society ensured enthusiasm. The same can be said, though even more so, about another aspect of the propaganda war, books representing the French war effort for British readers with time to assess it at leisure. There was a wave of these books, clearly an important aspect of Anglo-French cultural relations during the Great War. This chapter will review that forgotten literary war of 1914–18.

Just how big the literary war was is indicated by the accessions records of the British Library; between 1914 and 1919, the British Library acquired about seven hundred books that were wholly or predominantly about wartime France and the French war effort. The majority were naturally French language books published in France, and though the British Library's generous accessions policy for such books says a great deal about elite perceptions of France in wartime London, Francophone titles could have had only a negligible impact on the British reading public. About one-tenth of those seven hundred French war books were, though, published in English, some of them contemporary translations of recent French texts but mostly original titles in English, and these had a quite different potential. These seventy books constitute about half the total number of books in English on France's 1914–19 war that were listed in Enser's standard bibliography of 1979: as many books were therefore published in English on the subject in 1914–19 as over the following sixty years.[2] It is not possible now to discover print numbers for wartime books, but some comments are obvious. First, commercial publishers would simply not have continued to produce more than a book a month within a single genre unless they were experiencing healthy sales. Second, most of these publications were reviewed in such places as the *Times Literary Supplement* (almost invariably receiving positive reviews), but they were also prominent in trade publications like *The Bookseller,* which again suggests a thriving commercial market. Finally, copies now available for reading by scholars at the British Library seem generally to have been derived from provincial lending libraries, which clearly carried these same titles in large numbers, so making them available to poorer readers unlikely to purchase books.[3]

A number of general points can be made about the literature. It would usually have reinforced the picture of wartime France derived from the press, and several of the books were in fact derived from earlier press reports or written by war correspondents. Pearl Adam's *Paris Sees it Through* was mainly drawn from articles in the *Evening Standard* and the *Westminster Gazette*; W.E. Grey's *With the French Eastern Army* was a spin-off from articles published in the *Daily Telegraph*; Gerald Campbell's *Verdun to the Vosges* was by *The Times*'s man in Lorraine, while the existence of other books by *Times* correspondents attests both to the larger overseas staff maintained by *The Times* than by any other paper, and to the greater influence it therefore enjoyed in shaping British perceptions of foreigners. One of the most extravagant paeans of praise to the wartime French, *The Achievement of France,* reprinted articles that *The Times* published in June 1915, based on reports from its many (anonymous) correspondents in France.[4]

The Times was often regarded as a semi-official mouthpiece of the British government, but many of these books went out of their way to secure official endorsement, or at least the endorsement of celebrity figures. John Buchan, for example, while working for the Ministry of Information, contributed a foreword to Hilliard Atteridge's biography of Foch: the general was, wrote Buchan, 'without doubt' the war's 'greatest military figure', the man who had 'found in 1918 . . . a method to obviate the clumsiness of the modern military machine'. Foch and President Wilson were the war's two greatest personalities and the key to understanding why the allies were winning. (So much for both Douglas Haig and David Lloyd George.) W.E. Grey claimed his own official endorsement for the need to understand France, by quoting in his preface speeches by Lords Curzon and Kitchener; Curzon was pointing out early in 1915 that the French still held ten times as much frontline as the BEF. Hilaire Belloc, introducing Adrien Bertrand's war diary in translation, built up for English readers the importance of the Lorraine battles of 1914, of which he thought the British knew far too little, and helpfully establishes the author as a patriotic Frenchman by telling readers that he has died of his wounds since finishing the book. John St Loe Strachey of the *Spectator* assures readers of Philippe Millet that he tells his 'plain tale' with 'a very English sense of humour', for he knows both England and the British army well. Finally, Rudyard Kipling, in effect his own celebrity endorsement since he was the biggest selling author of the day, precedes his *France at War*, also based on previous articles for the press, with the poem 'France', the country which has been 'First to face the Truth . . . '. Significantly, the Kipling book was produced along with a dozen of his earlier titles by Macmillan, in a special edition sized to fit into a soldier's tunic pocket. France was, wrote Kipling for this audience of British soldiers, 'manning the frontier of civilisation'.[5]

The authors themselves were self-appointed intermediaries who seem to have seen it as their special wartime task to explain France to the British. Philippe Millet, for example, was a liaison officer who had familiarised himself with the British army during visits to prewar manoeuvres, and who was then attached to an Indian cavalry division in wartime. By the time that he wrote his book he was working with the British department of French military censorship, which may explain why *En Liaison avec les Anglais* became the far more evocative *Comrades in Arms* when translated. An Englishman who was equally untypical of his nation was M. Macdonald, who even enlisted as a private in the French rather than the British army in 1914, and then wrote of his experiences in *Under the French Flag*. Another Frenchman, Ernest Vizetelly, had already written widely on Anglo-French affairs, including his *With Zola in England* (1899),[6] and now contributed an explanation of Alsace-Lorraine for the British market. Sidney Dark, a journalist who found his lifelong sympathy for France underlined by equal hatred of Germans, followed up his wartime writing with the even more laudatory *Child's Book of France* in 1921.[7] His *The Glory that is France* – the title shamelessly lifted from J.C. Stobart's bestseller *The Glory that was Greece* – is dedicated to 'my 19-year old son, now fighting in France for France and Britain'. Dark's dedication to France is particularly notable from such a convinced Protestant, the future editor of the *Church Times*, just as another wartime Francophile writer, Leslie Church, went on to edit the *Methodist Recorder*. France could be viewed as either secular or Roman Catholic, Catholicism being a reason for viewing her as an enemy in the 1750s, while atheism fulfilled the same purpose in the 1790s; but never could it constitute the Protestant alliance that Kaiser Wilhelm had offered Britain in 1900. Just how ambiguous this aspect of the relationship was is indicated by reports that French opinion generally had welcomed Britain's belated wartime acceptance of a diplomatic representative from the Vatican – representation which anti-clerical France still did not have herself. M.E. Clarke reported meeting a fiercely lachrymose French priest in 1914, deeply regretful that British soldiers who fought so well as allies would nevertheless go to Hell, since they had only the same false religion as the Germans. For Charles Dawbarn 'Parisophile' might be a better description than Francophile; Dawbarn was from 1900 onwards Paris correspondent successively of the *Pall Mall Gazette*, the *Observer* and *The Times*. He wrote several supportive books on wartime France, one of which prompted the *Liverpool Post* to dub him 'the literary ambassador of the *Entente*', while the *Pall Mall Gazette* wrote of his 'profound and instructive sympathy for France'.[8]

The sustained objective of all these writers was the promotion of better mutual understanding. M.E. Clarke conceded that this was necessary because 'we are after all historical enemies', while Dawbarn wrote elliptically that his books were needed because 'French people have a peculiar facility for being misrepresented'. It was vital to achieve harmony between the wartime allies, for 'the barriers of our national characteristics are difficult things to adjust comfortably'.[9] Beyond the problems created by past antagonism and different national characteristics, it was argued that each country was from 1914 onwards understandably preoccupied with its own war effort and hence ignorant of what its allies were doing for the common cause. The *Times Literary Supplement* reviewer welcomed Perris's *The Campaign in France and Flanders* in June 1915 as explaining French 'achievements of which too little has been heard in England'. Even those British readers who thought they knew France from peacetime holidays were targets for these earnest wartime writers; the *TLS* also welcomed Clarke's *Paris Waits*, because it showed 'the dear, delightful happy France that most of us thought we knew so well, under a new guise – that of the grim, watchful defender of her hard-won liberties'.[10]

Some Britons resident in Paris attributed the continuing failures of mutual comprehension to the misdirection of British information campaigns in France, which tended to concentrate on abstruse issues like the constitutional structure of the British Empire, while 'we *should* have been better employed telling [France] why we don't mention our feelings, and why we are embarrassed when she mentions hers'.[11] This problem was thought to have reduced over time, though it was often said that the United States was better at explaining itself to the French than were the British (how unlike our own dear times). This was though probably a consequence of British jealousy when American 'doughboys' were feted as saviours by French crowds in 1917–18, one of General Pershing's officers having cannily proclaimed that they had come to repay the debt owed by the Americans to France since Lafayette's efforts for US independence – from Britain – in the 1780s. American authors were, however, sometimes thought to offer a useful slant on Anglo-French wartime relationships, a reviewer for example responding to E.A. Powell's *Vive La France!* that 'some of the hints on occasional little misunderstandings which arise from time to time from dissimilarity of national manners may be read with profit by ourselves'.[12]

The single overriding impression given by these writers was of French wartime unity, patriotism and self-sacrifice, a situation often implicitly and sometimes explicitly compared to lesser British commitment to the war. It was widely noted how quickly pre-war French political antagonisms had disappeared in 1914, as oppositional figures like Gustave Hervé and Georges Clemenceau rallied to the *union sacrée*. Along the same lines, class divisions were said to have lessened, and even to have disappeared altogether in the enforced unity of frontline trenches. 'All personal ambition, all personal grievances, have been swallowed up in one great emotion, La France!'.[13] Having travelled widely through France for his book, and not limited his investigations to Paris as did so many other writers, Kipling reported in 1915 that 'every aspect and detail of life in France seemed overlaid with a smooth patina of long-continued war – everything except the spirit of the people, and that is as fresh and as glorious as the spirit of their own land and sunshine'. The French were, he wrote, 'a people transfigured', and then adds that he wished that he could bring British strikers over to witness all this French self-sacrifice for themselves.[14] Women in particular were said to have thrown off their prewar role and adapted to wartime privations, much more quickly indeed than their sisters in Britain, but a special prominence was allotted to the deportees of the occupied regions. Henriette Celarié, in a scene eerily prefiguring the film *Casablanca* from the next world war, describes how teenage girls deported from Lille to work in German factories marched away singing the *Marseillaise,* with such fervour indeed that their brutal German captors dared not intervene to punish their defiance.[15]

More often, such reports were about French soldiers, united in uninhibited dedication to their country. Several writers recycled the heartfelt dictum of a single French soldier, originally heard and reported by the military correspondent of *The Times*, Colonel Repington: 'Mon corps à la terre, mon âme à Dieu, mon cœur à la France', a phrase which Sidney Dark thought to encapsulate 'the spirit of France'.[16] Such a spirit certainly enlivened the translated diaries of Adrien Bertrand, a young cavalry officer who fought in Lorraine in 1914. Bertrand and his fellows experience 'real pain' when they hear of the first French defeats ('I am thunderstruck'), and are 'crushed' by the news that Paris may fall to the Germans, then overjoyed by the victory on the Marne: 'it is the greatest moment of my life. We weep'.[17] Charles Dawbarn tells his readers that the British people must understand such patriotism, even if it goes against their national character to express anything like this themselves: French patriotism is 'a desperate, blind, falling in love with one's country'.[18] He certainly had a point, for it is quite impossible to imagine any British writer, even so patriotically uninhibited a figure as Kipling, signing a public letter 'yours patriotically', as did Anatole France. British reviewers were indeed not even sure that it was quite proper for Monsieur France himself to do so, arguing that by abandoning for the duration his customary gentle irony he had ceased to be true to himself and adopted an essentially false tone. Reviewers had real difficulties when responding to the issue of national character in wartime. One account of the Marne has French soldiers rushing into battle shouting 'Vive La France!' while nearby the British were advancing with cries of 'This way for the early door! Sixpence extra', as if queuing for a music hall. 'British reserve', noted the reviewer, 'sometimes feels the need of frivolity as a mask for deep emotion. The French, who at ordinary times are frivolous about some matters which it is our habit to treat gravely, admit no appearance of levity at the supreme crisis of their fate'.[19] There were however touches of humour reported in French patriotism too, though perhaps served up specially for the British readership. M.E. Clarke clearly enjoyed reporting that the shop of a Parisian mattress maker in September 1914 bore the notice, 'Dormez en paix. Le Matelassier est à la Frontière'.[20]

It was often argued that French patriotism derived from French history, though in order to explain this to the British, French history itself had to be rather thoroughly filleted. Those who sought to argue that French history was central to the entire history of Western Christendom – Reuben Saillens claimed the words and concepts of 'Liberty, Equality and Fraternity' to be biblical – tended to avoid recent examples of anti-Semitism such as the Dreyfus affair; this was a recent episode that was almost entirely purged from the record – though, oddly, biographers of Marshal Joffre pointed out his luck in being in Madagascar and the Sudan throughout 'that black and poisonous period', so escaping the need to choose sides.[21] Few went as far into the past for inspiration as Madame Drumont, whose diary records her emotions on hearing that French soldiers were in 1915 going to the Dardanelles to attack the Turks, inspiring her with dreams of revenge for the French knights slain during the Crusades. Though by comparison with young British officers like Rupert Brooke and Ernest Raymond, who welcomed Gallipolli since it allowed them to fight over the lands of Homer and to gaze at the roadsteads where Agamemnon had moored his thousand ships, Mme Drumont was positively up to date.[22] More often, inspiration from French history had a less historic vintage. Sidney Dark had no doubt that it was since 1789 that France had been 'the mother of European freedom'. He wrote of the nineteenth century as an extended struggle between 'the Prussian idea' and 'the French idea'. This was again a rebuke to Britain, in this case to the British left, for to Dark, Karl Marx was of course part of that 'German idea' of state worship, and even contemporary Fabians like Sidney Webb were essentially German in their thinking, while the French left had been more individualistic, more committed to personal freedom.[23] Along similar lines, Charles Dawbarn argued that France 'held aloft the banner of freedom' since 1789, though he necessarily said little about the hostile British response to the French Revolution at the time. Since 1789, France had developed for the whole of Europe the new civic virtues of courage and discipline. Dawbarn seems though hardly to have expected that his readers would be convinced by this: 'Ah, you say, discipline is a new quality to give the French!' He cannot have been much more confident when claiming that French patriotism had never been aggressive, never a threat to France's neighbours, though he did assert that Napoleon had only sought to 'dower foreign peoples with the liberty which France had owned for herself'. That 'only' must indeed have been hard to swallow for British readers educated on a diet of Nelson and Wellington. More often, writers simply ignored these earlier Franco-British wars, just as the historians of Alsace-Lorraine did not highlight the fact that France had conquered the provinces in the sixteenth and seventeenth centuries. Writers on General Foch were however delighted to learn that his father had been called Napoleon, as they were by the fact that the name 'Foch' was itself a corruption of *fioch*, the Basque word for 'fire'; Marshal Joffre could be similarly celebrated as the son of a barrel cooper, the same trade as the father of the legendary Marshal Ney.[24]

As this suggests, French leaders were an important part of the story, but since France was being offered to British readers as an example of a democratic country (by implication, more a democracy than Britain itself), the leaders of wartime France had to be unrelentingly offered as representative Frenchmen as well as dynamic leaders. In that process, these writers had to suggest that the hugely different personalities of Raymond Poincaré, Georges Clemenceau, Albert Thomas, Joseph Joffre and Ferdinand Foch were each quintessentially French. These five were probably the only leading Frenchmen ever to register on the radar for British people in 1914–18, though the fact that there was no account of General Robert Nivelle (who still indeed awaits a British biographer) is surely significant; there was also no account of the French army mutinies that were prompted by the failure of his 1917 offensive.[25] Of President Poincaré it was therefore argued that 'it is a great thing for France that in her day of ordeal she has for Chief of State one who by birth and education, as well as by temperament, is the type of man which the majority of Frenchmen would like themselves and their sons to be'. Alexander Kahn thought that Joffre was typical of the rural craftsman stock of France – actually he was of Catalan ancestry – those social classes for whom since Napoleon a military career was 'a treasured dream'. He was more generally seen as incarnating a deep sense of Frenchness through the unlimited patience and absolute unflappability of 'Papa Joffre', an image that was hard to reconcile with the idea that the excitable, theatrical Foch was also in some sense an incarnation of deep Frenchness. In part this was simply a matter of changing needs as the war developed, for by 1918 Foch rather than Joffre was being credited as the real victor of the Marne battles in 1914. If, as Grey suggested, Joffre never hurried over a meal in all his time in command (a characteristic that Britons saw as very French indeed), then it was in that way that he showed that France would be calm, when we British expected of them 'public clamour'. This in turn was hard to reconcile with the idea of Clemenceau, whose entire public life had epitomised 'public clamour', also somehow being 'a typical Frenchman' in 1918. Few writers rocked this particular boat, a belief that French leadership, actual Frenchness and national unity were indissolubly linked, even if H.M. Hyndman (though significantly publishing only in 1919, when the war had been won) did suggest that Clemenceau's earlier incarnation as the man who could wreck a new government each day had not exactly helped to strengthen the Third Republic before its great test in 1914–18.[26]

The effect of history and leadership had been to make the French army a formidable fighting force, most effective because it relied on discipline voluntarily accepted by 'a society of free men' – a surprising claim for British writers to make when France had conscription and Britain did not, though Dark explained to his readers that since 1790 the French had realised that national service had a 'pacific value' as well as instilling martial ardour into the people. French soldiers were notable for their 'heroic tenacity', as on the Marne and at Verdun, a claim often reinforced in the British editions by quoted endorsement from neutral Swiss, Dutch or American reviews of the original French editions of the same books. Bertrand writes that French soldiers' courage 'amounts almost to madness', and the *Daily Telegraph*'s 'Dixmude, the epic of the French marines' came to a similar conclusion. Alongside tenacity, which French writers were ready to concede also to the British army, French *élan* was thought to be a special military quality. Mme Drumont, acknowledging that the British had 'steadfastness' and an 'iron will', thought too that 'they have not perhaps got our spirit and dash'.[27] These military strengths were, though, acknowledged to have been used for the *Entente*, not simply for France, since France had, wrote Grey, 'borne the brunt of the war'; Gerald Campbell was one of many who stressed 'the greatness of the debt that Britain owes to France'. The French army, argued Warner Allen in 1916, had been 'the buckler behind which the allies have developed and organised their resources for the final victory. Never, even in the days when she overran continents and conquered nations has France played a part in a more glorious epic'.[28] It was perhaps inevitable that such generous tributes tended not to be paid after the summer of 1916; it was hard to think positively of *élan* after Nivelle's offensive, and even the quality of tenacity was harder to celebrate after the 1917 mutinies. There were however rather fewer British books of any kind depicting France's war in 1917–18, Britain now having less gratitude to spare as her own casualty list mounted during the Somme and Passchendaele battles. Nevertheless, the reiterated assertion that the French army was literally unconquerable, a conviction rooted in memories of Verdun and the Marne, was clearly still present in British minds in 1939–40, hence the deep shock in Britain during France's rapid defeat in Hitler's *Blitzkrieg*. 'Thank God for the French Army' was Winston Churchill's cry in the early 1930s, as he denounced British weakness.

French failings were rarely referred to in wartime books, and then usually only after the event. There were for example accounts of the panic in Paris in August–September 1914: Mme Drumont noted in her diary that 'some say the Prussians will be in Paris in a week. Everyone is in a funk'. Yet, this was not to be published until well after victory on the Marne had shown that panic was not necessary; by 1915 it was even being argued that the Government's panic flight to Bordeaux had been a masterstroke of policy, since it allowed the military to conduct a brilliant defence of the capital without having to worry about their political masters. Still, there were some critical references to French bureaucracy, always a source of bafflement to Anglo-Saxons. The American writer Richard Harding Davis, for example, waxed lyrical about the difficulty of getting embarkation papers at Le Havre when his mission took him on to Britain. M.E. Clarke, on the other hand, really let herself go when describing civil servants' treatment of foreigners queuing to get passports in order to return home in August 1914:

> The officials flourished their pens, twirled their moustaches and gave vent to their *bon mots* and their sarcasm with the utmost *sang froid*. They retired for their meals with great regularity, and announced the fact personally to their victims. Two hours for luncheon and a pause for an occasional *apéritif* made pleasant intervals for them; but for the crowds outside in the drenching rain . . . they merely perhaps prolonged torture. To humiliate further the people they were supposed to be helping, these 'Jacks in Office' took every opportunity to sharpen their wits on the ignorance of foreign women both in the language and in the laws of the land . . . Their behaviour was all the more noticeable in that, elsewhere, politeness and courtesy are the inviolable rule.

The final sentence barely modifies the resentment conveyed by the story as a whole, a resentment which Clarke as a long-term resident in Paris had no doubt been building up over years. It does indicate though how far such anecdotal evidence was susceptible to the viewpoint of the author. When Marshal Joffre refused to hurry his lunch it became proof of his refusal to panic, rather like Drake playing bowls as the Spanish Armada approached, but when the Paris passport office did exactly the same thing, it was seen as demonstrating its contempt for foreigners. Such stories were in any case not to be heard after the first few months, as either the censorship tightened or the French bureaucracy learned to wage war more sensitively.[29] Far more typical of those writers who acknowledged French failings was Henry Dugard: logistical failures described in his account of Verdun are merely the excuse for a hymn of praise to the French soldiers who stuck it out despite being let down by the authorities – a Third Republic version of the 'lions led by donkeys' myth on the British side in the Great War. Charles Dawbarn too turned criticism into praise, noting that France was not hypocritical and knew well her own faults (once again an implied comparison to the less self-aware British). France 'has many faults . . . She is too vital not to have them; she touches life at too many points not to feel sometimes the contamination of earth'.[30]

The overriding aim was of course greater allied unity: Philippe Millet hailed in 1916 the fact that 'the soldiers of the British Empire and of France [are] fighting side by side': they stood 'shoulder to shoulder once more on both banks of the Somme'.[31] Many writers emphasised even if unintentionally the shared experience of war which meant that Britain and France were undergoing the same experience – sons gone into battle, deprivation and rationing, xenophobia and enemy atrocities, failure to understand the trenches, maiming, bereavement and loss. Sometimes it was more overt: it was reported by Parisians that Zeppelin raids on London would make Britain really 'grasp' the war, now it had come home to the civilians, as it already had in eastern France months earlier. Similarly, accounts of the Lille deportations demanded that British readers imagine their own feelings if their teenage daughters were hauled off to a foreign land to do heavy manual work for a brutal enemy; late in the war, the British government invited its people to make exactly the same comparison, when a propaganda film showed German conquerors treating Chester exactly as they had apparently treated Lille. Publishers made the same equation between British and French experiences, Heinemann issuing Marcel Dupont's book in the series in which British 'Soldiers' Tales' were appearing, while the publisher brought out Kahn's biography of Joffre in the series that already included books on Drake, Cromwell, Nelson and Wellington.[32]

It could hardly be denied, though, that the French had not invariably thought as highly of the British war effort as in the interests of allied unity these writers would have liked. M.E. Clarke remembered 'bad hours' for British residents in Paris while the Asquith government decided between peace and war in early August 1914, and Pearl Adam recalled that 'we British had more than one awkward moment with our French friends'. Once again such memories were published only long after the event; as soon as Britain declared war, there was relief for the expatriates of what *Le Figaro* now hailed as 'La Loyale Angleterre'. M.E. Clarke noted that after that bad moment French workmen gave up their seats for her on the Paris Metro, as they had never done in peacetime. There were many reassuring accounts of British soldiers being feted on arrival, cheered through the streets of French towns, hence perhaps the jealousy when Americans received the same welcome in the final year of war. H.M. Alexander reported that French crowds were especially welcoming to troops from the British Empire, in both Marseilles and Orleans, cries of 'Vive l'Angleterre' mingling with 'Vive les Hindous' when the Lahore Division disembarked. This was to be understood, it was explained, in the misconceptions that French people had previously held of the Empire: having been taught to see it only as a great engine of exploitation, the arrival of Australians and Canadians to aid the mother country in her hour of need took the French completely by surprise, for 'loyalty at such a moment was the last thing they expected' (which rather suggests that propaganda lectures on the constitution of the Empire were not wasted after all). Pearl Adam's account described similar celebrations in Cambrai, in which 'every child wanted to shake the hand of an English soldier', and adds that 'one man declining to be kissed by a youth of about fifteen was a wonderful sight'. Few went as far in their pro-British sentiments as the Drumonts, though here tributes to the allies were once again a rebuke to their own country: 'the Master', as Mme Drumont, humbly described her extremely right-wing, anti-Semitic husband-writer, was reported saying 'how noble and chivalrous a race are these Allies of ours, who have not been corrupted by a Republic . . .'.[33]

There was an uneasy awareness, though, that, apart from these demonstrations of welcome, French people never adequately appreciated what Britain was doing for the alliance. There was, for example, no real understanding of the work of the Royal Navy; one writer speaks of the 'silent service' remaining rather too silent, and several record the amazement that Jutland had not been a decisive victory in 1916 (French children also having been educated for decades as to the historic fighting power of the British Navy). Clarke reported that 'if England expects every man to do his duty, France expects every Englishman to do two men's duty. It is a great compliment to us, but it is not an easy matter to fulfil the mission'. In this context, there had been real French criticism of the Christmas truce of 1914, after which it was being said that 'Britain has many men available; few are here; those that are here shake hands with Germans'. British readers would therefore have been reassured to know that there were also

French troops involved in a Christmas truce; they might though have expressed equal amazement to learn that when reprimanded, these same soldiers celebrated New Year 1915 by firing off champagne corks at the Germans in the trenches opposite.[34]

Above all, French opinion was disappointed by Britain's slowness in introducing conscription – to French thinking a normal part of democratic life, in Britain an unprecedented extension of state power over the citizen. Here the writers, proclaiming the (French) nation in arms, were almost invariably issuing a wake-up call to their British readers. Charles Dawbarn, reporting that many Frenchmen were saying 'that England has forgotten all about the war in her desire to make money' (not far from contemporary British views of the USA), added that 'the Frenchman's eye is always being caught by the headline "another strike in Wales"'.[35] Despite the enthusiasm expressed on their arrival, French observers were also said to find the ordinary British soldier odd in his behaviour: 'he likes tea and drinks it all day long, he almost lives on jam and biscuits, and . . . his chief recreation is not sport but shaving'; when in tight corners the British soldier was noted to sing rather a lot. The general perception was that the British soldiery concentrated on order, discipline, spit and polish and appearance, while the French soldier (who was, after all, called a 'poilu' – a *hairy* one) had very likely not shaved for some time and was dressed, thought Dawbarn, in a uniform 'made for the march, not the parade ground' (though of course British soldiers were seen by the French only on parade, not when slumming it in the trenches). Emotional gaps were also perceived still to count, between what Pearl Adam called the 'hard-headed expressive French' and the 'sentimental, inarticulate English'. Dawbarn noted that while the French government had banned the publication of casualty lists as likely to lead to panic and the French philosophically accepted the appearance of newspapers with blank spaces indicating the vigilance of the censor, in Britain it was the other way round, for the public accepted the casualty lists (at that early state of the war, only rather short ones, though), but would have been deeply upset if reminded too often of the loss of their civil rights. Philippe Millet, despite years of experience of the British army, did quite a bit to perpetuate such stereotypes. He describes in *Comrades in Arms* a series of emotionally stunted British officers, who 'speak of their fear as if it were toothache'; one even says that while it is better not to get killed in action, if it is necessary then at least it should be done in a way that would not undermine the men's morale. Another says calmly that 'it is better not to lose one's head' when under fire, since it tends to discourage the men, and they all face death bravely. Millet concludes that 'Turenne would, I fancy, have commended them for it' – but how many of his English readers had even heard of Turenne?[36]

Experience of fighting as allies encouraged in this group of Francophiles real optimism for the post-war world. Gerald Campbell wrote of the French in 1918 in terms of approbation beyond which an English gentleman and a *Times* correspondent simply could not go:

> The French have played the game; they have fought the good fight like knights and gentlemen. That, more than anything, is the reason why Englishmen have come to look upon them as something more than allies. Because of it they have forged a bond with us, and our children's children which Time itself will hardly be able to weaken. They are our brothers, not only in arms, but in all that civilisation stands for. The Germans are – different.

Others were, though, a good deal less hopeful, recognising even in their wartime writings that they constituted a core group of true believers in Anglo-French amity, surrounded by an English Channel full of scepticism. Clarke wrote that the problem continued to be mutual ignorance of each other's ways. The two armies did after all mainly fight in separate battles, or in separate sectors of the same battlefields, so that intermingling of the nationalities was always limited – far more limited than was the case, for example, when so many Americans trained in Britain in 1942–44. Hence it could be believed even by Clarke, a strong supporter of the *Entente* and long-term resident in France, that 'If you are French you are volatile. Always there is a little reserve behind our admiration, however sincere our admiration may be. The war will certainly wipe out many misunderstandings between Frenchmen and Englishmen, but it will strengthen some of the barriers.' Such barriers no doubt became a little higher when the tide of English language books on France's war ebbed in 1917–18, and even more so when the wartime publication rate of one book a month became about a book a year during the next half century. In the second half of the Great War, reviewers too were less committed to the literary *entente* than they had been in 1914–15. When the *TLS* reviewed in 1918 Edmund Gosse's *France et Angleterre* – note the French title, though the book itself was in English – a plea for better intellectual understanding for the post-war period, it was actually rather anti-French in its tone, or at least unwilling to meet France halfway as to future cultural relations:

> While French novelists of all kinds find a large number of appreciative readers in England, the English novel is understood and read little in France. And, though Mr. Gosse is courteous enough not to insist overmuch on this point, he hints clearly enough that it is the French public which has to make up for its sins of omission, while in England there is a real danger of excessive enthusiasm for the latest literary novelty from Paris.

This carping reference to one-way cultural traffic, it should be recalled, was written when Scott Moncrieff had barely even begun his translation of Proust, the first volume of which appeared only in 1922 and sparked off another great wave of literary Francophilia among the British elite. But that was, as our writers had feared, an admiration for all things French that did not permeate beyond the literary, and had no influence whatsoever on British international policy. After 1918, despite the literary *entente*-building of 1914–18, it was to be mainly business as usual in Anglo-French misunderstanding.[37]

Select list of 1914–19 books in English on France at war

Anon. *The Deportation of Women and Girls from Lille* (London: Hodder & Stoughton, 1916).

Anon. *Letters of a Soldier* (London: Constable, 1917).

Anon. *Raymond Poincaré* (London: Duckworth, 1914).

'A French Gunner'. *General Joffre* (London: Simpkin Marshall, 1915).

Adam, Pearl. *Paris Sees it Through, a Diary* (London: Hodder & Stoughton, 1919).

Alexander, H.M. *On Two Fronts* (London: Heinemann, 1916).

Allen, Warner. *The Unbroken Line* (London: Smith Elder, 1916).

Atteridge, Hillard. *Marshal Foch and his Theory of Modern Warfare* (London: Skeffington, 1918).

Behnvet, (Capt.) F. *A Crusader of France* (London: Melrose, 1916).

Bertrand, Adrien. *The Victory of Lorraine* (London: Nelson, 1918).
Brittain, H.E. *To Verdun from the Somme* (London: John Lane, 1917).
Burke, Kathleen. *The White Road to Verdun* (London: Hodder & Stoughton, 1916).
Campbell, Gerald. *Verdun to the Vosges* (London: Arnold, 1916).
Celarié, Henriette. *Slaves of the Hun* (London: Cassell, 1918).
Church, Leslie. *The Story of Alsace-Lorraine* (London: Kelly, 1915).
Clarke, M.E. *Paris Waits, 1914* (London: Smith Elder, 1915).
Dark, Sidney. *The Glory that is France* (London: Eveleigh Nash, 1916).
Davis, Richard Harding. *With the French in France and Salonika* (London: Duckworth, 1916).
Dawbarn, Charles. *France at Bay* (London: Mills & Boon, 1915).
Dawbarn, Charles. *Foch and his Army* (London: Mills & Boon, 1916).
Drumont, (Mme) E.A. *A French Mother in Wartime* (London: Arnold, 1916).
Dugard, Henry. *The Battle of Verdun* (London: Hutchinson, 1916).
Dupont, Marcel. *In the Field* (London: Heinemann, 1916).
France, Anatole. *Sur la Voie Glorieuse* (Paris: Éditions Champion, 1915, but in French and English).
Gosse, Edmund. *France et Angleterre* (London: Hayman, Chrity, Lilly, 1918).
Grant, Margaret. *Verdun Days in Paris* (London: Collins, 1918).
Grey, W.E. *With the French Eastern Army* (London: Hodder & Stoughton, 1915).
Hyndman, H.M. *Clemenceau, the Man and his Time* (London: Grant Richards, 1919).
Kahn, Alexandre. *The Life of General Joffre* (London: Heinemann, 1915).
Kipling, Rudyard. *France at War* (London: Macmillan, 1915).
Le Goffic, Charles. *General Foch at the Marne* (London: Dent, 1918).
McCabe, Joseph. *Georges Clemenceau, France's Grand Old Man* (London: Watts, 1919).
Macdonald, M. *Under the French Flag* (London: Scott, 1917).
Millet, Philippe. *Comrades in Arms* (London: Hodder & Stoughton, 1916).
Perris, George The Campaign in France and Flanders (London: Hodder & Stoughton, 1915).
Powell, E.A. *Vive La France!* (London: Heinemann, 1916).
Saillens, Reuben. *The Soul of France* (London: Morgan & Scott, 1916).
The Times, *The Achievement of France* (London: Methuen, 1915).

Vizetelly, Ernest. *The True Story of Alsace-Lorraine* (London: Chatto & Windus, 1918).
Wharton, Edith. *Fighting France* (London: Macmillan, 1915).
Whitton, F.E. *The Marne Campaign* (London: Constable, 1917).

Notes

1. Peter Buitenhuis, *The Great War of Words: Literature as Propaganda, 1914–18 and After* (London: Batsford, 1989), p. 59.
2. British Museum (Library), *Bibliography of Books on the Great War Acquired between 1914 and 1919* (Unpublished. London: British Museum (Library), 1919); A.G.S. Ensor, *A Subject Bibliography of the First World War: Books in English 1914–1978* (London: Deutsch, 1979).
3. See for example the *Times Literary Supplement*, 21 December 1916; among the provincial libraries whose de-accessioned stock provided material at the British Library during research for this chapter were Paisley, Salford, Gateshead, Rotherham, Merthyr Tydfil and Rochdale. These books were clearly available for borrowing and reading all across Britain, and in most cases seem to have remained on the shelves for more than half a century after 1918.
4. The various contemporary books on France mentioned in the text are listed with full publication details at the end of the chapter.
5. Atteridge, ii; Grey, 5–6; Bertrand, i–ii; Millet, vi–vii; Kipling, 1–5.
6. Ernest Vizetelly, with Zola in England (London, Chatto and Windus, 1899)
7. Sidney Dark, The Child's Book of France (London, Chapman and Hall, 1821).
8. Dark, i; Clarke, 104–5, 283; Dawbarn, reviews on book jacket.
9. Clarke, 98; Dawbarn, 31.
10. *Times Literary Supplement* [hereafter *TLS*], 18 February 1915, 24 June 1915.
11. Adam, 52.
12. *TLS*, 16 March 1916.
13. Clarke, 3.
14. Kipling, 43, 66, 69.
15. Celarié, 39.
16. Dark, 138.
17. Bertrand, 21, 80, 99–100.
18. Dawbarn, 11.
19. *TLS*, July 1915, 21 December 1916.
20. Clarke, 19.
21. Saillens, vi; Kahn, 50.
22. Drumont, 141.
23. Dark, 13, 16–18.
24. Dawbarn, ix, 70, 112; Kahn, 1–4; Dark, 80–1; Atteridge, 12.

25. A.G.S. Enser does, though, allow himself in his bibliography the pointed cross-reference, 'Mutinies, *see* French Army'.
26. *TLS*, 24 September 1914, 27 February 1919; Kahn, 5–6, 70, 97; Grey, 33–4; 'A French Gunner', 13–14, 62–3; McCabe, v, 2, 88; Dawbarn, 73.
27. Dark, 112; Dugard, v; Dupont, preface; Bertrand, 98; Drumont, 43; *TLS*, 26 April 1917.
28. Grey, 9; *TLS*, 4 June 1916; Allen, 324.
29. Drumont, 23; Davis, 217–8; Clarke, 30–31.
30. Dugard, 26; Dawbarn, viii.
31. Millet, xvii.
32. Celarié, 195.
33. Alexander, 33; Clarke, 5–6, 8, 106; Adam, 20, 24; Drumont, 43–4.
34. Clarke, 98; Adam, 49–50; *TLS*, 18 December 1919; Dupont, 302–7.
35. Dawbarn, xii, 107–8.
36. Clarke, 101, 108–9; Dawbarn, 31; Adam, 51; Millet, 149–50, 215–23.
37. *TLS*, 4 June 1916, 28 February 1918; Clarke, 284.

2
Lloyd George and Clemenceau: Prima Donnas in Partnership

Kenneth O. Morgan
The Queen's College, Oxford

David Lloyd George and Georges Clemenceau, leaders of their countries in the First World War, are the supreme symbols of the *Entente Cordiale* in its most momentous phase. Both were imperishably portrayed in Keynes's hostile vignettes during the Paris Peace Conference in 1919. Both were highly image-conscious. Lloyd George was silkily loquacious (though also an excellent listener), instantly recognisable with his long mane of hair, his Inverness cloak and his almost feminine pride in his feet. Clemenceau, at least in Keynes's version, was brusque, usually almost silent, insensitive to his colleagues and his surroundings, equally identifiable with his cape, his cane, his black leather boots with a buckle at the front and always grey suede gloves to hide his eczema.

Their style as politicians was utterly different. Lloyd George, in personal conversation, was subtle and beguiling with men and women alike, a man who 'could charm a bird off a bough'. Keynes's *Essay in Biography* saw him as 'a *femme fatale*'. Clemenceau was aggressive and confrontational, in parliamentary debate and the world outside, famous for his skill in duels with pistol and sword. This took a dramatic form in a sabre duel with the otherwise obscure Paul Deschanel, who understandably, kept up a permanent retreat until Clemenceau gave up, observing contemptuously 'J'avance, il recule'. No magnanimity in victory here. Keynes condemned both prime ministers with equal vigour. Lloyd George had become at Paris the tool of the chauvinists who won the 1918 'coupon election', the 'hard-faced men who looked as if they had done very well out of the war', in Baldwin's celebrated phrase. In Keynes's famous description, he was a man 'rooted in nothing', 'a vampire and a medium in one'. Clemenceau, the most intellectually eminent of the Council of Four (including Woodrow Wilson and Orlando, the Italian premier, as well), was in Keynes's view rooted in ancient enmities and hatreds, permanently fighting Europe's ancient civil wars.

Arguably, Keynes seriously misjudged both. His view of Lloyd George as devoid of principle or consistency was a travesty; his account of Clemenceau's wilful and negative nationalism was exaggerated. At any rate, throughout the two climactic years 1918 and 1919, the relationships between these two men (Clemenceau being born in 1841, twenty-two years before his Welsh colleague) were crucial to the world. Each was hailed, for a brief period, as 'the man who won the war': the world that emerged after Versailles was really their world. Indeed, in their emphasis on ethnic nationality, it is, in Europe at least, even more their world today.

They had met only once before 1914, through the agency of the Irish Nationalist MP, T.P. O'Connor at the German spa town of Carlsbad in 1910, when Clemenceau was an ex-premier and Lloyd George at the Treasury. They offered very different recollections of it. Clemenceau believed that their conversation was very brief, and was notable only for showing Lloyd George's immense ignorance of international affairs. Lloyd George thought it had lasted much longer, and that Clemenceau rebutted at some length his own views which favoured an Anglo-German rapprochement, especially on naval matters. He had in 1908 made a notable visit to Germany to investigate its social welfare programmes, and had spoken to the press in favour of closer Anglo-German relations. Both agreed at least that the meeting was not a success.

Both were maverick politicians, both natural outsiders. Lloyd George, Welshman, Baptist, man of the people, at least operated within the broad limits of Liberal party politics until 1916; then his earlier penchant for coalitions, variously demonstrated in Wales in 1904 and in British politics generally in 1910 at the height of the Lords crisis, saw him become head of an all-party coalition, his own Liberals fatally divided. Clemenceau, who had actually been prime minister for three years in 1906–09, remained determinedly out of office during the First World War, until persuaded into the premiership in November 1917. In 1918, it could be said that the leaders of both Britain and France were prime ministers without a party.

Each had much regard for the other's country, free from those traditional animosities dating back to the reign of Louis XIV. Lloyd George grew up as an admirer of the French Revolution and of Napoleon, also an enthusiast for Victor Hugo's *Les Misérables*, an admirer of the French Riviera and especially of Nice, where the Promenade des Anglais offered ample opportunity for companionship. He had spoken in favour of good relations with Republican France even at the time of the Fashoda crisis in the Sudan in 1898, and warmly applauded the conclusion of the *Entente* in 1904. There was an interesting dualism in his complementary enthusiasm for Germany. The German Empire, industrially thriving, Protestant and the land of Bismarckian social reform, appealed to Lloyd George the New Liberal, the apostle of social welfare. His National Insurance Act of 1911 was heavily shaped by what he had seen in Germany in 1908, and his wider social and economic outlook was influenced by that obsessive Germanophile W.H. Dawson, who worked for him at the Board of Trade. Germany pushed Lloyd George in the direction of the creed of 'national efficiency'.

France, by contrast, appealed to Lloyd George the Old Liberal – democratic, republican with a unique revolutionary tradition, anti-aristocratic, anti-militarist, anti-clerical. As a child he was excited to hear of the Paris Commune of 1871 (with which Clemenceau had himself been entangled as mayor of Montmartre). He was particularly stirred by the passage of the disestablishment of the Church in France in late 1905, shortly before a general election in Britain in which Welsh Liberals would campaign for a similar disestablishment of the Church of England in Wales. As time went on, however, especially after his visit to Germany in 1908, this sympathy for France was challenged by his enthusiasm for Bismarckian social reform (a passion he shared with another social radical with whom he enjoyed a mutual admiration, Theodore Roosevelt, the prophet of the progressive New Nationalism in the United States). Germany, not France, was his main overseas inspiration thereafter, arguably for the rest of his life, two world wars notwithstanding.

Clemenceau, unlike Lloyd George, was a serious intellectual and lover of the fine arts, whose close friends included Claude Monet of whom he became a notable patron. He rescued the ageing Monet's career at the end of the war with his support for his great project of mural-sized water landscapes, the *Décoration des Nymphéas*, eventually placed in the Orangerie. He devoted part of his retirement to writing a work on the Greek orator Demosthenes. Like Léon Blum and François Mitterrand, he was a genuine intellectual in politics. He actually wrote a novel, *Les Plus Forts* – of which Maurice Barrès derisively observed that all Clemenceau needed to be a good novelist was to find something to say.

Unlike Lloyd George also, he had a serious interest in political ideas. He spent much time in England in the 1860s and acquired a good knowledge of the language: at Paris in 1919 he was the only world leader to understand both the languages of the conference. His approach to the Anglo-Saxon world came through its liberal theorists, notably John Stuart Mill. He also became an enthusiast for English versions of Social Darwinism and an admirer of the work of Herbert Spencer and his positivist followers. He spent some time in America during the Civil War – he would recall later his personal reactions to the assassination of Lincoln in 1865 – and married an American woman, though not happily. Later in his career, his English political and financial connections were used by political opponents to attack him – in the 1893 elections, he was pursued with ironic cries of 'Aoh, yes!'. He became a strong supporter of an Anglo-French alliance, and had vain discussions with the pro-German Joseph Chamberlain to this end. He strongly supported the *Entente* in 1904, despite his later breach with its main French architect, the Foreign Minister Théophile Delcassé. When prime minister, he tried hard to give military substance to the *Entente* during the aftermath of the Moroccan crisis, and was dismayed when the British Prime Minister Campbell-Bannerman, showed great reluctance to admit that Britain had accepted any continental commitment at all.

For all that, Lloyd George and Clemenceau shared in many ways common traditions and common values. Like Lloyd George after 1906, Clemenceau too had been a strong advocate of a positivist liberalism that gave a high priority to social reform. He wrote extensively on poverty and social inequality. He urged that the Third Republic should become a social republic and not narrowly political. While he was never a Socialist, his ideas had much influence on Socialist leaders like Jean Jaurès and the youthful Léon Blum. It was ironic that in 1906 Clemenceau, a man hitherto regarded as being on the further reaches of the left, became known as a fiercely anti-labour prime minister who used the army to put down strikes by syndicalist trade unionists. Lloyd George, by contrast, made his name not only as a social reformer but also as a patron of labour during his time as president of the Board of Trade in 1905–8 (as in his famous settlement of the national rail dispute in October 1907) and at the Treasury (witness his securing agreement on a miners' national wage in 1912). In December 1916, his good relationship with the TUC was a vital component of his capture of power as prime minister. Even in the class-war atmosphere in 1918–21, he retained close ties with union leaders, and created (in the language of the 1960s) a kind of 'beer and sandwiches' access to No. 10 which the TUC later regretted losing in the years of Baldwin and MacDonald.

Both Lloyd George and Clemenceau were supremely skilful and ruthless practitioners of politics. Both made ample use of the newspapers as political weapons. Lloyd George spent time on his relationships not only with journalists but also with friendly editors (A.G. Gardiner and Robert Donald for a time), and also with owners like Lord Riddell and later Lord Beaverbrook. He contemplated buying up *The Times* as a pro-government newspaper when Alfred Harmsworth, Lord Northcliffe, retired to die in 1922, and he subsequently became wealthy through the sale of United Newspapers in 1925. Clemenceau, by contrast, owned his own newspapers, notably *La Justice* in the 1890s and *L'Homme Libre* and *L'Homme Enchaîné* during the First World War, as platforms of a highly personal kind. Both leaders also were singly unfussy in the kind of allies they enlisted. Each was casual in money matters. Clemenceau's career was almost ended when he was tainted by the Panama bonds and bribes scandal in 1892–93; Lloyd George was close to political obliteration during the Marconi affair in 1912–13. The Lloyd George fund, accumulated in large measure through the venal sale of titles, became highly controversial after 1918. Each of them had one highly useful and highly dubious ally, the arms manufacturer Sir Basil Zaharoff, a French citizen of Armenian origin, who used his money to finance Clemenceau's newspaper enterprises in the 1890s and acted as an unofficial intermediary for Lloyd George in Eastern Europe and Asia Minor in 1917–20. He was widely claimed to have been responsible for the immensely pro-Turkish thrust of British politics in the lead-up to the Chanak crisis in October 1922. Some murmured that Zaharoff must have had a hold on both leaders. Certainly another similarity that both Lloyd George and Clemenceau could claim was of having complicated relationships with women. Clemenceau had

Mme Baldensperger as his *amitié amoureuse* in his last years; Lloyd George had Frances Stevenson as well as his wife, Dame Margaret, the two of them taking care of his political needs in Westminster and in Wales. Not for nothing was Lloyd George known as 'The Goat'. As for Clemenceau, 'The Tiger', we need only recall James Agate's perhaps apocryphal story of Clemenceau's remark when he spotted a pretty girl on his eightieth birthday – 'Oh, to be seventy again'.

On balance, there was more than enough similarity of outlook, ideology and style between Clemenceau the intellectual and Lloyd George the intuitive Celt to make for a good working relationship between the two during the war years and later. They were both socially minded, radical Liberals, strongly devoted to the Revolution and champions of Dreyfus in recent times. Both combined a vivid regard for their own national interests with enthusiasm for the *Entente* as each understood the idea. There is a touching scene recorded during a lull at the Paris peace negotiations when both Lloyd George and Clemenceau (with Woodrow Wilson joining it) recorded their deep devotion to the values and achievement of Abraham Lincoln. In Lloyd George's case (and he was later to deliver a powerful address on Lincoln at Springfield, Illinois in a lecture tour in 1923) he was, after all, the nearest that Europe could offer as a cottage-bred man who advanced from log cabin to president, or in the title of an early admiring biographer, trod the primrose path 'from Village Green to Downing Street'.

Lloyd George and Clemenceau, of course, became inextricably associated in the last twelve months of the First World War, after Clemenceau became premier in November 1917. It was a critical time, with the French army still recovering from the prolonged ordeal of Verdun and the dangerous mutinies of 1917, and the British reeling after the massive losses at Passchendaele in August–September 1917. From the start, major differences emerged. Lloyd George was always an Easterner, the advocate of a more peripheral strategy, notably in the Balkans and in the war with the Turks. Clemenceau was always the supreme Westerner, anxious for the maximum of force to be brought to bear on the Western Front, along France's eastern frontier, to protect the territorial base. He found the British slow to take the point; Lloyd George countered by emphasising the supreme importance of the naval side of the war for food and raw materials, where Britain's commitment was supreme and where he himself had pushed on with the convoy system to neutralise the threat of the U-Boats. This aspect, he felt, Clemenceau underestimated.

Along with this, Clemenceau wanted the British under Haig's command to take over more of the line. Britain, he argued, had only 487 fighting units, as against France's 662, a statistic which Lloyd George did not dispute. Lloyd George, by contrast, was inclined to hold back British troops until the Americans could throw in a decisive force, probably not before the later summer of 1918. Lloyd George, later accused in the Maurice debate of 9 May of deliberately holding back British reserves in the aftermath of Passchendaele, complained that he would have to incorporate 'nigger' soldiers in his army. Clemenceau's riposte was that the French army had no problem with 'niggers': they had enlisted Moroccan and other Africans, and would take 'Ethiopians' if necessary. A related issue was Clemenceau's demand that the British played their full part in building up a strategic reserve on the Western Front. Lloyd George insisted on the prior needs of the Turkish campaign in Palestine, which would probably necessitate the withdrawal of British divisions from France.

Despite these tensions, relations between the two prime ministers appear to have steadily improved, especially in their close collaboration during the major German offensive in the Amiens sector in late March and early April 1918. In any case, Lloyd George and Clemenceau had one fairly constant enemy in their sights at this time – namely the British generals. Clemenceau rejoiced when Lloyd George succeeded in removing General 'Wully' Robertson as chief of the Imperial General Staff in February 1918, in a tense political crisis which almost cost him the premiership. After a conference at Beauvais in early April, the two prime ministers worked together in implementing the old objective of unity of command. Foch assumed titular authority over the Allied forces on the Western Front, Haig accepting the situation with some grace. According to Lloyd George's hugely exaggerated account, the main stumbling block here was not the British commander-in-chief but rather the old free-thinker Clemenceau's distaste for Foch's devout Catholicism. Certainly Clemenceau and Foch had a tense long-term relationship, but the roots were strictly secular. The later stages of the war saw the Anglo-French partnership probably working more effectively than at any other time. The lead-up to a post-war peace conference in the autumn of 1918 was marked by agreement on many key issues, other than the settlement with the Turks. In the end, a brisk realism ensured that the future of the Ottoman empire was partially resolved on the basis of the French being given Syria and the British the ominous legacy of Mesopotamia, later Iraq. Palestine became a British mandate while France assumed military control of Cilicia.

From Keynes onwards, observers of the Paris peace negotiations have focussed on the *Sturm und Drang* of conflicts between Clemenceau and Lloyd George on their approach towards the defeated Germans. Certainly there was much to record. Lloyd George, indeed, became deeply concerned at the way in which Clemenceau's national prejudices and insistence of curbs on a post-war Germany were taking over the entire agenda. The outcome of his anxiety was the celebrated Fontainebleau Memorandum, prepared with Lloyd George's aides and colleagues in the woods near that town, notably Philip Kerr and General Smuts of South Africa, in mid-March 1919. It was very much the personal statement of the British prime minister.

The Memorandum was the first formal document arguing the case for the appeasement of the defeated Germans. It had two main themes. The major one in the Fontainebleau document was a call for moderation in the frontier arrangements to try to ensure that large swathes of German people were not placed under foreign occupation. Lloyd George particularly mentioned the Saarland, Danzig, Upper Silesia and above all the Polish Corridor that should not be placed under alien rule. There should be 'no more Alsace-Lorraines'. Later in the conference negotiations, he showed his alarm at placing the Sudeten Germans under the governance of the newly created hybrid state of Czechoslovakia. The Czechs he never trusted, especially their leading statesman, 'that swine Benes' for whom Lloyd George was to show scant sympathy during the time of Munich in 1938. Here, Lloyd George had only limited success though he did achieve the triumph of forcing through a local plebiscite in Upper Silesia which in 1921 voted to stay in Germany.

The other main pivot of the Memorandum, though taken up far more prominently later on in the Paris negotiations, was the demand for German post-war reparations to be kept flexible so that Europe's economic recovery would not be held back by Germany's being undermined as a great manufacturing and trading nation. Here, Lloyd George was erratic. He later was to add widows' and orphans' pensions to the possible bill, which almost doubled it. But in the end he succeeded in pushing the reparations issue into the long grass. It was handed over to a Reparations Commission for long-term deliberation which ensured that most of the money would never be paid. The blame fell largely not on the British prime minister but on the British representatives, Lords Cunliffe and Sumner. Keynes could never fathom Lloyd George's strategy here – but, then, Keynes was not a politician!

Clemenceau, naturally, was deeply unsympathetic to the Fontainebleau *démarche*. He noted cynically that it dealt only with issues worrying to France. On issues that concerned Britain, such as freedom of the seas, it was silent. He and Lloyd George had inevitably many fierce arguments on the Memorandum's themes, notably the reparations issue. The two prime ministers also diverged sharply on the Middle East, where France tended to be pro-Turk whereas Lloyd George was as an old Gladstonian Liberal, passionately, even fanatically pro-Greek and a supporter of the Greek Prime Minister Venizelos. At one time, reportedly, the two premiers seemed likely to come to blows. Even though Clemenceau was by now almost seventy-eight, he was still combative and combustible.

And yet the Paris Peace Conference is far from only being a story of Anglo-French (or Gallo-French) conflict. In particular, Lloyd George, far more clearly than Wilson, recognised the need for long-term protection of French territorial security. He saw the force of Clemenceau's demand for a British 'continental commitment' and actually offered a serious proposal of a British military guarantee against future German aggression. He promised that his country would 'place all her forces at [France's] disposal'. He even threw in the exciting vision of a Channel Tunnel as part of this – the first time this idea ever emerged in an international conference. In the end, Lloyd George backed down, citing, correctly, the failure of the Americans to offer any kind of assistance themselves – indeed by this stage the USA was lurching fast into parochial hemispheric isolationism. But after the build-up, Clemenceau felt justifiably angry and let down.

Yet Lloyd George was serious about this issue, as no British prime minister had been since the end of the Napoleonic Wars – the Peninsular War against Napoleon had been the last 'continental commitment' to engage a British government. At the conference in Cannes in January 1922 he again proposed a long-term British treaty of guarantee to the current French Premier Aristide Briand, with whom he had struck up a good relationship, better than with Clemenceau. It would be ratified with other major proposals at a forthcoming international conference in Genoa in April. But, after the famous and much-derided game between Lloyd George and Briand on the seaside golf course at Cannes, Briand's government was summarily overthrown, and his successor Raymond Poincaré, a stern man of Lorraine and bitterly anti-German, refused all Lloyd George's overtures. But the coming together of Lloyd George and Clemenceau did show that the Welshman was perhaps the one international leader of the time who seriously tried to balance charity towards the defeated Germans with security for the victorious French.

After the signing of the treaty in the Hall of Mirrors at Versailles, Clemenceau had a far shorter political shelf life than Lloyd George. He was defeated for the presidency by no less than his old duelling adversary, Deschanel. He lived on for a further ten years, writing his war memoirs, and also significant books on Monet and on Demosthenes. He visited the House of Commons in June 1921, while receiving an honorary degree from Oxford University. Here he met Lloyd George once again, rather briefly. Direct as ever, Clemenceau told the British Premier, 'Dès le lendemain de l'Armistice, je vous ai trouvé l'ennemi de la France'. To which Lloyd George cheerfully replied, 'Eh bien, n'est-ce pas notre politique traditionnelle?'. Their last meeting was not a success any more than their first had been in 1910. Clemenceau wanted a firm adherence to the letter of the peace terms, not a revision of them. He rejoiced at the news of Lloyd George's downfall in October 1922. In his extreme old age, he loved to walk in the woods of his native Vendée. He is supposed to have said that one of their charms was he would never encounter Lloyd George there – only squirrels.

Lloyd George remained the dominant figure in world politics for almost another three years. He worked hard for international reconciliation through revision of the treaties. Keynes now changed his opinions radically and applauded Lloyd George's endeavours. Lloyd George sought peace with Germany, a deferring and scaling down of reparations payments. He withdrew all British troops from Russia. He still focussed on keeping the *Entente* with France alive, in partnership with Briand, until his fall from power. But in the end, French nationalism as voiced by Poincaré, American hemispheric isolationism, Russian commitment to world revolution and German unreliability shown by their Treaty of Rapallo with the Russians, were all too much for him. The Genoa Conference dragged on inconclusively. A provocative British challenge to the Turks in the Middle East then threatened war in the Chanak Crisis. Poincaré shouted at Curzon, the British foreign secretary, at their meeting in Paris. Curzon retaliated by bursting into tears. The dominant Conservative element in the coalition government turned against Lloyd George. Bonar Law wrote that Britain could not alone act as 'policeman of the world'. Appeasement was growing apace, Baldwin denounced the prime minister as 'a dynamic force', Lloyd George was overthrown on 19 October 1922 by a Tory revolt, and he never returned to office.

In the remainder of his career, down to his death in March 1945, he was constantly critical of France for its intransigence as he saw it. His wish to accommodate Germany through a pact of mutual guarantee reached a disastrous level when he had a friendly visit to Hitler in Berchtesgaden in 1936. Photographs of their meeting were as disastrous as those of Pétain and Hitler at Montoire in 1940. Although Lloyd George assisted mightily in the fall of Neville Chamberlain in 1940, he continued to advocate a possible negotiated peace with Germany during the war. Churchill in 1941 savagely compared him with Pétain, pleading for peace in the last days of the Reynaud government. At the end, Lloyd George was indeed being compared with the French – but the wrong French, the militaristic, neo-fascist French of Vichy, not the democrats and Jacobins of the Revolution of 1789. There was a final *démarche* on 1 January 1945. Wales's great commoner ended up an earl.

In the aftermath, it was Clemenceau's reputation which was to prove the stronger. Lloyd George was tarred for ever by his post-war coalition government of 1918–22 with the Tories. His Liberal Party was divided and defeated for ever, and never again returned to power. Not until his papers were opened up to historians at the Beaverbrook Library, run by A.J.P. Taylor in 1967, did a revision of his reputation take place, in which the present writer took some part. Clemenceau, by contrast, emerged as the one acknowledged hero of recent French history prior to de Gaulle, the epitome of Republican France. Only in late 2005 has money been found for Lloyd George's statue in Parliament Square in London, and it is hoped that in 2008 the great man will have his monument installed there, near the House of Commons he dominated for so long, close to that of Churchill, Britain's other great war leader. Just as Churchill's statue was targeted by anti-capitalist demonstrators three years ago, it is nice to think that Lloyd George's statue may in future attract the interest of the pheasant-shooting branches of the Countryside Alliance, the voice of the landlords he despised.

By contrast, Clemenceau stands tall on the Champs-Elysées as the indisputable 'Père la Victoire', dressed as in 1917 in his cape and high boots and brandishing a cane. Pierre Nora's *Lieux de Mémoire* notes that his statue is the only one in Paris that most Parisians may be expected to know, along with that of Joan of Arc in Place des Pyramides. That is Clemenceau in French legend and memory. David Lloyd George, for all his extraordinary achievements and his efforts in his war memoirs (brilliant but less effective than Churchill's in self-glorification), is recalled as a man who promised a land fit for heroes and failed to deliver. In Britain's public memory, the Second World War, Churchill's war, is a symbol of the national identity, Britain fighting alone in our finest hour. The first war, Lloyd George's, is remembered for senseless slaughter, 'lions led by donkeys'. The Cenotaph is non-triumphalist, Armistice Day is an ambiguous Celebration of unknown heroes, pain, pride and shame intermingled. To adopt the title of Joan Littlewood's 1960s satire, 'Oh! What a lovely war'.

For all that, Lloyd George and Clemenceau enjoyed a great, if temporary, partnership. They had different views of the international interest and their personal relationship was never easy. But they appreciated each other's qualities. Lloyd George's vivid sketch of Clemenceau in his war memoirs praised him as the greatest statesman of his day, courageous and strong. He told his newspaper proprietor friend, George Riddell of the *News of the World*, that Clemenceau was 'a wonderful old man' full of humour. Clemenceau, while finding Lloyd George baffling as an intuitive, mercurial Welshman, saw him nevertheless as capable of rising, as few others could, 'à la hauteur des grands événements'. Theirs was the most important Franco-British partnership, comparable with that of Churchill and Roosevelt in 1941–45 and far better than that between Churchill and de Gaulle in the Second World War. Together, they provided the historic high noon of Britain's most enduring special relationship – the *Entente Cordiale*.

For further reading

Agulhon, Maurice. 'Paris', in Pierre Nora (ed.), *Realms of Memory III* (New York: Columbia University Press, 1998).

Agulhon, Maurice. 'Symbols', *ibid.*

Clemenceau, Georges. *Grandeurs et misères d'une victoire* (Paris: Librairie Plon, 1930).

Duroselle, Jean-Baptiste. *Clemenceau* (Paris: Fayard, 1988).

George, David Lloyd. *War Memoirs*, 2 vols, new edn (London: Odhams, 1938).

George, David Lloyd. *The Truth about the Peace Treaties*, 2 vols (London: Gollancz, 1938).

Keynes, J.M. *Essays in Biography*, new edn (London: Hart-Davis, 1951).

Lentin, A. *Lloyd George and the Lost Peace* (Basingstoke: Palgrave, 2001).

Macmillan, Margaret. *Peacemakers* (London: John Murray, 2001).

Morgan, Kenneth O. *Lloyd George* (London: Weidenfeld & Nicolson, 1974).

Morgan, Kenneth O. *Consensus and Disunity* (Oxford: University Press, 1979).

Morgan, Kenneth O. *Rebirth of a Nation: Wales 1880–1980*, new edn (Oxford: University Press, 1982).

Watson, D.R. *Clemenceau* (London: Eyre Methuen, 1974).

3
Behind the façade of the *Entente Cordiale* after the Great War

Robert Boyce
London School of Economics

The relationship between Britain and France after the Great War has been described not unfairly as a *mésentente cordiale*.[1] In the early 1920s the two powers diverged radically over the basis of European security and the place of Germany in the post-war world order. In the later 1920s the relationship was further strained by differences over commercial policy, the operation of the gold standard, war debts, disarmament and a host of other issues. Two features of the bilateral relationship stand out. One is the extraordinary number of issues on which the two countries differed. The other is the one-sidedness of the anger this caused. In France, there was evidence of impatience, frustration, even cynicism at Britain's aloofness from the Continent and its efforts to see Germany freed from the constraints of the Treaty of Versailles. After the Treaty was signed and the promised Anglo-American guarantee to France failed to materialise, several Paris cabaret acts caricatured David Lloyd George, the British prime minister, as a trickster or conman. The acts attracted the notice of the French ambassador in London who demanded the intervention of the police on account of their potential damage to relations with Britain.[2] Subsequently, efforts by Raymond Poincaré, the French premier, to hold Britain to its Treaty commitments encouraged the impression of hostility. Yet nowhere in the French diplomatic record or national press in the 1920s can one find evidence of sustained hostility towards Britain. On the contrary, with the exception of a few individuals on the extreme left or right of the political spectrum, French politicians, statesmen and publicists sought only to revive the *Entente Cordiale* and were disappointed when their efforts proved unavailing. The contrast with British attitudes towards France could not have been more marked. Almost immediately after the armistice, British leaders substituted France for Germany as their chief target of loathing. So intense was their hostility that specific sources of disagreement, British calculations of balance of power or Britain's war weariness come nowhere near to explaining it. Indeed, the specific sources of disagreement seem better understood as symptoms of a more fundamental malaise.

One vivid illustration of this claim appears in *Goodbye to All That*, the memoirs of Robert Graves, the poet and novelist, published in 1929. Graves, just out of public school, joined the British army in the summer of 1914 and spent the next two years as a junior officer on the Western Front before being invalided out in 1917. He describes the horrors of the front, the killing techniques of German raiding parties and their preference for bowie-knives, the frequent occasions when prisoners on both sides were killed by their captors, the instance where German soldiers raised a white flag only to open fire on the British troops who approached to take their surrender. He includes a few unflattering descriptions of French civilians in Béthune and elsewhere in the British sector, which he presents as venal and coldly indifferent to the sacrifices that British soldiers were making to defend them from the enemy. But he also mentions fondly the occasions when he played with children in the villages were he was billeted.[3] And like most British officers, he had scarcely any contact with the French army. Demobilised in 1919 and still only 23 years old, he went up to Oxford to study English literature. There he found

> Anti-French feeling among most ex-soldiers amounted almost to an obsession. [His contemporary and fellow poet] Edmund [Blunden], shaking with nerves, used to say at this time: "No more wars for me at any price! Except against the French. If there's ever a war with them, I'll go like a shot". Pro-German feeling had been increasing. With the war over and the German armies beaten, we could give the German soldier credit for being the most efficient fighting-man in Europe. . . . Some undergraduates even insisted that we had been fighting on the wrong side: our natural enemies were the French.[4]

Paul Fussell warns us that Graves's account of his war experience takes considerable liberties with the evidence.[5] But there is little reason to doubt his reference to post-war Oxford and Edmund Blunden's reaction to the conflict. Even while he was fighting the Germans, it seems, Blunden took the view that 'the War was a great crime'.[6] Siegfried Sassoon, another poet and veteran of the Western Front who came to regard the war as a form of madness, confirms that Blunden reacted to it by becoming apologetic towards Germany and that until the very eve of the Second World War he remained 'strongly imbued with the German point of view, and seems unable to realise the meaning of Nazi aims and methods'.[7] Since at the same time as Graves and Blunden were in Oxford, British statesmen regularly stood alongside French colleagues at commemorative ceremonies to honour their fallen soldiers, and British and French army units jointly occupied parts of the Ruhr, the explanation for this hostility must be sought at a deeper level of collective memory or emotion. This paper offers one such explanation which, if speculative, at least has the merit of being consistent with British behaviour throughout the post-war period.

In August 1914, Britain went to war against the Central Powers. Its reason for doing so was straightforward enough. As Sir Eyre Crowe, the assistant secretary of the Foreign Office, reminded ministers in 1907, the cardinal principle of British foreign policy had long been that no foreign power should be allowed to dominate the North Sea and Channel ports. He added that whereas in previous times Britain had had the leisure to decide when and where to respond to such a threat, the mobility of modern armies meant that it could no longer afford to wait until the threat arose, but must act immediately if a major power threatened to seize the ports.[8] Leading members of the Campbell-Bannerman and Asquith governments accepted this principle. Thus, when Germany spurned Britain's approaches and threatened to annihilate Belgium and France, Britain entered commitments not far short of an alliance with France and eventually entered the war.

Yet if the strategic logic of Britain's involvement is clear enough, the same can hardly be said of the language used by contemporary British observers to describe the international scene. The term nation was commonly used in public discourse. But the terms people and race were also frequently employed, often interchangeably with nation. Thus, A.F. Whyte, MP, RNVR, speaking to an audience at King's College London in July 1916 on the moral basis of the war, referred to the 'oppressed races' of Europe, but also to the 'liberation of nationalities', to Austria-Hungary as an empire of 'a dozen races', 'the Southern Slav race' and 'the Serbo-Croat race', and to 'the Slavic nationalities' and the 'ethnical unit' of Southern Slavs.[9] Ernest Barker, professor of politics at King's College, in a public lecture after the war, expressed regret that racial categories, so 'greatly in vogue to-day', should be applied in such an unscientific way. 'A culture or civilization', he affirmed, 'is something distinct both from race and from language', and nations were commonly 'a blend of races'. Yet even while insisting that 'race is not destiny', he accepted that at one remove it played a vital part in shaping destiny. Thus, 'race is a material substratum or stuff which has to be shaped by the mind; and the mental shaping is a greater thing than that which has to be shaped. But every artificer and craftsman must know the qualities of the material on which he works'. Accordingly, it was 'of practical importance, and a matter of civic duty to understand the racial basis of national life . . . and . . . it may also be no less important, and no less a matter of duty, to control that composition by deliberate policy'. To illustrate his point, he added, 'We do not know why empires fall and states decay; but we can at any rate conjecture, with no little justice, that a disturbance of the racial composition of the effective core of the Roman Empire was one great cause of its fall'.[10]

The equation of nation with race, while far from new even in the nineteenth century, appears to have reached its zenith in Britain in the years surrounding the First World War, owing in part to the recent scramble for overseas empire. But as Whyte's and Barker's lectures illustrate, British observers did not apply racial categories only or even mainly to the non-white parts of the world. They also applied them to America and Europe. In Europe they identified, albeit in a loose and frequently inconsistent way, three dominant white races. These were the Anglo-Saxons, the Latins and the Slavs, and as with all such categorisation its proponents acknowledged, implicitly if not explicitly, a hierarchy of value. In 1914, numerous voices were raised in dismay at the idea that Britain, an Anglo-Saxon country, should go to war with its Germanic cousin, and especially in alliance with its traditional Latin and Slavic enemies. Thus at the outbreak of war a group of writers and academics, including J.A. Hobson, J.L. Hammond, G.M. Trevelyan, Graham Wallas and Gilbert Murray, appealed for British neutrality rather than siding with 'only partly civilised' Russia against Germany, 'highly civilised . . . with a culture that had contributed enormously in the past to Western civilisation' and 'racially allied' to Britain.[11] In September, T.B. Strong, the vice-chancellor of Oxford, expressed regret that Britain should find itself at war against Germany, 'the one power in Europe with which we have the closest affinity'.[12]

For the majority in Britain, to be sure, Germany's decision to expand its navy had posed a serious challenge, and war seemed necessary once Germany launched its offensive in the West. But for those who supported the war as well as those who opposed it the justification was frequently framed in racial terms. Thus William Beveridge, the administrator and social reformer, wrote on 3 August, 'The whole thing is an incredible nightmare come true. I can't of course . . . help feeling relieved that apparently we are to join in (because it seems necessary and in a sense our duty) but it's all against the grain with me to go in against the Germans with French and Russians'.[13] Thus Sir Nevile Henderson, British ambassador to Germany from 1937 to September 1939, recalled that 'in the [Great] war it was the Prussians rather than the Germans whom we regarded as our real enemies and . . . not the Germans as a race'. He had nothing but respect for 'the great qualities of order and efficiency, probity and kindness of the purer German of Northwest, West and South Germany, with whom an Englishman on his travels abroad finds himself in such natural sympathy'. The trouble arose from the Prussians, whose character was corrupted by a 'considerable admixture of Slav blood', and who dominated the country through the emperor and military high command. '[T]he Prussians, of whom even Goethe spoke as barbarians, are a distinctive European type, which has imposed itself and its characteristics upon the rest of Germany.'[14] It followed that once the Prussians were removed from power, there would be no basis for further Anglo-German enmity. The 'two-Germany' thesis remained very common in Britain.[15] Among many others who shared this view was J.L. Garvin, editor of *The Observer*, who repeated during the period of the Paris Peace Conference that only 'rabid vengeance confounds the whole German people with its former militarist-political system and with the crimes of that system'. Significantly in his weekly appeals for generosity to be shown the 'German race', he never mentioned the plight of other 'races' whose fate was being settled at the Conference.[16]

British diplomacy at the Paris Peace Conference conformed closely to these prejudices and suspicions. Britain had already secured control of the German navy as well as most of its merchant marine, its colonies and leased territories in China, its coaling and telegraph stations, its submarine cables and other overseas assets. Thus the British Empire was safeguarded, and for the sake of their taxpayers British statesmen entered a demand for huge reparation payments. Largely to appease Woodrow Wilson, the American president, they also agreed to place the proposal for a League of Nations at the top of the Peace Conference agenda. But once agreement was reached on the League and discussion turned to the German question, they quickly dug in their heels. They refused to listen to Marshal Foch's warning that the security of Eastern and Western Europe was indivisible and that Germany must be permanently weakened by the removal of the Rhineland from Berlin's direct control. They were scarcely more enthusiastic about piecemeal measures for addressing French security, such as the transfer of Luxembourg and the Saar to French control and military occupation of the Rhineland, and they vigorously resisted concessions to Poland that placed Germans under Slavic rule. Instead, they favoured the minimum of penalties or restraints on Germany, now that the Kaiser and his Prussian circle had been removed.

Lloyd George, who led the British delegation, took as his closest adviser Jan Smuts, the South African foreign minister, who alone of Dominion statesmen had occupied a seat in the Imperial War Cabinet. Smuts's best-known contribution to the peace was a memorandum on the League of Nations proposal, which he circulated to the British delegation in December 1918, encouraging their support. Throughout the Paris Peace Conference he seemed the embodiment of enlightened liberalism, advocating reconciliation between the victor powers and Germany for the sake of Europe and humanity itself. His appeal for reconciliation reflected the formative experience of his life when, having led the Boers in the war against the British, he secured a peace settlement that enabled the Dutch and British settlers to live amicably under the British crown. For narrow political reasons he was anxious to see Germany treated generously, for the war had created tension between Boers and British in South Africa, and a harsh peace would compromise his own authority. In advocating South Africa's participation he had hoped to hasten the war's end. He saw it as a racial struggle in which the Germans had unwisely taken on not only Latin and Slav powers but also their British cousins. But the war had gone on far longer than he anticipated, and the Peace Conference threatened to end in the elevation of Latin and Slav interests over those of the German people. To him the Poles were a Kaffir – or black – nation.[17] The Russians similarly were unsuited to western democracy and perhaps better off under Bolshevik control.[18] It worried him that even before the Conference began the Habsburg Empire had broken up, leaving the Austro-Germans shipwrecked in a Slavic sea. Initially he was more hopeful that Germany would survive defeat: as he put it, 'that the great racial homogeneity and the education and political discipline of Germany will in the end keep her from disintegration'.[19] But when delegates agreed to remove Danzig from German control and accord Poland large swathes of German territory, he importuned Lloyd George to reject 'this monstrous instrument', as he described the draft treaty in a letter to a like-minded opponent, John Maynard Keynes.[20]

Lloyd George, while obliged to disregard Smuts's more radical advice, nevertheless shared his general point of view. He strenuously opposed a territorial settlement that favoured Poland at Germany's expense, although French delegates believed it was necessary to Poland's long-term survival. When delegates of the leading powers failed to agree on its post-war frontiers, they formed a commission of experts to devise a solution. But when the commission, including the British member, agreed upon a new frontier incorporating German territory into Poland, Lloyd George rejected their work and insisted upon reopening negotiations.[21] Perhaps he was wise to do so, since German resentment at Polish control over former German lands and people became a running sore throughout the inter-war years. But the tendency of British statesmen to favour Germany at Poland's expense, indeed to regard the whole of the Slavic world as beyond the pale of civilised society, was a common feature of the time. James Headlam-Morley, a leading member of the Foreign Office Intelligence Bureau during the war and member of the British delegation at Paris, became incensed at French insistence upon reducing German territory in the East – 'they bargain like Jews and generally are Jews', he wrote of the French delegation – and described their support for a strong Poland as 'a disastrous policy'.[22] Another Foreign Office official warned that the proposal to place the largely German town of Danzig under Polish control 'would be like handing over a Scottish town to its Irish population'.[23] So common was this bias that a British diplomat in Warsaw protested to London. His colleagues, he complained, should not be so ready to assume that Germany was the sole bearer of civilisation in this region or to ignore the cultural attainments of the Slavic people.[24] His protest was evidently ignored.

Lloyd George's conflict with Clemenceau over Poland might have been less acute had he shown greater recognition of France's security requirements. Instead, he treated France as the chief obstacle to peace and indirectly as the cause of the war. Late in March 1919 he retreated with seven advisers to Fontainebleau for a weekend of reflection on the direction the negotiations were taking. The outcome of their deliberations was a memorandum that emphasised the importance of respecting the national principle and the desirability of holding out for peace terms acceptable to victors and vanquished alike. The document has been cited by many historians as evidence of the reasonableness and far-sightedness of British policy. One historian describes it as 'a blueprint, wise and far-sighted';[25] another as 'a notable memorandum . . . an eloquent demand for moderation; perhaps the first positive blow struck for appeasement in the post-war period'.[26] Generally overlooked, however, is the historical analogy that Lloyd George used to justify his position. According to the memorandum:

> France itself has demonstrated that those who say you can make Germany so feeble that she will never be able to hit back are utterly wrong. Year by year [after its defeat by Prussia in 1870] France became numerically weaker in comparison with her victorious neighbour, but in reality she became ever more powerful. She kept watch on Europe; she made alliance with those whom Germany had wronged or menaced; she never ceased to warn the world of its danger and ultimately she was able to secure the overthrow of the far mightier power which had trampled so brutally upon her. You may strip Germany of her colonies, reduce her armaments [armies] to a mere police force and her navy to that of a fifth rate power; all the same in the end if she feels that she has been unjustly treated in the peace of 1919 she will find means of exacting retribution from her conquerors.[27]

The warning in the last sentence was perhaps prescient, but the history itself was remarkably self-serving. In the first place, the claim that France had grown stronger after 1870 and eventually prevailed over Germany ignored the fact that France had made no effort to regain Alsace-Lorraine for forty years, and had only done so in a war brought on largely by Germany itself. There seems little reason to think that France would ever have regained its lost provinces had Germany not made the mistake of going to war in 1914. In fact, Lloyd George was baldly suggesting that the Great War had been a war of revenge instigated by France. Perhaps this was merely an unfortunate use of language, and perhaps he meant simply that where states dispute territory there is bound to be conflict. But Lloyd George was to repeat the claim that French *revanchisme* over Alsace-Lorraine caused the war many times in the next few years without correction from colleagues.[28] Placed in context, there are compelling grounds for thinking his words were deliberate.

The Fontainebleau memorandum was revealing in other ways as well. The suggestion that France was now playing a dangerous game in its oppression of Germany hardly squared with the evidence adduced to support it. In the first place, Germany's territorial losses in Europe, now blamed on France, were virtually unavoidable if justice was to be done to the nations surrounding Germany and to the principle of national self-determination that formed the centrepiece of Wilson's Fourteen Points. Second, it was Britain, rather than France, that had insisted upon stripping Germany of its colonies and reducing its navy to that of a fifth-rate power, and Britain that was chiefly responsible for inflating reparation demands to an unrealistic level. If the Fontainebleau memorandum revealed anything it was the tendency of British observers to view the recent war as a quarrel among the continental powers, and to regard Britain itself as the arbiter, standing outside the ring rather than bearing its share of responsibility as one of the competitors for empire and markets. Racial bias was also present. Whereas the Germans were characterised as 'one of the most vigorous and powerful races of the world', the Latins and Slavs were represented essentially as troublemakers who could hope for security only once German 'rights' were satisfied.[29]

Most historians of inter-war Britain accept that calculations of balance of power prompted its statesmen to shift their attention from Germany to France after the war. Certainly, there is no shortage of realist language in the Cabinet record and elsewhere in official archives. But the assumptions that underlay British calculations of balance of power are altogether another matter. The lack of 'realism', or in laymen's language rational thinking, becomes clear in Cabinet deliberations on the proposal for a Channel tunnel and its decision to build up the Royal Air Force (RAF) to meet a possible attack from across the Channel.

Proposals for a Channel tunnel had been regularly debated since the 1880s. Merchants on both sides of the Channel favoured the construction of a tunnel. At the official level, France raised no objections, and in Britain something like a hundred members of Parliament supported the idea. But the British Admiralty and War Office adamantly refused to accept the risk that a tunnel seemed to present to Britain's security, so construction was blocked.[30] Lloyd George revived the proposal at the Paris Peace Conference when, without consulting other members of the British delegation, he promised the construction of a tunnel along with the British guarantee to France against an unprovoked attack from Germany. The proposal became the subject of debate in the Cabinet and Parliament in 1920.

In light of the experience of the recent war, when congestion in the Channel ports seriously delayed the movement of men and goods and tied up a large amount of shipping that could have been profitably deployed elsewhere, the army and the navy cautiously favoured construction of a tunnel. Not so, however, ministers and senior Foreign Office officials. Arthur Balfour, the chairman of the Committee of Imperial Defence (CID) and former prime minister, offered a commonsense objection: that Britain might come to rely upon the tunnel and hence become vulnerable to the sabotage of this lifeline.[31] Lord Curzon, the foreign secretary, warned more pointedly of the dangers emanating from France. In his opinion, the British and the French were two different people who could never be expected to understand one another or bury their differences. While for the time being their relations were good, this could not be expected to last, since the French were an inherently self-interested, short-sighted, aggressive people:

> It must be remembered that until a century ago France was England's historic and natural enemy, and that real friendship between the inhabitants of the two countries has always been very difficult owing to differences of language, mentality and national

> character. These differences are not likely to decrease. The slightest incident may arouse the resentment or jealousy of the French and fan the latent embers of suspicion into a flame. [. . .]
> Nothing can alter the fundamental fact that we are not liked in France, and never will be, except for the advantages which the French people may be able to extract from us.
> These considerations point conclusively to the imprudence, and even danger, of increasing at enormous cost the facilities of communication with France by means of a tunnel under the Channel which may have to be destroyed at any moment as a military measure to secure the safety of this country in the event of France assuming a hostile and aggressive attitude. [. . .] The Foreign Office conclusion is that our relations with France never have been, are not, and probably never will be, sufficiently stable and friendly to justify the construction of a Channel tunnel, and the loss of the security which our insular position . . . continues to bestow.[32]

Lord Curzon, it is fair to say, was given to overstatement and acute sensitivity to imagined slights by French officials. But Lord Hardinge, the permanent under-secretary of the Foreign Office, was equally opposed to the construction of a Channel tunnel and for the same reason. Appearing before a Cabinet committee on the proposal, he was queried by a minister who suggested that the age of flight had increased the risk of sudden invasion, making fear of invasion through the tunnel exaggerated. Hardinge replied that air flight was precisely what made a tunnel so dangerous. With aircraft, an enemy could swiftly land troops and seize the British end of the tunnel, thus opening the way to sudden invasion. Such a claim begged at least two large questions: first, how an enemy power could without detection concentrate a sufficiently large military force near the Continental entrance to the tunnel to be able to exploit its seizure; and second, whether such a threat could plausibly arise except as the culmination of a major crisis, when security precautions would naturally be taken. Clearly the enemy he had in mind was France, since only France could concentrate an invasion force near the Continental entry to the tunnel without alerting British observers. Indeed, he made no secret of his belief that France remained Britain's hereditary enemy and a permanent threat to its security. The very idea that France threatened Britain then or at any time in the foreseeable future beggared belief. As head of the Foreign Office, Hardinge should have known better than anyone that scarcely a Frenchman in a position of authority was not fixated by the menace of a resurgent Germany just across the Rhine, and looked to Britain for help. Hardinge's warning added another nail in the coffin for the tunnel proposal, which as it happened had already been sealed by the Treasury and the military chiefs of staff.[33]

For similar reasons, the Cabinet the following year called for a review of Britain's defences against sudden aerial attack from France. A CID sub-committee on the Continental Air Menace, as it was called, was formed in the summer of 1922. In August the government approved plans for a metropolitan air force of 500 aircraft. And in March 1923, after the breakdown of Lloyd George's coalition government, the Conservative government of Andrew Bonar Law instituted a new committee to review national and imperial defence, largely out of fear that existing defences against France were inadequate.[34]

The impetus for a larger air force derived partly from inter-service rivalry and the ambitions of Air Marshal Sir Hugh Trenchard to strengthen the RAF. He and other partisans of a larger air force naturally made the most of the fact that France continued to build bombers, especially as some military strategists currently claimed that the next war would be won by air strikes alone. But the suggestion that Britain must prepare for a possible French air attack verged on the absurd. Lord Derby, the secretary of state for War and former ambassador to France, pointed out to the Committee of Imperial Defence that so long as France faced a larger, potentially menacing German threat across the Rhine, it was hardly likely to attack the one ally capable of ensuring its survival.[35] In any case, France had already savagely reduced spending on aircraft production, making it only a matter of time before its current air force would become obsolete.[36] Lord Balfour nonetheless persisted in arguing the worst-case scenario:

> He [agreed] with Lord Derby that . . . the possibility of France attacking this country was decidedly remote, but he was doubtful if we possessed sufficient confidence in the French nation, who were at present in a somewhat hysterical condition, which would enable us to say, "We throw down our weapons; you can stab us in the back if you wish, but we are certain that you will not". He

did not consider that the country could accept such a position of defencelessness.[37]

In fact, of course, Britain was far from defenceless. Without a single warplane, the Royal Navy could retaliate against a French air attack by bombarding vulnerable coastal towns such as Dunkirk, Calais, Boulogne, Le Havre, Cherbourg and Brest. It made no sense to prepare for every possible threat, without regard in each case to intentions and exposure to counter-attack, since otherwise preparations would have to be made against even small powers. Given their common strategic interests, British statesmen would have been wiser to regard a strong French air force as grounds for *reducing* defence spending rather than increasing it. But such was the Francophobia in British political circles that most ministers sided with Balfour. Borrowing the principle applied to the navy of a one power standard while allowing for the need for economies, they agreed to build a Home Defence Force of 52 squadrons, comprising 'in the first instance' 394 bombers and 204 fighters. In June 1923 Parliament accepted this without challenge.[38] Sir Eyre Crowe, now permanent under-secretary of the Foreign Office, was left to observe the tendency in Whitehall and Downing Street 'towards the substitution of an Entente with Germany in place of that with France'.[39]

Throughout the inter-war years, the Foreign Office possessed the reputation of being pro-French in outlook. One reason is that the diplomats favoured the granting of a unilateral British guarantee to France in place of the joint Anglo-American guarantee that collapsed when Washington refused to ratify the Versailles Treaty. Subsequently they favoured British participation in the Rhineland Pact and offers to France of diplomatic or military conversations, which were made at times of crisis over the next thirteen years. But the purpose in every instance was to gain some purchase over French external policy and usually to induce France to make concessions to Germany. They did not reflect an identity of outlook. Towards Germany, they broadly shared the policy of 'hear no evil, see no evil'. Towards Eastern Europe, they favoured a policy of benign neglect.[40] Towards France, their policy was essentially one of containment of a potentially dangerous alien power. In January 1921, two months after becoming ambassador in Paris, Lord Hardinge recorded in his diary, 'no sane Englishman could possibly be tempted by the idea of being dragged at the wheels of the Chauvinism and pseudo-Imperialism of France. We would suffer more and have to condone more'.[41] The British were Anglo-Saxons, the French were Latins, and '[w]ith Latin races it is essential to stand up to them, the only thing that really matters being the question of form'.[42]

Hardinge was by no means alone in harbouring such extreme views. Sir George Graham, the chargé d'affaires at the Paris Embassy, confidently stated in April 1920 that the French had no cause to worry about Germany 'in our lifetime' and probably for much longer. In his words, the French occupation of the Ruhr would 'have Germany at their mercy for all time; and then, as sure as winter follows summer, they, feeling themselves absolute masters of the Continent, will turn round on us'.[43] Sir Eyre Crowe, Hardinge's successor as permanent under-secretary and reputedly a friend of France, dissented from this extreme view. But he shared his colleague's racial outlook. Difficulties with France, he wrote in December 1921, arose

> partly from the traditions of French diplomacy, but still more from the mentality of the French race, and it represents a difference both of outlook and methods, as compared with the British, which is fundamental. Perhaps the difference can be best defined as a contrast between the British habit of endeavouring to deal with the current problems of diplomacy, as they arise, on the merits of the particular case, and the French practice of subordinating even the most trivial issues to general considerations of expediency, based on far-reaching plans for the relentless promotion of French prestige and the gratification of private, generally monetary and often sordid, interests or ambitions, only too frequently pursued with a disregard of ordinary rules of straightforward and loyal dealing which is repugnant and offensive to normal British instincts. [. . .]
> [I]t cannot honestly be said that there is a good prospect of the French changing their ways in this respect, however sincere their friendship for this country. They are not really conscious of the extent of their shortcomings and therefore not amenable to argument or capable of responding to remonstrance.[44]

Oddly, Crowe included this pessimistic portrait of the French nation in a Cabinet paper recommending a guarantee to France against unprovoked aggression. Not surprisingly, ministers were more impressed by the dangers of closer relations with France than the advantages of extending it a guarantee.

Between 1925 and 1933 Crowe had three successors as permanent under-secretary of the Foreign Office. Sir William Tyrrell, who occupied the post from 1925 to July 1928, avoided stereotyping and made none of the hostile remarks about the French character that had been common before him. (Was it perhaps linked to the fact that he was a Catholic and Irish?) Sir Robert Vansittart, who succeeded to the post in 1930 after the brief tenure of Sir Ronald Lindsay, was a greater puzzle. As a young diplomat he had been posted to the British Embassy in Paris shortly after the signing of the *Entente Cordiale* in 1904. He immersed himself in Paris society, wrote a play in French that ran for six weeks at the Théâtre Molière and regretted his recall from the city. Yet in the 1920s he displayed all the same political and race prejudices against France as his contemporaries. He regularly accused France of blocking progress to peace, and as the new head of the Foreign Office in 1930 he portrayed France to the Labour Cabinet as a nation of short-sighted, self-interested, unreliable people, interested only in their narrow material advantage – the usual characterisation of the Latin race. France, he affirmed in a Cabinet paper in May 1930, was backward looking, hysterical and foolish in pushing Germany towards extremism.[45] As late as 1932 his advice to the Cabinet was to gain some purchase over the French by holding out a unilateral guarantee, in order to persuade them to abandon all the Versailles Treaty restrictions on German rearmament. He combined this with an unrestrained attack on France for its 'short-sighted and disappointing' policy, its 'ill-faith, obstinacy and discourtesy' in recent disarmament negotiations and its grotesque pursuit of power:

> No one, of course, contemplates any avoidable friction with France. We are, in any case, in no position for high words or dudgeon with our nearest and most powerful neighbour, who has of late attained the very thing that we have traditionally sought to avoid in Europe, hegemony, if not dictatorship, political and financial.[46]

After Hitler gained power in 1933, Vansittart acquired a reputation as an opponent of appeasement. It hardly helped his cause that in the fourteen years before then he presented Germany as a victim and France as the chief obstacle to peace in Europe.

Between 1925 and 1928 the Franco-British relationship remained as one-sided as ever, with French statesmen looking anxiously for any sign that Britain was prepared to accept some responsibility for European security. But at least the confrontations that reached crisis point during the Ruhr occupation had given way to more stable relations. This owed partly to the efforts of Aristide Briand, whom the Foreign Office described patronisingly as the only good European in France,[47] and partly to his British counterpart, Austen Chamberlain. Chamberlain did not rule out the possibility of future conflict with France, but he did at least make a show of friendliness towards France. The good relations however lasted only until the latter half of 1928, when new tensions arose, this time chiefly over economic issues rather than foreign policy and defence.

Britain's economic performance in the 1920s was by far the worst of any developed country in the world, with low economic growth and exceptionally high unemployment. But its political and business élites could at least console themselves that the pound sterling remained as prestigious as ever. For in 1925 with great difficulty Britain had restored sterling to the gold standard, and moreover restored it without having to devalue it a penny from its pre-war exchange rate. France, in contrast, had allowed inflation to soar and the franc to fall at one point to barely 10 per cent of its pre-war rate, and had only managed to stabilise it in 1928 at a mere fifth of its former parity. Until then, France's financial turmoil had obscured the remarkable success of its real economy, but once the franc was stabilised this immediately became evident. The contrast between France's economic growth and Britain's relative stagnation attracted widespread envy in Britain and numerous allegations that the one was the cause of the other.[48] Moreover, the franc now became the strongest currency in Europe and attracted much of the speculative capital that had earlier fled France for the security of London and New York. As a result, the Banque de France was forced to intervene in the foreign exchange market, to mop up demand for the franc. While its holdings of gold and foreign exchange grew to massive proportions, the Bank of England was forced to raise interest rates and discourage foreign lending, to stop the pound sterling from slumping below its gold export point and perhaps being forced off the gold standard.

Sterling's weakness was in fact due to several factors: the huge burden of debt carried by the government and industry since the war, the decline in demand for exports from Britain's older industries, the growth of 'hot money' that washed about in the world financial system, the over-valued exchange rate adopted in 1925, the secular decline in world commodity prices since 1925 and the boom – not crash – on Wall Street since 1927, which attracted liquid funds from London to the high interest rates offered by New York banks. The stabilisation of the franc at a slightly undervalued rate in 1928 was only one, and by no means the most important, reason for the Bank of England's chronic problems. But to Britain's élites, sterling symbolised the country's status as a world power and the strength of national character as well as the underpinning for the City of London, which was by far the greatest source of Britain's wealth. They found it intolerable to see the pound driven to the wall, while France, a country of supposedly lax morals and narrow self-interested policies, acquired gold reserves second only to the United States. British newspapers therefore mounted a campaign against France in the summer of 1929, suggesting baldly that it was deliberately driving down sterling for political reasons.[49]

The press campaign ceased after the crash on Wall Street eased pressure on sterling, but it resumed in May 1930 when sterling's weakness led to a renewed outflow of gold from the Bank of England. For eight months, until January 1931, British newspapers drew attention to the intermittent flow of gold from London to Paris. Hardly had it ceased when the financial markets were shaken by the crisis over news of an Austro German customs union proposal. City of London bankers, who had close links with Germany and had tied up huge balances in Central Europe, reacted with horror when France refused to bail out the Austrian National Bank until Vienna formally renounced the customs union scheme. The Bank of England stepped in, but it was well known that its current reserves were insufficient to hold the situation for long. City bankers became even more annoyed when the financial crisis spread to Germany in June, and France delayed the implementation of the Hoover Moratorium on intergovernmental debts until Germany offered assurances on the payment of the so-called unconditional *tranche* of reparations. Their annoyance reached fever pitch when the financial crisis spread to London in July. So general were the reports that France was behind the run on the pound that Tom Johnston, a British Cabinet minister, visited Paris to interrogate Pierre Laval, the president of the Council, and Pierre-Étienne Flandin, the minister of Finance, about their involvement.[50] He returned reassured, and indeed the French government and the Banque de France did everything they could to assist Britain in its hour of need. It made no difference.

By 5 July, Ramsay MacDonald, the prime minister, was convinced that France was prepared to destroy Germany for its own benefit. As he wrote in his diary,

> France has been playing its usual small minded & selfish game over the Hoover proposal. Its methods are those of the worst Jews. To do a good thing for its own sake is not in line with French official nature. So Germany cracks while France bargains.[51]

A week later he had become almost frantic:

> The behaviour of the French has been inconceivably atrocious. . . . [S]uch pettiness & implacability. [. . .] Another war is inevitable if an independent nation in Europe is to exist. The immediate outlook is black; the more remote one still blacker.[52]

Several times that summer, Vansittart denounced the French as 'bullying', 'singularly short-sighted', 'selfish and avaricious'.[53] The Banque de France contributed to two large loans to the Bank of England and the British government. When they did not stem the run on the pound, the French government offered further support. Yet, when the pound sterling was driven off the gold standard on 21 September, France was singled out for ferocious attack by members of Britain's political and business élites. Lord Robert Cecil, the former Tory Cabinet minister and adviser to the Labour government on disarmament, wrote to Lord Reading, the foreign secretary, that day from Geneva of the urgent need for Anglo-Saxon solidarity:

> It must be remembered that the French have no finer feelings. They pride themselves on dealing with all affairs from a strictly business point of view. In spite of Napoleon they believe very little in imponderables, which has been the source of most of their troubles in their history and is the cause of their great tenacity on

> the question of material security. On their own terms and in their own medium they are charming people to negotiate with because they are so intelligent and, in my experience, so direct; but if you try to deal with them from the Anglo-Saxon point of view you merely prepare yourself for disappointment. [. . .] The reason they are so contemptuous of us now is because they believe we no longer have any financial strength and that we have no industrial future. Quite a foolish opinion, I believe, but apparently held by such men as Flandin. If, by some assurance from Washington, they were led to understand that the two English-speaking Powers were going to stand together, they would see their mistake and immediately become more reasonable.[54]

The allegations about Flandin were wholly fanciful, but Cecil's sense of humiliation was not. Nor was it untypical of those in British political circles. Even two months after sterling was forced off the gold standard, the diplomat Sir Charles Mendl found that feelings in England were still inflamed. After visiting London, he wrote to a colleague in Vienna:

> The feeling in England of intense 'gallophobia' really frightened me. I have never seen anything like it & lunching at one of our new Under-Secretaries (not Duff Cooper) someone alluded to the 'lousy French' which drew my goat & I was quite offensive. After all, when we did go off the gold standard, Laval offered [us] an instant short-term loan to be followed by a very large long termed one 'to the limit of their resources', while the Yanks couldn't or wouldn't do anything except express grief. No one in England seems to know this, although we have sent it over time and again.[55]

Mendl and Lord Tyrrell in Paris did their best to explain France's position. But by now the National Government was determined to pursue a policy of imperial protectionism, and to detach Britain so far as possible from Europe. For the foreseeable future, there was no hope of reviving the *Entente Cordiale*.

If the foregoing account seems one-sided in its treatment of the Franco-British relationship, this is because the relationship itself was one-sided. For, as might have been expected, France remained constantly hopeful of reviving the *Entente* after the Great War, while

Britain constantly refused to do so. The explanation offered in this paper for Britain's refusal is necessarily speculative, since the picture of national and racial prejudice must be assembled from the slim fragments scattered about in the archival record. Decisions on public policy are invariably set out in rational terms and justified by reference to the national interest. Irrational prejudices, as James Joll put it thirty years ago, are the 'unspoken assumptions': the motives that often, as Joll wrote, 'go without saying'.[56] Yet they may be all the more important for being unspoken and therefore largely unchallenged. In the case of racial prejudice, it seems that historians of the first half of the twentieth century have made an egregious error to assume that it shaped the behaviour only of the aggressor powers, or that among the democratic powers it arose only in the form of anti-Semitism or colour prejudice. It was on the contrary omnipresent and widely influential in the shaping of international relations. In the case of Britain, it profoundly affected attitudes towards Europe, and naturally therefore it affected the *Entente Cordiale* as well.

Notes

1. See for instance, André Avice, *Mésentente cordiale: La politique séculaire de l'Angleterre* (Paris: Éditions du Scorpion, 1964); Christine Geoffroy, *La Mésentente cordiale: Voyage au cœur de l'espace interculturel franco-anglais*, préface de Claude Hagége (Paris: Grasset; Le Monde de l'éducation, 2001); François Kersaudy, *De Gaulle et Churchill: La mésentente cordiale*, nouvelle éd. (Paris: Perrin, 2001).
2. France, MAE, Europe 1918–1940, Grande-Bretagne 48, Préfet de Police to Briand, 26 November 1921. The cabaret acts are described in Sisley Huddleston, 'Great Britain according to the French stage: A word of advice to our French citizens', *The Illustrated London News*, 10 December 1921.
3. Robert Graves, *Goodbye to All That*, rev. edn (Harmondsworth, Middlesex: Penguin, 1960), pp. 140, 191.
4. *Ibid.*, p. 240.
5. Paul Fussell, *The Great War and Modern Memory* (Oxford: University Press, 2000), pp. 204–20.
6. Edmund Blunden, *Undertones of War*, rev. edn (London: Cobden-Sanderson, 1930), pp. 204–5; Barry Webb, *Edmund Blunden: A Biography* (New Haven: Yale University Press, 1990), p. 171.
7. John Stuart Roberts, *Siegfried Sassoon, 1886–1967* (London: Richard Cohen Books, 1994), p. 274.
8. G.P. Gooch and Howard Temperley (eds), *British Documents on the Origins of the War, 1898–1914*, vol. III (London: HMSO, 1928), Appendix A,

'Memorandum on the present state of British relations with France and Germany', pp. 397–420.

9. A.F. Whyte, 'The outlook of a good European', in Francis Younghusband (ed.), *For the Right: Essays & Addresses by Members of the 'Fight for the Right Movement'* (London: T. Fisher Unwin, 1916), pp. 163, 165, 170, 175, 181, 182, 185.
10. Ernest Barker, *National Character and the Factors in its Formation* (London: Methuen, 1927), pp. 21, 23, 44, 46, 47.
11. Stuart Wallace, *War and the Image of Germany: British Academics, 1914–1918* (Edinburgh: John Donald Publishers, 1988), p. 25.
12. Samuel Hynes, *A War Imagined: The First World War and English Culture* (New York: Collier Books, 1990), p. 68.
13. Lord Beveridge, *Power and Influence* (London: Hodder & Stoughton, 1953), p. 133.
14. Nevile Henderson, *Failure of a Mission: Berlin, 1937–1939,* 2nd edn (Toronto: Musson Book Company, 1940), pp. 4–5, 23.
15. Wallace, *War and the Image of Germany*, p. 31.
16. 'First steps to the real settlement', *The Observer,* 18 May 1919, p. 10; also 'How to mend it', *ibid.*, 25 May 1919, p. 10; 'Second thoughts at Paris', *ibid.*, 15 June 1919, p. 10.
17. Margaret MacMillan, *Paris, 1919* (New York: Random House, 2002), p. 220.
18. W.K. Hancock and Jean Van Der Poel (eds), *Selections from the Smuts Papers,* vol. IV, *November 1918 – August 1919* (Cambridge: University Press, 1966), p. 272.
19. *Ibid.*, p. 13.
20. *Ibid.*, pp. 157–8, 183–9, 215–7, 219–21, 223.
21. James Headlam-Morley, *A Memoir of the Peace Conference, 1919,* Agnes Headlam-Morley, Russell Bryant and Anna Cienciala (eds) (London: Methuen, 1972), p. 170; Harold I. Nelson, *Land and Power: British and Allied Policy on Germany's Frontiers, 1916–19* (Newton Abbot: David & Charles, 1971), p. 174.
22. Headlam-Morley, *A Memoir of the Peace Conference, 1919*, pp. 174, 163.
23. National Archives, Kew (NA), FO371, f. 3787, fo. 534, minute by George Saunders, 27 March 1919.
24. DBFP, series 1, vol. VI, doc. 83, memorandum by H.J. Paton, 27 February 1919.
25. Anthony Lentin, *Lloyd George and the Lost Peace: From Versailles to Hitler, 1919–1940* (London: Palgrave, 2001), p. 5.
26. Kenneth O. Morgan, *Lloyd George* (London: Weidenfeld & Nicolson, 1974), pp. 133–4.
27. David Lloyd George, *The Truth about the Peace Treaties,* vol. I (London: Victor Gollancz, 1938), p. 405.
28. See, for instance, House of Lords Record Office, Lloyd George papers, F/89/2/23, Kerr to Lloyd George, 18 February 1919; *ibid.*, F/30/3/40, Lloyd George to Bonar Law , 30 March 1919.
29. Lloyd George, *The Truth about the Peace Treaties*, vol. I, p. 406.

30. NA, FO371/3765, 18704, Committee of Imperial Defence (CID), 'The Channel Tunnel', memorandum by M.P.A. Hankey, Secretary, 23 October 1916.
31. NA, *ibid.*, 'The Channel Tunnel – 1920', memorandum by Mr Balfour, 5 February 1920.
32. *Ibid.*, 'The Channel Tunnel', by Curzon of Kedleston, 1 May 1920.
33. Charles Hardinge, *Old Diplomacy: The Reminiscences of Lord Hardinge of Penshurst* (London: Murray, 1947), p. 264; Keith M. Wilson, *Channel Tunnel Visions, 1850–1945: Dreams and Nightmares* (London: Hambledon, 1995), pp. 150–1; Richard S. Grayson, 'The British Government and the Channel Tunnel, 1919–39', *Journal of Contemporary History*, 31 (1996), 127–9.
34. N.H. Gibbs, *Grand Strategy*, vol. I, *Rearmament Policy* (London: Her Majesty's Stationery Office, 1976), pp. 47–8.
35. NA, CAB 16/47, N.D. 31, General Staff Note on French Air Situation, May 1923.
36. Immediately after the war, two-thirds of French squadrons were dissolved, and the aircraft industry, which employed 200,000 in 1919, was reduced to 10,000 employees by 1920: Jean Doise et Maurice Vaïsse, *Politique étrangère de la France: Diplomatie et outil militaire, 1871–1991*, rev. edn (Paris: Seuil, 1992) p. 360.
37. NA, AIR 8/63, Committee of Imperial Defence, Sub-Committee on National and Imperial Defence, minutes of the 10th meeting, 16 May 1923.
38. *Hansard*, HC Deb. 5 s., vol. 165, 2142.
39. DBFP, series 1, vol. XVI, no. 747, fo. 7, Crowe minute, 30 November 1921.
40. The advice of the Permanent Under-Secretary, Sir William Tyrrell, on the Polish-German problem corresponded exactly to that of the foreign secretary and may well have formed the basis of it: 'Let sleeping dogs sleep – or if they won't, let us try to make them sleep'. DBFP, ser. 1A, vol. I, no. 151, memorandum by Huxley, 17 December 1925, minute by Tyrrell, 21 December 1925.
41. Quoted in Briton Cooper Busch, *Hardinge of Penshurst: A Study in the Old Diplomacy* (South Bend: Archon Books, 1980), p. 298.
42. *Ibid.*, p. 305.
43. Lentin, *Lloyd George and the Lost Peace*, p. 64.
44. DBFP, series 1, vol. XVI, no. 768, Memorandum by the Marquess Curzon of Kedleston on the question of an Anglo-French Alliance, 28 December 1921. On the origins of the memorandum, see Crowe and Corp, *Our Ablest Public Servant*, p. 413.
45. NA, FO371/14350, C3358/3358/62, memorandum by Vansittart, 1 May 1930.
46. NA, CAB 24/227, C.P. 4(32), Vansittart memorandum, 'The British position in relation to European policy', 11 January 1932.
47. NA, FO371/14366, W5585/451/18, memorandum by A.W.A. Leeper, 30 May 1930.
48. R.W.D. Boyce, *British Capitalism at the Crossroads, 1919–1932: A Study in Politics, Economics and International Relations* (Cambridge: University Press, 1987), p. 177.

49. *Ibid.*, pp. 207–8.
50. Thomas Johnston, *The Financiers and the Nation* (London: Methuen, 1934), p. 198.
51. NA, 30/69/8/1, MacDonald diary, 5 July 1931.
52. NA, 30/69/8/1, MacDonald diary, 25 June, 5 and 11 July 1931.
53. NA, FO371/15182, C4391/172/62, minute by Vansittart, 22 June 1931; NA, FO371/15183, C4549/172/62, minute by Vansittart, 29 June 1931; NA, FO371/15187, C5176/172/62, minute by Vansittart, 12 August 1931; NA, FO371/15195, C7119/172/62, minute by Vansittart, 5 September 1931; NA, CAB 21/350, memorandum by Vansittart, 4 September 1931. Ironically, Vansittart had only recently circulated a memorandum to Cabinet deploring the tendency to make France the scapegoat for Europe's ills: NA, CAB 24/221, 'An aspect of international relations', 14 May 1931.
54. British Library, Add. Ms 51,082, Cecil papers, Cecil to Reading, 21 September 1931.
55. NA, Phipps papers, vol. 1, 2/21, Mendl to Phipps, 20 November 1931.
56. James Joll, *1914: The Unspoken Assumptions*. An Inaugural Lecture delivered 25 April 1968 at the London School of Economics and Political Science (London: Weidenfeld & Nicolson, 1968).

4

Entente and Argument: Britain, France and Disarmament, 1899–1934

Andrew Webster
Murdoch University, Perth, Western Australia

If there was one subject in particular on which decades of Anglo-French entente, or at least cordiality, never produced anything like real harmony, it was disarmament. From one point of view, this was hardly surprising: the island naval power and the continental land power were inevitably going to possess entirely different conceptions of disarmament's strategic implications on their European and world contexts. Yet, from another point of view, the very asymmetry of their armed forces and strategic concerns might instead have allowed for productive trade-offs in terms of their relative maritime and terrestrial forces. In essence, and particularly in the years after the First World War, Britain would be 'top nation' at sea and France on land. This outlook had more resonance in Paris than in London. In the former, General Maurice Gamelin told the British military attaché that he considered 'the British fleet and the French army as the two stabilising factors in Europe'.[1] In the latter, Gilbert Murray complained that 'One of the most advanced French advocates of the League once said to me that the true guarantee of peace in Europe was a strong French Army and a strong British Navy. The sort of man who thinks that is the sort of man who ought never to be allowed to touch international affairs'.[2] The conflict between such different perspectives would produce constant tensions in the Anglo-French relationship. In early 1930, just as the French Prime Minister André Tardieu was insisting to the Senate that 'France, so far as land disarmament is concerned, is in the lead. She is in the same situation as is Britain with naval disarmament', the British Prime Minister Ramsay MacDonald was exclaiming to the British delegation at the London

Naval Conference that 'besides the navy they now demanded, France had a huge land army and a great air force, large enough to blow London to bits'.[3] Given that Britain and France were nominally close partners, the inability to harmonise their disarmament policies in order to promote European stability demonstrated that the existence of *Entente Cordiale* could not overcome a continuing legacy of wariness between London and Paris.

The modern era of disarmament can be dated from the First Hague Conference of 1899, the product of an initiative of Tsar Nicholas II of Russia. However, the actual outcome of the Conference fell far short of the Tsar's ambition to check the steady growth of land armaments and armies: merely three prohibitory declarations on the use of certain types of weaponry, namely expanding bullets, projectiles diffusing asphyxiating gases and (for five years) the discharge of explosives from balloons. An anodyne resolution stated that 'the restriction of military charges, which are at present a heavy burden on the world, is extremely desirable for the increase of the material and moral welfare of mankind'. Governments, it went on, 'may examine the possibility of an agreement as to the limitation of armed forces by land and sea, and of war budgets'.[4] While it was the German delegation that took the lead in resisting anything more exacting and in upholding the sovereign rights of states, the British and French in particular were not unhappy to let it do so. Lord Salisbury, the British prime minister, was not alone in considering that modern weapons 'and the horrible carnage and destruction which would ensue from their employment on a large scale, have acted no doubt as serious deterrent from war'.[5] French fears that the Conference would endorse existing European territorial boundaries and so make permanent the loss of Alsace-Lorraine led Foreign Minister Théophile Delcassé to proclaim that 'France still remembers - it is her principal *raison d'être* and she would be less respected if it was felt that she was ready to forget'.[6]

While armies and land warfare were central to the 1899 conference, the crux of the Second Hague Peace Conference in 1907 was navies and naval warfare. The British Liberal government proposed reductions in arms expenditure, hoping to halt its naval race with Germany at a favourable point. The British Foreign Secretary, Sir Edward Grey, stressed that his aims were limited and should not alarm Berlin: 'You may observe that the phrase I use is not "Limitation of Armaments" or "Disarmament" but "Expenditure on Armaments"'.[7] Grey correctly anticipated that the Germans would once more carry out the unpopular task of defeating his proposal, helping him win support from Liberal backbenchers for further naval increases. The German Naval Secretary Admiral Alfred von Tirpitz told the British naval attaché: '[Y]ou, the colossus, come and ask Germany, the pygmy, to disarm. From the point of view of the public it is laughable and Machiavellian, and we shall never agree to anything of the sort'.[8] In fact, the French also wanted to expand their navy and furthermore were keen to back their Russian ally's desire for land forces expansion. In the end, the total amount of discussion given over to disarmament was twenty-five minutes. All the Conference achieved was a renewed resolution on the limitation of military expenditure stating that 'it is eminently desirable that the governments should resume the serious examination of this question'.[9] Instead of disarmament, what followed over the next years was a massive growth in naval and military spending, followed in 1914 by world war.

The cataclysm of the First World War profoundly changed attitudes towards disarmament. It was no longer possible for governments to assert forthrightly that armaments were a necessary factor in creating security. On the contrary, for many people, hopes for lasting peace now were invested in the disarmament ideal, drawing upon the belief that arms races inevitably caused wars. This was famously encapsulated in the much-quoted verdict delivered by Grey in his memoirs: 'The enormous growth of armaments in Europe, the sense of insecurity and fear caused by them – it was these that made war inevitable'.[10] Part V of the Treaty of Versailles mandated the disarmament of Germany on land, sea and air; its provisions reflected British and French national interests that were competitive as well as complementary. (The Americans mostly remained on the sidelines during the negotiations over Part V at the Peace Conference in Paris.) In broad terms, Britain had the primary role in designing the naval clauses of the peace treaty whereas Britain and France had more equal roles in drawing up the land clauses. The interaction between the powers would in fact make the settlement harsher than if any one of the victors had drafted it alone.[11]

The naval clauses were relatively straightforward in inspiration as the British Admiralty sought to use the peace treaty to make permanent the favourable conditions created by the armistice, under which Germany had surrendered all its submarines and its most powerful surface ships. Mindful of the power ratio between Britain and its wartime allies, the Admiralty preferred to see the German navy scuttled rather than redistributed among the victors. There was thus private satisfaction when the Germans in fact sank their own ships in Scapa Flow on 21 June 1919. The German navy was permanently restricted in its numbers of surface ships and personnel, and forbidden to possess submarines. The Admiralty (supported by the Americans) in fact favoured a universal ban on submarines, but ultimately it had to defer to opposition from the French, who wanted submarines to compensate for their inferiority in surface vessels. In the words of the French representative, Admiral de Bon, only 'certain maritime powers sufficiently rich to maintain enormous fleets of war' wanted abolition.[12] Consideration of the land clauses evolved within an ongoing debate over what was needed in order for the Allies to be able to impose their peace terms; as they steadily demobilised their armed forces, fears grew that the Germans perhaps remained strong enough to renew hostilities. British demands for deep cuts to the German army were thus motivated by a desire to reduce the demands on Britain but also to remove a key obstacle to large-scale French disarmament, to pave the way for an end to French conscription and to weaken the justification for French demands in the Rhineland. For French Prime Minister Georges Clemenceau, treaty limits on German armaments were not a particularly high priority. His overriding concern was the Rhineland, for he believed that only a physical guarantee could save France from permanent vigilance; disarmament would be insufficient protection. The draft clauses proposed by the military commission headed by Marshal Ferdinand Foch made deep cuts into German forces. Tanks, heavy artillery and aircraft were carefully restricted, a general staff was prohibited and arms manufacture was heavily controlled. The army was to be sufficient only to keep internal order, comprising a maximum of 9,000 officers and 200,000 conscripted men. (Contrary to British hopes to abolish conscription, the French delegation were firm that universal service 'appears to France to be a fundamental issue of democracy'.)[13] British Prime Minister David Lloyd George objected both that the limit of 200,000 men was too high and that the army should instead be comprised of more expensive volunteers rather than cheaper conscripts. Foch insisted a long-term service volunteer army would in fact create a core of thousands of trained officers and

NCOs, perfectly suited for a future rapid expansion of the army. The final compromise was that the German army would be all-volunteer, but its size would be capped at 100,000 men. Fewer soldiers of course meant less equipment was needed, so this was also cut back. The idea had been to allow a German force adequate only for internal order, but there was now serious doubt among the British whether the German army could even secure its own borders. The effect of Anglo-French compromise was thus to ratchet Germany's army down to a lower level than either country's military would have favoured on their own.

By the later 1920s, the German violations of the Versailles disarmament clauses were creating additional tensions between London and Paris. The British considered the infractions to be relatively minor and felt it was better to ignore them in order not to undermine the 'Locarno era' atmosphere of reconciliation. In contrast, the French were constantly anxious about the facts of German deceit. French military intelligence had become fixated with an idea of German potential power and industrial efficiency, going so far as to report in 1929 that Germany would be able to field an army of approximately 1.5 million trained and fully equipped soldiers within about a month of war breaking out – a massive exaggeration. French generals insisted that the German violations had to be illicit preparations for war, with even the Chief of Staff Maxime Weygand apparently believing 'a surprise attack by Germany against France possible under certain circumstances and feasible, notwithstanding the grave political dangers to Germany of such an act'.[14] British assessments of these fears were dismissive, for example by the British ambassador in Berlin, Sir Horace Rumbold: 'I told [British ambassador in Paris, Lord Tyrrell] that French fears of an *attaque brusquée* on the part of Germany merely made us here smile'.[15] As the Quai d'Orsay would only follow through with diplomatic intervention if it was done jointly with London, which the British steadfastly refused, no action was ever taken.[16]

International disarmament was laid down as a fundamental task of the new League of Nations in Article 8 of the Covenant. The story of the League's pursuit of such disarmament during the inter-war period is a long and tragic one, though not so tedious or futile as is frequently charged.[17] The disarmament talks ultimately foundered on underlying differences between Britain and France reflecting the gap between the perspectives of a maritime and a land power. The British, safe behind the Channel moat guarded by the dominant Royal Navy, argued that with peace now restored to Europe, significant cuts to continental armies were possible, which would in and of themselves create an even stronger ethos of peace and security. They dismissed all demands for an extension of their military obligations to Europe. The French, though now the dominant continental land power, remained fixated upon the potential threat from Germany. Before any reductions could be made to their relative military superiority enshrined in the Versailles Treaty clauses, new mechanisms of security were required to make good the difference. The gap in outlooks between London and Paris was aptly summarised by an official in the French War Ministry:

> For us, disarmament can only be the consequence of security organised through a pacific system compulsory for all disagreements and an automatic mutual assistance, effective and immediate, against a future aggressor. It is the organisation of security alone that permits disarmament. For our adversaries and notably for the Anglo-Saxons, disarmament in itself creates security. ... But for them security is only a question of sentiment, of spiritual *detente*, sufficiently assured by agreements of a general type such as the Briand-Kellogg Pact and for which the sanctions required by our thesis are not merely useless, but harmful.[18]

The League-sponsored disarmament process thus found itself condemned to repeated stalemates, whether in the debates at the annual League Assemblies or in the long negotiations in the Preparatory Commission for the World Disarmament Conference (1926–30) and at the World Disarmament Conference itself (1932–34). Without pressure from a common Anglo-French front, there was no way to overcome the resistance of Germany to accepting the permanent inferiority in armaments contained in the Versailles clauses. Nor was there any chance of pressuring the smaller European powers into accepting less-than-maximised force levels. The differences in outlook in Paris and London as to their relative needs for armaments, land and naval respectively, and what constituted a suitable *quid pro quo* for compromising on those needs, were never bridged over years of argument.[19]

The repeated British demands for cuts to French land forces were based upon assessments in London that France was 'over-armed'. Analysing France's construction of frontier fortifications in 1930, the War Office concluded that, despite the increase in French security since the war, the military budget was also going up 'by leaps and bounds', without any serious protest in the French parliament or from French public opinion. 'It is difficult to discover in these formidable preparations any real intention to disarm, although the French appetite for further "security" and paper guarantees remains unappeased'.[20] Similarly, a contemporary War Office analysis of the state of the French army insisted that 'the steady and progressive increase' in French military expenditure led to an 'irresistible' conclusion: 'it is plain that the most formidable military power in the world is not yet satisfied that her armaments are sufficient to ensure her military security'.[21] Only isolated individuals like the iconoclastic Winston Churchill actually supported the maintenance of a strong French army. 'I am not at all sure that if the French were to disarm completely thereby placing themselves in a defenceless position ... that the peace of Europe would stand upon a more secure of solid foundations than it does today', he told an audience in Montreal.[22] But such opinions were very much in the minority. What stood out by the end of the 1920s were the amazingly narrow-minded attitudes about French intentions and mentality on display among British policy-makers. The Cabinet Secretary Maurice Hankey wrote to Prime Minister Ramsay MacDonald in October 1931 that 'France is so situated as to be able, in the last resort, to injure us more than any other nation. Submarines operating from French ports could inflict terrible losses on our commerce. London is extremely vulnerable to air attack from France. Diplomatically and financially they are in a position to harm us'.[23] Hugh Dalton, at the peak of the 1931 financial crisis, noted in his diary that in London, 'the anti-French virus is widespread and almost unreasoning – not only in the Cabinet, but in all parts of the House of Commons, in the City and in the press'.[24] Lord Thomson, minister for Air in the second Labour government, believed that France could best be influenced by keeping her 'in a healthy state of fear and uncertainty'. 'The French are essentially feminine', he went on, 'and firmness is the only way to handle them'.[25]

Speaking to the French Chamber of Deputies about naval disarmament on 19 December 1929, Jacques-Louis Dumesnil, the minister of

Marine, referred to the British as 'our friends of today, our allies of yesterday'.[26] It was an interesting distinction: the ties of wartime alliance had certainly been severed and even the friendship was now of questionable ardour. There was real frustration in Paris at the continual British attacks on France as heavily and even aggressively armed. They found it hypocritical that the British should claim their naval superiority as a necessity and right while labelling the French desire for (as they saw it) a parallel military preponderance on land as militarism. While France might spend more on its army, this was natural as a land power; Britain certainly spent much more on its navy, as was natural for a sea power. The anger in Paris over apparent British attempts to press for greater restrictions on land armaments, combined with suspicions of Anglo-American collusion on naval disarmament, was reflected in the insistence by General Édouard Réquin of the War Ministry that it had to be made clear to London 'that we will create difficulties for them in naval discussions unless they finally abandon their perpetual attacks against our land forces'.[27] In the naval sphere, policy-makers in Paris were deeply frustrated at the British refusal to recognise that France, as an imperial power with worldwide interests just like Britain, required a large and modern fleet. They certainly did not wish to see their own naval power, particularly *vis-à-vis* their great maritime rival Italy, casually overturned simply to protect British superiority. As the chief of the French naval staff complained: 'little does our colonial empire matter, little do our justifications matter – only one thing counts, the language of the Lion'.[28] Thus, when France ultimately refused to sign the 1930 London Naval Treaty, the Chief of the French Naval Staff, Admiral Louis-Hippolyte Violette could celebrate (on the way to Dover in the railway coach of Foreign Minister Aristide Briand) the outcome as a victory:

> 'This is just like on board a ship after a hurricane,' Admiral Violette said, 'when everybody likes to get together and check up on the damage, and drink to the future. But today it is even better – there is no damage! The French Navy emerges intact from the greatest naval battle in current history. Three cheers for Admiral Briand!'[29]

On the British side, in contrast, MacDonald revealingly noted in his diary about the same events that 'the disquiet of the discovery of the genuine war mentality of France still clouds my mind'.[30] Where MacDonald saw a gap in the Treaty left by the refusal of French militarists to accept strict limits on the size of their navy, Violette saw a narrow escape from an 'Anglo-Saxon' trap to keep France in permanent naval inferiority.

It is true that there was some degree of Anglo-French cooperation over managing the disarmament process; the governments of both powers had to deal with a mobilised domestic public opinion that steadily came to view success in disarmament as the vital element in securing stable and lasting peace. The final meeting of the Preparatory Commission for the World Disarmament Conference, for example, saw the formation of a noticeable Anglo-French front as the British delegate (Lord Cecil) became increasingly annoyed by the stubborn obstructionism of the German delegate (Count Bernstorff) and made common cause with the French delegate (René Massigli). Cecil, who repeatedly clashed with Bernstorff during the debates, reported that 'I have become great personal friends with Massigli, who is certainly delightful to work with. He really is a fair-minded Frenchman, with all their extreme alertness and intelligence and more than their usual honesty'.[31] For his part, Massigli could report after a critical day's discussions in which Cecil backed the French stance, that 'the line of action that I have followed since the start of the [meeting] in order to maintain, as far as my instructions permitted it, solidarity with the Anglo-Saxon representatives found its justification in this debate'.[32] On almost all the contentious issues, Cecil and Massigli voted together against the German positions. Still even Cecil knew that such allegiances would be tested when final decisions had to be made at the World Disarmament Conference itself. 'I have very little doubt the French at present do not mean to accept any substantial reduction of their existing armaments', he wrote to Gilbert Murray. 'But I cannot help hoping that when we get to the conference the pressure of opinion will be so great that they will be forced to do something, and in future conferences – which I hope will take place at least once every five years – they may be induced to go further.'[33]

It is doubtful if the World Disarmament Conference of 1932–34 could ever have succeeded. While the five major naval powers had taken three conferences to obtain only partial success in the single sphere of naval armaments, the Geneva Conference included over fifty nations involved in negotiations covering all spheres of armaments (land, sea and air). The sum of the Conference was thus long discussions, lasting over the next two years, without any decisions. Its many complexities, with proposals and counter-proposals, defy any brief description. The key point was that the basic state of Anglo-French incomprehension continued, neatly encapsulated in a surreal vignette from the Conference's opening day. Britain was represented by its Minister for the Dominions, the working-class stalwart Jimmy Thomas. When he met the cultured André Tardieu, now serving as minister for War, he was treated to a lengthy and eloquent sermon in French on the usual theme that security must precede disarmament. When Tardieu at last finished, Alexander Cadogan, Britain's chief disarmament expert, gave Thomas the fullest translation he could manage. Thomas' only response was to splutter, 'Oh 'ell!'. Whipping round to Cadogan, Tardieu demanded to know what the British minister had said. Having only two syllables to work with, Cadogan could only hurriedly reply 'that Mr. Thomas had listened with great attention and interest and would of course report faithfully to his government'. The British official recalled: 'Monsieur Tardieu eyed me with scarcely veiled mistrust'.[34]

The events of the succeeding months did not do anything to enhance the level of Anglo-French common cause. French threats to expose German violations publicly at the Conference were met only with exasperation by the British, who opposed German rearmament but feared that confronting the Germans would only destroy any chance of a successful outcome. Following the German unilateral withdrawal from the Conference in mid-1932, it was considered in London that securing Germany's return was the most important priority, as one official colourfully explained: '[the conference] without Germany is like (if not *Hamlet* without the Prince) at least *The Merchant of Venice* without Shylock'.[35] There had to be negotiations with Germany to reach agreed arms limitations, otherwise the Germans might well declare themselves free to rearm without restriction, sparking a new arms race in Europe. But the result was not pressure on Berlin to compromise, but on Paris to make concessions. Massigli commented in exasperation at the end of the year that 'the British government more than ever persists . . . in assuming a position of arbiter between Germany and ourselves'.[36] A deal was finally struck that brought Germany back to the Conference, but only by papering over the fundamental issues at stake. In any case, larger international events now took over. From early 1933 onward, with Hitler's accession to power in January and Japan's withdrawal from the League in March, the Conference for all productive purposes was effectively over. It would meet discontinuously until mid-1934, and though it continued to serve as a major focus of political, strategic and diplomatic attention, there was no longer the luxury of time: a fundamental shift had already taken place in the movement of Europe from peace to war.

In the pursuit of disarmament, both Britain and France pursued policies based upon self-interest. The desire to ensure that the nation was properly defended and capable of protecting its interests was just as strong in London as it was in Paris. The naval regime established at the London Naval Conference ensured British maritime security, yet at the same time it became an assertion of British leadership in disarmament. It was an argument that Prime Minister MacDonald ceaselessly repeated: 'we had not waited for this conference at Geneva [to disarm]. The London Naval Treaty had been meant to be our own very substantial contribution to paving the way for the conference'.[37] The lack of a direct European threat or overwhelming internal pressure gave British policy-makers more leeway than was open to their French counterparts, allowing them publicly and genuinely to support disarmament via cuts to land and air forces while ignoring the depth of French anxieties. What policy-makers in Paris found so hard to accept was this belief in London that British policies were somehow thus inherently virtuous, and indeed beneficial for international stability as a whole, while their own policies were labelled as simply militarist and even potentially hegemonic. French claims at least possessed a kind of honesty in their open recognition that France's armed forces were only as low as the existing state of security allowed. To release Germany from the restraints of Versailles would be to seriously compromise the peace, they believed. Germany's dishonesty, General Gamelin wrote in January 1932, demanded 'not only a constant vigilance, but a sustained effort to safeguard a level of military strength already reduced to the strict minimum necessary for our security'.[38] The French consequently protested unhappily at British condemnation of France's stance and at British agitation for land disarmament while naval armaments were protected: 'France, disposed to accept the minimum conditions laid down by Britain for her maritime security, asks nothing more than an equal recognition of the needs of her terrestrial security'.[39] It was a lament that never found a comforting response across the Channel. The theme that perhaps emerges most clearly from this contrast in perspectives on disarmament is the extent to which the Anglo-French relationship was, in many aspects, not bilateral but trilateral: it forever involved Germany. Berlin was the constant presence that so often stood between London and Paris and kept them in argument rather than in *entente*.

Notes

1. Memo by Waterhouse (military attaché, Paris), 3 December 1931, Kew, The National Archives (TNA), FO 371/15708, W13999/47/98.
2. Gilbert Murray, *The Ordeal of this Generation: The War, the League and the Future* (London: George Allen & Unwin, 1929), p. 88.
3. Speech by Tardieu, 26 March 1930, *Journal Officiel (Sénat)*, 46, 512; meeting of British delegation, 16 February 1930, TNA, CAB 29/128.
4. James B. Scott (ed.), *The Reports to the Hague Conferences of 1899 and 1907* (Oxford: Carnegie Endowment for International Peace, 1917), p. 21.
5. Quoted in Frederick W. Holls, *The Peace Conference at the Hague and its Bearings on International Law and Policy* (New York: Macmillan, 1914), p. 15. See also David Stevenson, *Armaments and the Coming of War: Europe, 1904–1914* (Oxford: University Press, 1996), pp. 106–7.
6. Quoted in Christopher Andrew, *Théophile Delcassé and the Making of the Entente Cordiale* (London: Macmillan, 1968), p. 121.
7. Quoted in André T. Sidorowicz, 'The British government, the Hague Peace Conference of 1907 and the armaments question', in B.J.C. McKercher (ed.), *Arms Limitation and Disarmament: Restraints on War, 1899–1939* (Westport: Praeger, 1992), p. 13.
8. Quoted in Arthur J. Marder, *From the Dreadnought to Scapa Flow: The Royal Navy in the Fisher Era* (Oxford: University Press, 1961), vol. I, p. 131.
9. Scott, *Hague Conferences*, pp. 216, 892–7.
10. Sir Edward Grey (Lord Grey of Fallodon), *Twenty-Five Years, 1892–1916* (2 vols, Oxford: University Press, 1925), vol. I, p. 90.
11. The following discussion of the Versailles disarmament clauses is drawn from David Stevenson, 'Britain, France and the origins of German disarmament, 1916–1919', *Journal of Strategic Studies*, 29, 2 (April 2006).
12. Stephen Roskill, *Naval Policy between the Wars* (London: Collins, 1968), vol. I, p. 92.
13. Léon Bourgeois, quoted in Stevenson, 'German disarmament'.
14. Memo by Needham (military attaché, Paris), 23 October 1930, TNA, FO 371/14366, C7943/230/18.

15. Rumbold (Berlin) to Graham, 19 December 1930, Oxford, Bodleian Library, Rumbold papers, vol. 38, fos 124–6.
16. On French reactions to German evasions of Versailles, see Peter Jackson, 'French intelligence and Hitler's rise to power', *Historical Journal*, 41, 3 (September 1998).
17. The best examination of the interwar disarmament story as a whole is in Zara Steiner, *The Lights that Failed: European International History, 1919–1933* (Oxford: University Press, 2005), pp. 372–83, 565–97. For a more general overview, see Andrew Webster, 'From Versailles to Geneva: The many forms of interwar disarmament', *Journal of Strategic Studies*, 29, 2 (April 2006).
18. Memo by Lucien, 30 November 1929, Paris, Ministère des Affaires Etrangères (MAE), série SDN, vol. 723, fos 140–5.
19. For more on this, see: Andrew Webster, 'An argument without end: Britain, France and the disarmament process, 1925–1934', in Martin S. Alexander and William J. Philpott (eds), *Anglo-French Defence Relations between the Wars* (London: Palgrave, 2002).
20. Memo by Chief of Imperial General Staff (CIGS), 'The reorganisation of the French eastern frontier defences', 2 July 1930, TNA, CAB 4/19, CID paper 999-B.
21. Memo by CIGS, 'The French military budget for 1930', 5 June 1930, TNA, CAB 4/19, CID paper 994-B.
22. Speech by Churchill, Montreal, 13 August 1929, quoted in *Montreal Gazette*, 14 August 1929. This speech was read avidly in France; translated copies of it are in the archives of the Quai d'Orsay as well as the Tardieu and Painlevé papers.
23. Memo by Hankey, for MacDonald, 'Notes on the task of the National Government', 28 October 1931, TNA, CAB 63/44, fos 187–200.
24. Dalton diary, 20 July 1931, London School of Economics, Library of Political and Economic Science, Dalton papers, part I, vol. 14a, fos 33–5. Dalton continued, in a light-hearted vein: 'The Victorian view was that the French practised all sorts of occult forms of sexual intercourse and were the wickedest people on earth. The modern view was the same, only it had turned from the sexual to the political. If you went to Paris, you would catch some politico-venereal disease. They would infect you with their ideas, and their guarantees'.
25. Note by Basil Liddell Hart, 15 July 1929, King's College, London, Liddell Hart Centre for Military Archives, Liddell Hart papers, 11/1929/9.
26. Speech by Dumesnil, 19 December 1929, *Journal Officiel (Chambre)*, 116, 4490.
27. Memo by Réquin, 8 October 1929, Vincennes, Service Historique de la Marine (SHM), 1BB/2, vol. 191, in file 'Position de la Guerre'.
28. Memo by Violette, 31 March 1931, SHM, 1BB/2, vol. 193, in file 'Négociations Navales: 1 Mars–1 Avril 1931', pp. 118*bis-ter*.
29. Geneviève Tabouis, *They Called Me Cassandra* (New York: Charles Scribner's Sons, 1942), p. 97.
30. MacDonald diary, 23 April 1930, TNA, PRO 30/69/1753/1.

31. Cecil (Geneva) to Noel-Baker, 25 November 1930, British Library (BL), Cecil papers, Add. Mss. 51107, fo. 143.
32. Massigli (Geneva) to Quai d'Orsay, 27 November 1930, MAE, série Y, vol. 516, fos 199–207.
33. Cecil (Geneva) to Murray, 29 November 1930, BL, Cecil papers, Add. Mss. 51132, fos 122–4.
34. Alexander Cadogan, unpublished memoirs, draft chapter 'Geneva Disarmament Conference, February 1932', Cambridge, Churchill College Archives Centre, ACAD 7/1.
35. Note by Leeper, 12 September 1932, TNA, FO 371/15940, C7652/211/18.
36. Massigli (Geneva) to Herriot, 17 November 1932, *Documents Diplomatiques Français, 1932–1939* (Paris: Imprimerie Nationale, 1966) series I, vol. 2, doc. 6.
37. Meeting of British delegation to World Disarmament Conference (Geneva), 25 April 1932, TNA, FO 371/16429, W4914/10/98.
38. Memo by Gamelin, 6 January 1932, MAE, Tardieu papers, PA-AP 166, vol. 499, fos 361–402.
39. Memo by Quai d'Orsay, 2 July 1931, MAE, série SDN, vol. 863, fos 37–43.

5
British Communists and Anglo-French Relations, 1914–45

Andrew Thorpe
University of Exeter

Studies of the *Entente Cordiale* tend to focus on various aspects of Anglo-French inter-state relations. This is entirely right and proper: the *Entente* was, after all, an agreement between two states. It is to be expected that any volume covering the *Entente* historically will focus primarily, as this one does, upon relations between governments, statesmen, diplomats and soldiers. Nonetheless, these are not the sum total of the contacts between the two countries. In particular, many people in both countries considered themselves to be a part of a wider international movement of revolutionaries who were working together to overthrow capitalism and imperialism and build a 'better' world. From 1917 onwards, in particular, Communists believed that theirs was the ideology of the future, and that their success was only a matter of time. From 1919 onwards, the efforts of Communists were, in theory at least, directed from the Communist International (Comintern) in Moscow, a world party of which the British and French Communist parties were – again, in theory at least – only branches. This paper, then, sets out to analyse the importance of France for the British Communist Party in the era of the World Wars. It focusses on the impact that France itself had upon British Communists' views of the world, and also upon the nature of the British Communist Party's relationship with its French counterpart.

The Communist Party of Great Britain (CPGB) was formed in London in August 1920, by the combination of a number of smaller bodies to the left of the Labour Party. Its achievements were to prove limited. It never threatened to supplant the much larger

Labour Party as the dominant force on the British left. Its membership never exceeded 56,000 (at the height of 'Russomania' in the Second World War) and was often (and for much of the inter-war period) no more than a tenth of that figure. It only ever had two MPs at the same time, in 1922–23 and again in 1945–50; in 1929–35, which included the worst years of the depression, it had none at all. Only in its trade union work was the picture a little less bleak; but even here, the peaks of influence achieved in the mid-1920s and from the mid-1930s onwards never suggested anything like a Communist takeover of the trade union movement. Even so, the Communist Party was not irrelevant to British politics and society, least of all during the inter-war period.[1] Its membership was low, but not non-existent. Given its high membership turnover, many more people passed through it than were members at any one time; and given that the reasons people left were by no means confined to political disagreement with communism, it did have a wider influence than its bare membership figures would suggest.[2] The party also acted as a *provocateur* to the larger Labour Party. To some extent, Labour defined itself in contrast to the Communists. At the same time, the presence of the Communists to its left, ever eager to 'expose' any compromising tendencies, was a barrier to Labour's shifting too far away from the left and towards the political centre.

Literature on the history of British Communism has multiplied in recent years, with the opening of archives in Britain and Russia offering masses of new evidence.[3] There has also been, still more recently, a very lively debate about the subject, and particularly the nature of the CPGB's relationship with Moscow and Soviet Communism.[4] This debate has sometimes generated more heat than light, and there is a danger that it will overshadow important and interesting facets of Communist history. In particular, there is scope for study of the nature of the party's views of countries other than the Soviet Union, and of its relations with foreign Communist parties other than Communist Party of the Soviet Union and its predecessors.[5] This is a very brief initial attempt to offer such a study in the case of France, a country which, precisely because of its physical proximity to Britain and the development of inter-state relations following the 1904 *Entente*, was bound to feature significantly in British Communists' calculations.

I

France occupied a somewhat marginal place in the mindset of the British far left in the years prior to the Great War. In one sense this was strange. The great French Revolution of 1789 was the prelude to a significant upsurge in British radicalism, and for a time France was the model for British radicals. But this strong French influence soon waned. As war replaced revolution, British radicals became increasingly marginalised. By the time of Waterloo in 1815, few figures on the British left still drew inspiration from France. The series of revolutions that punctuated French history in the nineteenth century – in 1830, 1848 and 1871 – led to periodic upsurges of interest, but such interest tended to be fleeting. French revolutionaries were less likely to be forced into exile than their German or Russian counterparts, which meant that cheek-by-jowl cohabitation between French and British Socialists was not common. If France had been the model in the late eighteenth century, Germany had usurped that position by the end of the nineteenth. And, for most of the British far left at least, the 1917 Bolshevik Revolution in Russia represented a new and still better exemplar.

What of France itself? The Great War left two predominant images in the minds of those on the British far left: that France was an imperialist power, and that the French left – as it had existed in 1914 – was fatally compromised. The Third French Republic had never excited the British left as the First had: it was felt to have its roots in the crushing of the Paris Commune, and British left socialists had shared the outrage felt widely within the International regarding the decision of Alexandre Millerand, the French Socialist leader, to enter the cabinet of Waldeck-Rousseau in 1899. France's uncompromising attitude during the war, best characterised by demands for unconditional surrender to end the war and reparations to follow it, was repulsive to many British Socialists, who felt that it would merely guarantee a continuing cycle of conflict. Although few on the British left went as far as Lenin in arguing for revolutionary defeatism and the turning of the European war of nations into a civil war of classes, more people were influenced by ideas of a negotiated peace without annexations or indemnities. This group became increasingly prominent as the war developed, and especially following the expulsion of H.M. Hyndman and his super-patriotic acolytes from the leadership of the main British Marxist organisation, the British Socialist Party (BSP), in 1916. Shorn of the pro-French, anti-German revanchism of the Hyndmanites, the BSP moved much closer to the essentially anti-French positions already taken up by smaller left-wing groups like the Socialist Labour Party and the Workers' Socialist Federation. This in turn meant that the British far left totally rejected the peace treaties that followed the conclusion of the war. The Treaty of Versailles, in particular, was vigorously denounced, not just by those who would eventually become members of the Communist Party, but also by many in the more moderate Independent Labour Party (ILP), and also within the Labour Party proper. For such people, France was a state with few saving graces or virtues, and the idea of any Anglo-French *entente* was repulsive.

This was partly because they tended to be influenced by the view that the war had been caused in large part by the division of Europe into armed camps. In a sense, this was ironic, since it was essentially a liberal interpretation of the war's causes, which went on to have a significant influence in the creation of the League of Nations, upon which the British far left was to heap considerable abuse. However, it was possible to square such a view with a more Marxist interpretation that argued that the war had been caused by the development of rival imperialisms, since the bloc-formation that was described by the liberal view could be seen as an essential by-product of the imperialist tendencies of Europe's states. Indeed, this overlap between liberal and Marxist analyses would prove long-lived, and would enable the CPGB to profit for large parts of its history from what were essentially liberal positions. However, where they came into conflict – as in 1939 – the party would face problems.

The other notion that came out of the war was the idea that the French left was fatally compromised. As John Horne has shown, French Socialists had faced an unenviable dilemma as war with Germany had erupted, and ultimately the great majority had settled for the 'choice of 1914'. This was not simply a relapse into some visceral form of super-patriotism. Instead, it was calculated that, since war had come anyway, the labour movement would be better able to maintain its identity, and defend its interests, as part of a national war effort, rather than by trying to stand outside it. This was, in many ways, a sound calculation. However, it 'rendered official labour leaderships vulnerable to those who rejected the "choice of 1914" or who urged the full use of labour's power to protect its interests'.[6] In other words, the choice to support the war effort predetermined that there would be hostility from an anti-war minority. For British far leftists, the French Socialists had shown themselves no better than the Labour Party leadership. On the other hand, the breakaway of the independent Social Democrats (the USPD) and the revolutionary Spartakists seemed to suggest that there was still a strong strain of Socialist internationalism and revolutionary zeal in Germany. Meanwhile, the Russian Revolution offered fresh inspiration. The fact that the French appeared even keener than the British on smashing the Bolsheviks was enough – along with Versailles – to confirm France's perfidy, so far as the British far left was concerned. The fact that the French left seemed relatively inert, even supine, at a time when revolution was taking hold in many other parts of Europe – Germany and Hungary as well as Russia – suggested to many British revolutionaries that there was little to be gained at any level from close relations with France or the French.

II

The war ended in November 1918. Two months later, a new factor entered European revolutionary politics with the establishment, in Bolshevik Moscow, of the Communist International. At first, the new organisation was weak, isolated and poorly understood by many revolutionaries. But its first five world congresses (in 1919, 1920, 1921, 1922 and 1924) gradually stamped its authority over the Communist movement that was developing, at first mainly in Europe and then in the wider world. Both British Communist views of Anglo-French relations, and the relationship between the British far left and its French counterpart, would now be influenced by the outlook of the Comintern, and of the Soviet party leadership that came increasingly to dominate it.[7]

One of the first acts of the Comintern was to help in the formation of Communist parties in both Britain and France in 1920. The creation of the CPGB in August 1920 was the culmination of a long series of discussions between various far-left organisations. In the end, the new party amounted, at least initially, to little more than an aggrandised BSP. The rapidly expanding Labour Party was able to marginalise the new body with a degree of ease: Communist attempts to affiliate to the larger body were rebuffed, and steps were taken to ensure that Communists could not become candidates for, or members of, the party. At first, prospects in France looked brighter. The French Communist Party (PCF) was formed in December 1920, when, at the Tours conference of the French Socialist Party, the SFIO, a majority of the latter body voted to re-form as a Communist Party affiliated to the Comintern. The minority, however, then re-formed the SFIO, and in the years that followed the latter rapidly outstripped the PCF in strength and prestige.

From the outset, it was obvious that there was potential for the CPGB and the PCF to collaborate. After all, their respective states were doing so in the aftermath of the war, and would continue to do so, although on a less close basis, for most of the inter-war period. Specific issues, in short, drew the two parties together. Britain and France remained the two most important states in the League of Nations, from which the Soviet Union was excluded, and which was seen as a thieves' kitchen.[8] Secondly, the *Entente* States remained the world's leading imperialist powers – indeed, the League's mandates system had, in effect, added to their imperial possessions. This meant that there was much potential for greater collaboration on anti-colonial agitation, which was a particular enthusiasm of the Comintern. Still more vitally, of course, there was now a revolutionary state – Soviet Russia – to be defended against external aggression, of which Britain and France were the main purveyors in the early years of the new regime. Both had intervened in Russia against the Bolsheviks; both had supported the Whites against the Reds in the Russian Civil War. Although Britain's enthusiasm for such interventions had waned before that of the French, there was little doubt that both remained essentially hostile towards the new regime, the French to the extent of giving strong support to Poland in its war against Russia in 1920–21. Given that Lenin also believed that Britain and France were at a similar stage of capitalist development, there was even more logic in the Comintern seeking to ensure that its parties in both France and Britain were in close co-operation.[9]

The Third Republic continued to be seriously distrusted by British Communists during the 1920s and into the 1930s. Continuing French hostility towards Soviet Russia played a large part in this process. So did the fact that Paris became the favoured refuge of many white Russians in exile. The French were seen as trying to lead successive British governments in an anti-Soviet direction.[10] In addition, British Communists increasingly saw France as a state where capitalism was speeding up production, and rationalising industry, in ways that were inimical to the workers' interests.[11] The Bedaux system, a form of industrial speed-up against which many unions were fighting in Britain from the later 1920s onwards, was strongly associated in British Communist minds with France.

There was, for all these reasons, early interest in developing links between the Communist parties of the world's two leading imperialist powers. After the Fourth Congress of the Comintern, in November and December 1922, had criticised the CPGB for being too insular, it looked to thicken its links with the French and German parties in particular. The French invasion of the Ruhr in January 1923 led to the formation of a joint committee including British and French, as well as German, Czech and Polish Communists.[12] In April 1923, the French Communist Alfred Rosmer attended a CPGB central committee meeting to report on developments within the PCF.[13] The Communist MP J.T. Walton Newbold visited Paris that August to try to develop links between the British and French parliamentary fractions.[14] These forays were continued with the development of an ambitious plan for Anglo-French collaboration, which was approved by the political bureau of the British party in February 1924;[15] and later in that year, two French Communists came to Britain to speak on behalf of Communist candidates at the general election.[16]

However, this early momentum was not sustained. In part, this was simply due to events – the ending of the Ruhr crisis took a lot of the pressure out of the situation, and the parties' international gaze began to wander in different directions. But there were other reasons, too. The fact that the British responded to Comintern criticisms of slow progress by blaming the French did not help matters.[17] Nor did the frequent leadership changes in the PCF. A setback came when Newbold, who had led the British party's diplomacy towards the PCF, left the party in 1924.[18] He was one of a series of middle-class Communists to leave the party at this point, and this exodus depleted the number of francophone members that the party could boast.[19] The departure of the party's leading intellectual, Rajani Palme Dutt, to Brussels in 1924 – where he remained for the next decade – was a similar blow.[20] The PCF's electoral success in 1924, when it won almost one million votes and 26 seats in the Chamber of Deputies, would hardly have made it more likely to wish to collaborate with its relatively puny British counterpart, which won only one parliamentary seat at the October 1924 general election.

The Comintern did not help matters. The establishment of the regional secretariats (*Ländersekretariate*) in Moscow hindered co-operation. The CPGB was made answerable to an Anglo-American secretariat, which comprised the Communist parties of anglophone nations and some parts of the British Empire; and it was the Romance secretariat which oversaw the work of the Communists of France, Italy, Belgium, Luxemburg, Spain and Portugal.[21] In theory, the Comintern was a smooth and well-oiled machine; in practice, this bureaucratic division made it increasingly difficult to co-ordinate the efforts of the CPGB and the PCF. Their two countries might only have been a couple of dozen miles apart, but this counted for little against the realities of Comintern bureaucracy. The major mid-1920s campaigns of the two parties were rather like ships that passed in the night, therefore. The French were not particularly forthcoming in assisting the CPGB over the General Strike and miners' lockout in 1926. But then again, the British had done very little to help the PCF's campaign against the 'Rif War' (1920–26) in Morocco in 1924–25.[22] It was perhaps not entirely by chance that British Communist representatives in Moscow tended not to have many intimates among the French Communists there.[23] By the later 1920s one of the few commonalities between the two parties was that they shared a Comintern representative, in the person of Max Petrovsky, who, although living in Paris and working with the PCF, continued his role as advisor to the British party under the pseudonym A.J. Bennett.[24]

Relations between the two parties did not improve significantly in the later 1920s or the early 1930s, for a number of reasons. Firstly, they moved at differing speeds towards the anti-social democratic sectarian policies of the 'class against class' period. In France, the shift began early: the new approach began to be discussed in the spring of 1927, and by that November the party was embarked upon the 'new line', in time for the elections of April 1928. In Britain, by contrast, the line shifted well to the left around the end of the 1926 miners' lockout, but then reverted to a more centrist position, and it was only in early 1928 that the moves towards 'class against class' began in earnest. The British party – or at least a strategically placed section of its leadership – then fought a long and, for a while, partly successful rearguard action against the adoption of the line in all its implications. It was only with the Leeds convention of December 1929 that the leadership was finally changed in such a way as to remove – in some cases only temporarily – the leaders who had resisted the new line (see below).

Secondly, and partly as a consequence of this, there was very little stability in the leadership of either party for much of the period. The French party had been notable for frequent changes of leadership during the 1920s, and this process was not really arrested, at least initially, by the new line after 1927. Pierre Sémard, who had only been the party's general secretary since 1926, was ousted in April 1929 by the so-called 'youth group', who provided a collective leadership comprising Henri Barbé, Pierre Célor, Benoît Frachon and Maurice Thorez. However, their lack of success led to most of them being removed from the leadership in 1931. In Britain, the resistance to the new line led to significant changes in the party's leadership in 1928–29, with Andrew Rothstein being permanently, and John Campbell temporarily, removed from leading positions within the party. Harry Pollitt became the party's general secretary in the summer of 1929, but at first his position was not strong, as he had to cope with a group of youthful, Comintern-supported ultra-leftists; it was only in 1930 that Moscow recognised him formally as the leader of the party, and only in November 1932 that his authority as leader was finally established beyond question.[25]

Thirdly, neither party enjoyed much success during the class against class period. While many of the Comintern's predictions about capitalist economic crisis, and the behaviour of social democratic leaders in the face thereof, were proved at least partly true by the depression that began in 1929, the other side of the prediction – that there would open up a new period of worker militancy and Communist Party expansion, and that the collapse of capitalism was being driven forward 'with hurricane speed' – proved illusory.[26] The fact that the economic experience of the two countries varied at this point, with the downturn in France coming somewhat later than in Britain, also inhibited close collaboration.[27] Furthermore, far from expanding, both parties were struggling even to hold on to their existing members in the early years of 'class against class'. In this context, it was often a case of the parties doing what they could to remain in being, rather than moving in such exotic directions as the intensification of Anglo-French links.

In any case, Communist eyes were increasingly focussed on Germany in this period. The Comintern was certainly preoccupied with events in that country. And British and French Communists were hardly likely to be indifferent to what was happening there, either. The Communist parties in both France and Britain were at least publicly optimistic as to the fate of the German Communist Party. But, of course, those hopes proved illusory. The appointment of Adolf Hitler as chancellor of Germany in January 1933 signalled the start of a very different era in Anglo-French relations, both at the state level but also at the level of the respective Communist parties.

III

Soviet reactions to the rise of Hitler were mixed: so too were the reactions of the Communist parties around the world. It was possible, in theory, to take up any one of three positions. The first was that Hitler and the Nazis would prove to be short-lived phenomena, the last and most brutal gasp of a dying capitalist system. Communist parties should redouble their efforts along class against class lines, refusing to compromise, especially with the Social Democrats who would try to resist supposedly growing revolutionary impulses.[28] Second, it could be argued that although Hitler was not a flash in the pan, he was predominantly an anti-western politician, whose main target was Versailles and the Anglo-French alliance that had created it; that, while he was domestically anti-Communist, he was a foreign policy realist and would revert to a traditional alignment with Russia, continuing with the kind of policy that had been concluded by Weimar Germany in the 1922 Treaty of Rapallo. If this view was correct, then the Soviets could welcome his accession to power, and the task would be to persuade Communist parties abroad to keep their fire fixed on the British and French governments. Finally, it was possible to argue that Hitler posed a serious threat to Communism, not just in Germany, but everywhere, especially the USSR; and that therefore the best tactic was to resist him and Nazi Germany to the full. This would involve Communist parties in Britain and France agitating for full-scale military alliances between their countries and the Soviet Union, to counter any danger of German attack.

In 1933, all three of these views found influential supporters at the highest levels of Communist decision-making. By the end of that year, however, the third model was becoming increasingly persuasive. In the spring of 1934, Stalin appointed the Bulgarian, Georgi Dimitrov, as general secretary of the Comintern. Dimitrov had witnessed the rise of Nazism in Germany as head of the Comintern's Western European Bureau in Berlin; he had become an international celebrity as a result of being imprisoned and tried by the Nazis on false accusations of involvement in the 1933 Reichstag fire. Dimitrov was convinced that Nazism was a real threat to the workers of the world and also to the 'workers' state', the Soviet Union. Stalin knew this, and his appointment – and increasing favouring – of the Bulgarian marked the start of the temporary eclipse of hopes for Soviet-German co-operation in the immediate future.[29]

Increasingly, therefore, the French and British parties came to the centre of Comintern thinking. The German Communist Party, the KPD – up to 1933 the most important non-Soviet Communist party – was now discredited by its failure to prevent the rise of Hitler and its still more obvious inability to do much in terms of leading resistance to the new regime, while the continuing failure of the KPD and SPD in exile to reach any kind of agreement rang an increasingly discordant note in the new period of 'anti-Fascist unity'. At the same time, Soviet foreign policy was moving into a more pro-western direction. From being a semi-alliance of robber barons, of states that were enemies of the workers, Britain and France were now potential allies of the USSR against Germany. Indeed, the USSR joined the League of Nations in September 1934, and agreed a treaty with France the following May.

The French and British party leaderships, meanwhile, were increasingly instrumental in the development of a new, more inclusive, approach. United front initiatives in both countries had a degree of success. Although there was limited resistance within the British party, some moves were made towards united front work with the Independent Labour Party (ILP) in 1933–34. More spectacular were the events of 5–6 February 1934 in Paris, when Communists and Socialists came together spontaneously to demonstrate against the prospect of an imminent Fascist *coup d'état*. Thorez and Pollitt were in the vanguard of international Communists during the latter half of 1934 in terms of developing an even more inclusive approach.

Thorez, in particular, appears to have disobeyed the advice of at least some Comintern officials in travelling to Nantes in October 1934 to address the national congress of the Radical Party, which, as a lower middle-class and non-Socialist organisation, was beyond the pale of the united front, which was only meant to incorporate working-class bodies.[30] His successful appeal to the Radicals saw the practical beginning of a new, and even more inclusive, strategy: that of the broad anti-Fascist *front populaire* (popular, or people's, front). The place of the French party at the heart of the Comintern was now confirmed. The success of his action was also used explicitly by Pollitt to inspire his own party to move away from sectarianism.[31]

The Seventh World Congress of the Comintern met in Moscow in the summer of 1935. France, and to a lesser extent Britain, were at the hub of Comintern concerns, and the quest for better relations with Britain and France was at the core of Soviet foreign policy. The key party at the congress, as Dimitrov made clear, was the PCF. The eclipse of the KPD, and the fact that most other Communist parties in the world were illegal, further boosted it: so too did the continuing weakness of the CPGB, which could only muster 7,500 members at the end of 1935 as against the PCF's 87,000.[32] France, Dimitrov said, was 'a country in which the working class is setting an example to the whole international proletariat of how to fight fascism'. The French Communist Party was 'setting an example to all the sections of the Comintern of how the tactics of the united front should be applied; the Socialist workers [we]re setting an example of what the Social-Democratic workers of other capitalist countries should now be doing in the fight against fascism'.[33]

The experiences of the two parties began to move still further apart after the Seventh World Congress. At the November 1935 general election, the British party – largely in pursuit of better relations with the Labour Party, but also in recognition of its own miserable prospects – withdrew all but two of its candidates. When one of these – William Gallacher at West Fife – was elected to Parliament, the virtual euphoria of Pollitt and his colleagues must have seemed odd to the French party, which had long had a bloc of deputies in the French Chamber. For its part, the PCF was about to enter its *annus mirabilis*. It fought the elections as part of a popular front, which went on to win convincingly. A popular front government was formed under the Socialist, Leon Blum. Although the Communists decided, for various reasons, against taking ministerial office in the government, they were, for a time, of central importance to it. Indeed, it was largely through Communist intervention that the strike wave that followed the elections was ended amicably with the Matignon Agreement, which enshrined in law a series of important rights for workers, such as paid holidays. Electoral success and practical influence on government policy in the interests of the workers was not quite the revolutionary transformation for which the PCF still claimed to be working, but it was a long way ahead of anything that their British counterparts could achieve at the time. As Nina Fishman has argued, events in France 'greatly intensified British Communist expectations'.[34] It was no coincidence that, in May 1936, the first book published by the Communist-dominated Left Book Club was Maurice Thorez's *France Today and the People's Front*.[35] It was to be followed periodically by further volumes on France, such as one on the Paris Commune of 1871 in 1937, and a biography of the mid-nineteenth century French revolutionary Auguste Blanqui on the eve of the Second World War.[36] It is true that the CPGB was at the forefront of street protests against Sir Oswald Mosley's British Union of Fascists (BUF), and did find some political space opening up thanks to the Labour Party's reluctance to commit itself to armed support for the Republican forces in the Spanish Civil War (1936–39). But otherwise, 1936 was a year of disappointment. In particular, the failure once again of its attempt to affiliate to the Labour Party left hopes of emulating the French in their popular front efforts demonstrably unfulfilled.[37] In October 1937, while Communists in France, Spain and China appeared to be engaged in real struggles for power, Pollitt was reduced to bickering with Labour politicians about who could claim most responsibility for preventing marches by the relatively insignificant BUF in the context of the London borough council elections.[38] British party membership did expand somewhat in 1936 to 11,500. But this a poor showing at the side of the PCF's 288,000 reached in December of that year.[39]

And yet, at the same time, there were things that continued to bind the two parties together. At the bureaucratic level, the Seventh World Congress had abolished the old *Ländersekretariate*, replacing them with new more flexible secretariats under named individuals. The British party was now placed under the overall control of the secretariat headed by the French Communist, André Marty. This brought French and British Communists closer together than had been the case in recent years, although the results were not always positive.[40] More significantly, Spain pulled the two parties closer together. The Spanish Civil War broke out in July 1936, and over the next two years a great deal of each party's campaigning and resources was devoted to the struggle against Fascism there. Inevitably, this kept the question of France at the fore of Communist thinking. France was, with Britain, the chief proponent of 'non-intervention', by which they both did their utmost to avoid being drawn into the conflict, and still more into a general European war. This meant that they maintained, against increasing evidence, that the policy was, in effect, working, when in fact German, Italian and Soviet forces were all involved in one way or another. Naturally, British Communists were quick to attack what they saw as the duplicitous behaviour of the British and French governments which, they believed, were effectively encouraging Fascism. In addition, of course, the foreign volunteers who went to Spain were largely forced to travel though France and be organised to a large extent by French Communists, which meant that there were closer personal contacts between significant numbers of British and French Communists than ever before.[41]

As the prospects in Spain dimmed, however, the focus moved back to the direct threat posed by Nazi Germany. Both the CPGB and the PCF ran strong campaigns against the appeasement policy being favoured by the British government and its increasingly anti-left French counterpart. In one sense, they were well placed to lead the attack: two leading Communist parties could try to work together to change the common policy of their two governments. The logic became even more compelling when, in October 1938, the Munich Agreement broke any last lingering links between the French government and the PCF.[42] However, tensions between the two parties remained. The Comintern was encouraging all parties to do more to emphasise their national traditions: in early 1937 it told the CPGB to 'base the whole of [its] propaganda upon British traditions, fortified by international experience and support'.[43] But this approach held dangers. It was not hard to find 'internationalist' Communists who held some rather truculent nationalist prejudices: the long history of Anglo-French antagonism prior to, and indeed since, 1904 did not necessarily mean that emphasis on national traditions would lead to a reaffirmation of the *Entente Cordiale*. And, as the French popular front government withered, and prospects of any form of wider unity in Britain died away, Anglo-French Communist relations began to take on an increasingly acerbic air. By March 1939, Pollitt was expressing hostility towards the French combined with a defensive pride in his own party in correspondence with Campbell, who was then the CPGB's representative in Moscow:

> One thing let me say Johnny, you have no need to be ashamed of your section of the C[ommunist] I[nternational]. The more I see of some others when I attend conferences in Paris the more proud I am of our own Party. Forgive me for being British.[44]

It was in this mood that Pollitt entered the most significant controversy between the two parties during the whole of the period under discussion. This concerned conscription. Britain's armed forces had traditionally been based on volunteers. This principle had been breached during the Great War, but conscription had been phased out soon after the conclusion of hostilities. In March 1939, the Chamberlain government announced that it was to be reintroduced. If anything could be claimed as part of a 'British national tradition', it was hostility towards military compulsion, and the reaction of many Communists, including Pollitt and the party's sole MP William Gallacher was to denounce the proposal. However, the Soviets and the French saw it differently. They both had conscription: they believed that Chamberlain's declaration was a long-overdue recognition of the threat posed by Nazi Germany. Against this, Pollitt's objections looked like effete liberalism. The French Communist Gabriel Péri attacked the British party. At first, the CPGB leadership repudiated Péri.[45] But it soon became clear that he was in fact pushing the line favoured by Moscow; and eventually the party overturned its earlier opposition to conscription. As a result, on 20 May, Pollitt offered his resignation from the post of party secretary, although for the time being it was not accepted.[46] The next time he offered it, it would be. Anglo-French relations, both inter-state and inter-party, were beginning to have a significant impact on the CPGB and its leadership.

Meanwhile, the chances of the two parties achieving anything of immediate significance in the fight against Fascism were fading. The failure of the *Entente* powers to reach a military alliance with the Soviets in the summer of 1939 was merely the end of the process. By this stage, British Communists had a rather jaundiced view of France, and of Anglo-French relations. Their views of the Anglo-French *Entente* had changed considerably after the rise of Hitler. Between 1934–35 and 1939, many, perhaps even most, had hoped that it would form one side of the collective security arrangements that would protect the Soviet Union against attack, and even begin a counter-attack against Fascism. But many had continued to hold severe suspicions of the motives of both countries. Many found it hard to swallow the argument that Britain and France, with their extensive colonial empires, could be in any way regarded as defenders of 'democracy' against Fascism. When Pollitt praised the merits of a British democratic tradition that had given birth to the largest empire the world had ever seen, and Thorez defended the rights of France's Catholic schools even as they denounced 'godless Communism', some of their less gullible, or more experienced, followers looked askance at them. For these people, little had changed about Britain and France since the *Entente* had been agreed in 1904. What had originated as a deal to resolve various disputes about colonial possessions remained, for many British Communists, essentially a compromise between two rival imperialisms which might otherwise lack the strength to survive. They would soon have their say.

IV

The German invasion of Poland on 1 September 1939 was followed on the third, somewhat haltingly, by declarations of war on Germany by Britain and France. Initially, many Communists felt that there needed to be no change in line, even though the USSR and Germany had entered a non-aggression pact a week before the outbreak of war. Pollitt continued to push the line of 'war on two fronts' – against Hitler, but also against the Chamberlain government at home – and believed he had the support of his party members in doing so. However, many British Communists had become increasingly alarmed as Pollitt's position had moved further and further towards straightforward defence of Britain against Germany.[47] Other Communist parties, not least the French, were starting to alter their positions in the early days of September. Pollitt was unmoved. He suppressed at least one telegram from Moscow informing him of the need for a new approach.[48] But the return from the Soviet capital of the British representative to the Comintern, D.F. 'Dave' Springhall, brought the conflict out into the open. At a stormy meeting of the party's central committee on 2 and 3 October, Pollitt, Campbell and Gallacher found themselves isolated as, one after another, their comrades backed the alternative, Comintern-backed, line advocated by Springhall, ably backed by Dutt, a long-time Comintern loyalist. Pollitt was ousted from the leadership and replaced by a secretariat comprising Springhall, Dutt and William Rust.[49]

The new line rejected the view that the war was being fought to defend democracy against fascism. Instead, it was a conflict of rival imperialisms, whose outcome was a matter of indifference to the working class of all countries. There was nothing to choose, so far as the workers were concerned, between British and French imperialism on the one hand, and German imperialism on the other. If anything – so the more extreme versions went – British and French attitudes had helped to promote German revanchism, and so Britain and France could be seen as even more culpable than Nazi Germany. At one level, of course, this was palpable nonsense, so much so that it has usually been seen as nothing more than the naïve swallowing of Soviet self-interest by gullible British (and French) Communists. As I have argued elsewhere, there can be no doubt that the Comintern's imprimatur was an important influence on many British Communists, not least those who were relatively new to the party and for whom a direct and explicit Comintern intervention was a novelty with which they had little idea how to deal other than to obey.[50]

But the change also accorded with the existing views of many British Communists: it was not a wholly alien imposition. Firstly, there had been misgivings about the old line, as stated above. For most Communists, it took something of a suspension of disbelief to see Britain, or France, for that matter, as a bastion of freedom. The 'war on two fronts' line helped to obscure the issue, but the failure of the British government to reach an alliance with the Soviets over the summer, and the Labour Party's continuing hostility towards collaboration with the CPGB, had simply confirmed older prejudices. Secondly, the memory of 1914 weighed heavily with many Communists. Then, Europe had descended into a long and bloody war. The outcome had not been the end of war, but, rather, a recasting of rival imperialisms as a prelude to a further round of armed conflict. Pollitt argued that the situation was now transformed – that Fascism and Nazism were fundamentally different from anything that had been fought over, or against, in the earlier conflict. It would be difficult, in retrospect, to maintain that he was wrong to do so. But to many at the time, Pollitt's line sounded suspiciously like the 'choice of 1914' – in a different key, perhaps, but fundamentally the same tune. For such people, Pollitt's line was merely a reprise of the attitudes that Lenin had been quick to denounce as 'social chauvinism', whereby the moment the guns started firing, international Socialists emerged as national patriots. Linked to this, thirdly, many saw the crisis as a chance to remove Pollitt, under whose leadership the party had become increasingly centred on the fight against Germany and Fascism, to the exclusion of the 'larger picture' of trying to bring Communism to power. In the years that he had led the party Pollitt had made enemies, and not a few of them now saw their chance to be rid of him.

But France was also very much in the minds of British Communists in September 1939. As one British Communist put it many years later, 'the French government made war not on the Nazis but on the [French] Communists and their sympathisers'.[51] Even before war broke out, the French Communist press was closed down and the party was clearly under threat, a point emphasised by Dimitrov to Stalin at the time.[52] The PCF was banned on 26 September, about half of its deputies were arrested, and Thorez was forced into exile (he was to spend the war years in Moscow). This was scarcely the act of a 'democracy', a point made trenchantly by Dutt in a pamphlet published that November:

> If this were a genuine anti-fascist war, would the first act of the French Government be to suppress the French Communist Party, the principal party of the working class and the leader of the anti-fascist fight? This act alone reveals the true character of the war as a war against the interests of the working class and democracy.[53]

In this way, therefore, the fate of the French Communists was central to the way in which British Communists justified their change of line on the war.

In reality, though, the line of the British Communist Party changed less in practice than it did in theory. The party did not launch a strong campaign of revolutionary defeatism, or anything of the sort. While it did continue to press the 'peace' line, it also kept its head down to a certain extent, focussing on day-to-day issues rather than that of the war.[54] Pollitt, after 'admitting' his 'error' with an insincerity that was recognised on all sides, soon returned to the higher levels of the party, although it was not until 1941 that he returned to the leadership.

Even so, the fall of France in June 1940 did lead to a significant, if short-lived, change in the Communists' approach to the war. Suddenly, a new, defencist line began to be put forward. Ivor Montagu's book, *The Traitor Class*, was a best seller: Montagu, a Communist who was personally and politically close to Pollitt, argued that the fall of France was due to the treachery of its ruling class, and that the same could happen in Britain.[55] It was argued that 'Two Hundred Families' had dominated French society, economy and politics, and had effectively betrayed France to the Germans. Strong parallels were claimed with British society on the basis of earlier Left Book Club publications alleging close connections between the supporters of appeasement and big business.[56] The implication was obvious – that there *was* after all something to choose between German imperialism on the one hand and French (and indeed British) imperialism on the other. The *Daily Worker* referred to the defeat of France as 'this sad hour' – hardly in line with the view that there was nothing to choose between French and German imperialism so far as the French working class was concerned.[57] Once again, therefore, France moved to the centre of the CPGB's discourse about the war. However, the absence of Soviet approval for a more wholehearted change of line meant that there was, at this stage at least, no long-lived, overt return to Pollitt's earlier policy.

There remains much controversy about the PCF's performance in the period from the fall of France to the German invasion of the USSR the following year, the time 'between the Junes'.[58] For the CPGB, 'between the Junes' of 1940 and 1941 was difficult in one sense, in that it could not openly come out for gung-ho prosecution of the war effort; but, in another, it was quite profitable, as it took up issues like inadequate air raid shelters, pay, prices, rationing and service dependents' allowances to make something of an impact, not least through the People's Convention in January 1941. However, the banning that month of their newspaper, the *Daily Worker*, was a sign that state repression was never far away. Thanks to Hitler, however, the party was on the verge of a new era of apparent success.

V

The new era began on 22 June 1941, with the German invasion of the Soviet Union. At first, Dutt tried to argue for a nuanced view of the conflict which would have put the CPGB firmly behind the USSR while being strongly critical of the Coalition government under Winston Churchill. But neither the Soviets themselves, nor Pollitt, nor, it may be surmised, the great bulk of the CPGB's membership, felt that this was an appropriate moment for an outbreak of Dutt's sophistry and semantics. In 1939, in his great row with Dutt in the central committee, Pollitt had said that what he wanted most of all was to '[s]mash the fascist bastards once and for all'.[59] Now he had his chance to help achieve that: and this largely summed up the party's line over the next four years.

In this context, there was a curious duality about British Communist attitudes towards France. On the one hand, there was admiration of the French Resistance, and no mistaking, so far as the CPGB was concerned, that it was French Communists who were leading it. At the same time, though, a somewhat patronising air emerged. Pollitt, in particular, had never been much of a Francophile, and he clearly took the view that the British, by successfully resisting Germany, had proved a certain superiority over the French. As the CPGB's membership soared to new heights – 56,000 in December 1942 as opposed to the pre-war peak (1939) of 18,500 – it seemed that it might now, at last, take its 'proper' place at the head of western European Communism. There were high hopes of the party finally gaining affiliation to the Labour Party, which would have given it a bigger stage and a wider influence – although the Labour Party Conference voted against this by a large margin in 1943, the vote in favour was higher than on any previous occasion, and it was expected that there would be a more favourable verdict when Labour next discussed the matter. Plans for the first post-war election were on a relatively grand scale, but Pollitt also had hopes for a while of a permanent continuation of Coalition politics, in the context of a permanent collaboration between the victor powers, into the post-war world. In such a context, it seemed possible to adopt a fairly superior attitude towards the French. Significantly, the CPGB's statement welcoming the D-Day landings in 1944 made not a single mention of France.[60] The party did its best, though, to draw on the reflected glory of the Resistance and of German atrocities against French Communists: ironically, given events in early 1939, the party published a glowing tribute to Péri following his murder by the Germans in 1941.[61]

But the CPGB's high hopes came to very little. The Labour Party's rules prohibited a renewed discussion of Communist affiliation for three years following its defeat in 1943; by the time that period was up, it had changed its rules to permanently bar separate political parties such as the CPGB from joining. Communist Party membership deflated slowly after 1942. Ideas of permanent Coalition foundered on Labour's refusal to contemplate continuing association with the Conservatives; hopes of an electoral deal with Labour alone then came to nothing. The CPGB ran 21 candidates at the 1945 election, but only 2 were elected, while Labour's massive majority of 146 meant that the handful of fellow travellers who were elected as Labour MPs would have very little opportunity to help the Communists by pressuring Attlee's government.[62]

Conversely, the reputation of the PCF flourished. The party's role in the Resistance has, of course, aroused much discussion and debate, but it was real and significant enough not only to offer short-term glory to the party, but also to help forge a collective mentality and memory that would keep the party firmly united for more than a generation. Nothing that the CPGB experienced during the war could rival this – the nearest was probably the fight against the ban on the *Daily Worker*, which hardly compared, for all that the party tried to make of it, at the time and afterwards.[63] Even the fact that the party's leader, Thorez, had not been in France during the war probably helped the PCF, by ensuring that its leaders had close relations with the Soviet leadership. It was not insignificant that when the Soviets, having formally abolished the Comintern in 1943, wanted to denounce the American Communist leader Earl Browder for his dissolution of the Communist Party of the United States of America in 1945, they used as their mouthpiece a French Communist, Jacques Duclos. For a while after the war, the PCF even participated in the

French government. The contrast with the CPGB could not have been sharper.

The final insult came in 1947, when the Communist Information Bureau (Cominform) was formed by the Soviets as a rather pale successor to the Comintern. Unlike the earlier body, its membership was restricted to Communist parties within the Soviet sphere of influence, plus two other parties – the Italians and the French. Pollitt was 'privately somewhat annoyed' by the exclusion of the British.[64] It hardly helped his mood, or that of other British Communists, that the conduit through which Cominform communication was to reach the CPGB appears to have been the PCF headquarters in Paris.[65] Although there was some British support for the French miners' strike in 1948, there was otherwise not much *entente,* and even less cordiality, between the British and French Communist parties by the later 1940s.[66]

At the level of international relations more broadly conceived, British Communists now regarded the idea of an Anglo-French *entente* as being of little relevance to the modern world. The developing Cold War was at the centre of Communist thoughts, and the final exclusion of Communists from the French post-war government in 1947 left no room to doubt that, once again, Britain and France were united against the USSR. But they were now regarded by Communists, not as masters of their own fate, but as mere pawns of a much more sinister influence, namely, the 'Yankee Imperialism' of 'dollar-hungry American gangsters'.[67] Nor did early moves towards greater European integration, which culminated in the formation of the European Economic Community in 1957, appear to offer anything better. For British Communists, Britain and France were once again powers ranged against the USSR, but now in collaboration with the USA. And that was enough to condemn them.

VI

This account has not challenged the accepted view that British Communists were essentially unsuccessful in this period. It has, however, attempted to trace the relationship of the British Communist Party with its French counterpart, and its view of France in general, in order to shed new light on the nature of Anglo-French relations more generally in the period of the World Wars. Historical significance, after all, is not just a matter of success or failure. In the period under review, British Communists had a greater sense of France, and of the revolutionary movement there, than their immediate predecessors on the British left had had. At various points between 1918 and 1945, the issue of Anglo-French relations did come to the forefront of British Communist thinking. However, enthusiasm for a bilateral *Entente Cordiale* was minimal. In part, this was because France was mistrusted as being an imperialist, and indeed counter-revolutionary, state: only *in extremis*, in the popular front period, did this perception soften somewhat. It was also due, however, to mistrust, shading into sheer dislike, of French Communists. But it was also due to the Soviet factor. Given the centrality of both Britain and France to the considerations of Soviet diplomacy and statecraft, it was inconceivable that British and French Communists would either have wanted, or been allowed, to pursue an approach towards their own countries' foreign policies that did not prioritise Soviet interests. For a time, in the Second World War, it was possible to claim that all three countries were working together. But, all too soon, that period ended, and western European Communists found themselves in the much harsher political climate of the Cold War. That the PCF flourished, at least when compared with the CPGB, is just one minor illustration of the differences between the two countries that have made their broad cooperation since 1904 seem all the more remarkable.

Notes

1. Though for an alternative view, see Steven Fielding, 'British Communism: Interesting but irrelevant?', *Labour History Review*, 60 (1995) 120–3.
2. Andrew Thorpe, 'The membership of the Communist Party of Great Britain, 1920–1945', *Historical Journal*, 43 (2000) 777–800.
3. See e.g., Andrew Thorpe, *The British Communist Party and Moscow, 1920–43* (Manchester, 2000); Gidon Cohen and Kevin Morgan, 'Stalin's sausage machine: British students at the International Lenin school, 1927–1937', *Twentieth Century British History*, 12 (2002) 327–55; John McIlroy and Alan Campbell, 'The British and French representatives to the Communist International, 1920–1939: A comparative survey', *International Review of Social History*, 50 (2005) 203–40.
4. See, among others, Kevin Morgan, 'Labour with knobs on? The recent historiography of the British Communist Party', *Mitteilungsblatt des Instituts für soziale Bewegungen*, 27 (2002) 69–83; John McIlroy and Alan

Campbell, 'Histories of the British Communist party: A user's guide', *Labour History Review*, 68, 1 (2003) 33–59; John McIlroy and Alan Campbell, 'A peripheral vision: Communist historiography in Britain', *American Communist History*, 4, 2 (2005) 125–57.

5. One noteworthy recent addition to the literature in this area is John McIlroy and Alan Campbell, 'British and French representatives to the Communist International, 1920–1939: A comparative survey'. *International Review of Social History*, 50, 2 (2005) 203–40.
6. John Horne, *Labour at War: France and Britain, 1914–1918* (Oxford, 1991), p. 83.
7. Thorpe, *British Communist Party* pp. 19–90, Passim.
8. For an example of this kind of attack, from what was in effect a CPGB 'front' organisation, see National Left Wing Committee, *Towards a Labour Government: The Policy and Programme of the National Left-Wing Movement* (London, nd [1927]), esp. pp. 12–13, 16–17. See also J.T. Murphy, *New Horizons* (London, 1941), pp. 342–3.
9. See e.g., V.I. Lenin, 'Political report of the Central Committee RKP(b) to the ninth all-Russian conference of the Communist party', 20 September 1920, in *The Unknown Lenin: From the Secret Archive*, ed. Richard Pipes (New Haven and London, 1996), pp. 95–115; *Lenin on Britain* (London, 1934), p. 207.
10. Rajani Palme Dutt, *World Politics, 1918–1936* (London, 1936), pp. 61–3.
11. Rajani Palme Dutt, *Socialism and the Living Wage* (London, 1927), pp. 59–60.
12. Russian State Archive of Socio-Political History (RGASPI) 495/100/104, fo. 22, CPGB political bureau, 11 April 1923.
13. RGASPI 495/100/103, fo. 79, CPGB central executive committee minutes, 10 April 1923.
14. RGASPI 495/100/117, fos 60–1, 'Statement of Newbold's talk with Comrade Sellier in Paris', 7 August 1923.
15. RGASPI 495/100/159, fos 49–50, CPGB political bureau 29 February 1924; 495/100/147, fo. 102, political bureau 6 June 1924; 495/100/147, fo. 2, preliminary meeting of British delegation, 9 June 1924; 495/100/163, fo. 74, organisation bureau 10 June 1924.
16. CPGB, *Seventh National Congress* (London, 1925), p. 159.
17. RGASPI 495/100/104, fos 49, 78–9, CPGB political bureau, 7, 26 September 1923.
18. Newbold, 'Why I have left the Communist Party', *Forward*, 13 September 1924.
19. Thorpe, *British Communist Party*, pp. 80–1; see also Harry Wicks, *Keeping My Head: The Memoirs of a British Bolshevik* (London, 1992), pp. 53–4.
20. John Callaghan, *Rajani Palme Dutt: A Study in British Stalinism* (London, 1993), pp. 58–62.
21. Grant Adibekov and Eleonora Shakhnazarova, 'Reconstructions of the Comintern organisational structure', in Mikhail Narinsky and Jurgen Rojahn (eds), *Centre and Periphery: The History of the Comintern in the Light of New Documents* (Amsterdam, 1996), p. 68.

22. John Callaghan, 'The Communists and the colonies: Anti-imperialism between the wars', in Geoff Andrews et al. (eds), *Opening the Books: Essays of the Social and Cultural History of the British Communist Party* (London, 1995), pp. 10–11.
23. This can be seen from comments in Murphy, *New Horizons*, pp. 87, 274.
24. Thorpe, *British Communist Party*, p. 109.
25. *Ibid.*, pp. 200–1.
26. Rajani Palme Dutt, *Crisis: Tariffs: War* (London, 1931), p. 19.
27. Charles P. Kindleberger, *The World in Depression, 1929–1939* (Harmondsworth, 1987), p. 46.
28. A prominent British example of this viewpoint, published in the year before the Nazi takeover, was John Strachey, *The Coming Struggle for Power* (London, 1932).
29. Kevin McDermott and Jeremy Agnew, *The Comintern: A History of International Communism from Lenin to Stalin* (London, 1996), pp. 124–5.
30. E.H. Carr, *The Twilight of Comintern, 1930–1935* (London, 1982), pp. 198–201. The 'united front' was developed as a Comintern strategy in 1920–1, and essentially involved Communists seeking alliances with other Socialist and working-class organisations which would help to promote Socialism and, in the not-too-distant future, revolution. The 'popular front' emerged in response to Nazism, and was aimed to unite all anti-Fascists, including non-Socialists and those from organisations outside the working class. Although the long-term aim of revolution remained, the popular front was, effectively, a much more moderate and defensive formation than its predecessor.
31. CPGB, *Harry Pollitt Speaks: A Call to All Workers* (London, nd [1935]), pp. 4–5.
32. Julian Jackson, *The Popular Front in France: Defending Democracy, 1934–1938* (Cambridge, 1988), p. 219; Thorpe, 'The membership of the Communist Party of Great Britain', p. 781.
33. Georgi Dimitrov, 'United front of the working class against fascism', speech delivered at the Seventh World Congress of the Communist International, 2 August 1935, in *idem*, *The Working Class against Fascism* (London, 1935), p. 40.
34. Nina Fishman, *The British Communist Party and the Trade Unions, 1933–45* (Aldershot, 1995), p. 94.
35. Noreen Branson, *History of the Communist Party of Great Britain, 1927–1941* (London, 1985), p. 214.
36. Frank Jellinek, *The Paris Commune of 1871* (London, 1937); Neil Stewart, *Blanqui* (London, 1939).
37. See for example Emile Burns, *Communist Affiliation* (London, 1936).
38. Harry Pollitt, *Labour's Way Forward* (London, 1937), p. 5.
39. Thorpe, 'The membership of the Communist party of Great Britain', p. 781; Jackson, *The Popular Front in France*, p. 219.
40. See e.g., RGASPI 495/74/36, fo. 105, Marty to Dimitrov, 9 September 1937.
41. Branson, *History of the Communist Party of Great Britain*, p. 231.

42. Jackson, *The Popular Front in France*, p. 248.
43. RGASPI 495/100/1149, fos 12–15, 'Draft resolution of secretariat on report of Comrade Pollitt', 4 January 1937.
44. RGASPI 495/100/1040, fos 5–7, Pollitt to Campbell, 30 March 1939.
45. *House of Commons Debates*, 5 series, vol. 346, cols 1348, 1382, 1457, 1461, 27 April 1939. I am grateful to Kevin Morgan for this reference.
46. Thorpe, *British Communist Party*, pp. 247–9.
47. See e.g., John Attfield and Stephen Williams, *1939: The Communist Party and the War* (London, 1984), pp. 54–8, 99–109; Douglas Hyde, *I Believed: The Autobiography of a Former British Communist* (London, 1952), pp. 68–9; Malcolm Macewen, *The Greening of a Red* (London, 1991), p. 63; Bas Barker and Lynda Straker, *Free – But Not Easy* (Matlock, 1989), p. 70; Harry McShane and Jean Smith, *Harry McShane: No Mean Fighter* (London, 1978), p. 231.
48. Monty Johnstone, 'The CPGB, the Comintern and the war, 1939–1941: Filling in the blank spots', *Science and Society*, 61 (1997) 27–45, at 29–32; Thorpe, *British Communist Party*, pp. 257–8.
49. For this meeting, see Francis King and George Matthews, *About Turn: The Communist Party and the Outbreak of the Second World War: The Verbatim Record of the Central Committee Meetings, 1939* (London, 1990).
50. Thorpe, *British Communist Party*, p. 259.
51. Macewen, *Greening of a Red*, p. 62.
52. Dimitrov to Stalin, 27 August 1939, in *Dimitrov and Stalin, 1934–1943: Letters from the Soviet Archives*, ed. Alexander Dallin and F.I. Firsov (New Haven and London, 2000), p. 150.
53. Rajani Palme Dutt, *Why this War?* (London, 1939), p. 5.
54. Willie Thompson, *The Good Old Cause: British Communism, 1920–1991* (London, 1992), p. 68.
55. Ivor Montagu, *The Traitor Class* (London, 1940), p. 63.
56. See Simon Haxey, *Tory M.P.* (London, 1939), published by the Left Book Club.
57. *Daily Worker*, editorial on 'France and Britain', 6 July 1941, reprinted in *Daily Worker* Defence League, *The Daily Worker and the War* (London, nd [1941]), pp. 14–16.
58. David Wingeate Pike, 'Between the Junes: the French Communists from the collapse of France to the invasion of Russia', *Journal of Contemporary History*, 28 (1993), pp. 465–85.
59. King and Matthews, *About Turn*, p. 203.
60. Communist party, 'The second front opens', June 1944, in CPGB, *Documents for Congress: A Collection of the Principal Political Statements issued by the Communist Party between July 1943 and August 1944* (London, 1944), p. 30.
61. William Rust, *Gabriel Péri* (London, nd [1941/2]); see also Harry Pollitt, presenting central committee's report to CPGB national conference, May 1942, reprinted in CPGB, *The Way to Win* (London, 1942), p. 13; Harry Pollitt, *How to Win the Peace* (London, 1944), p. 59.

62. The two Communist MPs were Gallacher at West Fife, in the Scottish coalfield, and Phil Piratin, at Mile End in the East End of London.
63. William Rust, *Lift the Ban on the Daily Worker* (London, nd [1941]); *idem*, *The Story of the Daily Worker* (London, 1949), esp. pp. 83–96.
64. Noreen Branson, *History of the Communist Party of Great Britain, 1941–1951* (London, 1997), p. 157
65. Henry Pelling, *The British Communist Party: A Historical Profile* (London, 1958), p. 141.
66. *Ibid.*, pp. 153–5.
67. William Gallacher, *The Tyrants' Might is Passing* (London, 1954), pp. 37, 43.

6

Churchill and de Gaulle: Makers and Writers of History

David Reynolds
Christ's College, Cambridge

Winston Churchill and Charles de Gaulle bestrode Anglo-French relations in the mid-twentieth century. They were the Second World War analogues of Lloyd George and Clemenceau. In fact, Churchill and de Gaulle probably had greater significance for the *Entente* than any other pair of leaders in the whole century. This was partly because of their longevity and influence as national leaders – Churchill was prime minister in 1940–45 and 1951–55; de Gaulle led his country in 1944–46 and again, as president of his tailor-made Fifth Republic, from 1958 to 1969 – but their importance also derived from being historians, not just statesmen, shaping events through their writings as well as their deeds. This essay examines three facets of their wartime relationship – what happened at the time, how they wrote about these events in their memoirs, and the underlying vision of history that inspired them as statesmen and historians.[1]

Churchill, half-American, is renowned for his special relationship with the United States. He was, however, a warm friend of France and spent much more time there – 1447 days during his whole life, according to biographer Roy Jenkins, compared with less than 400 in the United States.[2] He was well acquainted with France's war leaders of the Great War era, when he was a British Cabinet minister, and kept in close contact with many of its politicians of the late 1930s, as part of his campaign for a 'Grand Alliance' against Nazi Germany. But his path did not cross that of Charles de Gaulle until the crisis days of June 1940. Born in 1890 and therefore sixteen years Churchill's junior, the Frenchman was a professional soldier and staff officer. His main claim to fame was a short book published in 1934 entitled *Vers l'Armée de Métier*, which advocated an elite force of motorised, armoured divisions to bring back mobility to the battlefield.

De Gaulle's ideas were not novel – he drew heavily on French and British military thinkers such as Doumenc, Fuller and Liddell Hart – but it took much courage for a young colonel to champion them against the defensive orthodoxy of the French high command, not least his patron Marshal Philippe Pétain. The book was not translated into English (under the title *The Army of the Future*) until 1940 and, although Churchill became vaguely aware of de Gaulle's ideas during a visit to Paris in March 1938, he did not take them seriously. They were in fact diametrically opposed to his own strategic thinking at the time. In a newspaper article in April, entitled 'How Wars of the Future will be Waged', Churchill extolled the 'glorious' contributions of tanks to victory in 1918 but doubted that they would play as decisive a part in the next war. 'Nowadays the anti-tank rifle and the anti-tank gun have made such great strides that the poor tank cannot carry a thick enough skin to stand up to them.' Churchill placed his faith in the defensive power of the French army, which he continued to laud as the greatest in Europe, and he was as shocked as anyone by the devastating German armoured breakthrough in May 1940.[3]

On 6 June 1940 Brigadier General de Gaulle was suddenly promoted to under-secretary for National Defence in the desperate endgame of Paul Reynaud's premiership. Three days later he was sent to London to show the British a general with aggressive spirit. Between 9 June and 16 June he had four meetings with Churchill, on both sides of the Channel, and played a role in the hasty declaration of Anglo-French union patched together in an effort to prevent the French surrender. By the time they met for the fifth time, on 17 June, Reynaud had resigned, Pétain was seeking an armistice and de Gaulle was a refugee in London. De Gaulle was amazingly, almost ludicrously, defiant. On the 17th, before leaving Paris, he was announcing calmly, as a matter of fact: 'The Germans have lost the war . . . France must keep on fighting'. But he could have done nothing in exile without Churchill's support. Overruling the Foreign Office and War Cabinet, who were still hoping to keep Pétain in play, the prime minister allowed him to use the BBC to broadcast a call for French resistance. Otherwise, de Gaulle's immortal 'Appel' of 18 June would have been impossible – a debt the General never forgot throughout all their subsequent altercations. And on 28 June the prime minister announced that the British Government recognised de Gaulle as 'leader of all Free Frenchmen, wherever they may be, who rally to him in support of the Allied cause'. Churchill, for his part, desperately needed to create the impression that Britain was not entirely alone. This was essential in his own bid to ensure that the country fought on and he made his own epic appeal to the French people, in French over the BBC, on 21 October. Each man needed the other, but necessity should not obscure the courage with which they reacted to the crisis of 1940. Truly this was 'their finest hour'.

If that phrase sums up the first phase of their wartime relationship, in similarly Churchillian vein, one may summarise the next period (1941–43) as the 'not-so-grand alliance'. The problem was that Churchill thought he was backing a military leader, who could serve an immediate purpose as a rallying point for resistance. But no politician of note fled to Britain so, *faute de mieux*, de Gaulle became a political figure as well – which was, of course, what the General intended. For the best part of three years, however, the British Government tried to avoid a total embrace: Churchill took the line that 'General de Gaulle was not France, but Fighting France'.[4] In 1940–41 the British kept open contacts with Vichy via the Madrid Embassy and intermediaries such as Professor Louis Rougier and also tried to rally alternative leaders in French North Africa. After the failure of the attempt to seize Dakar in September 1940 – which the British blamed partly on leaks from de Gaulle's forces – they kept firm control of subsequent operations, such as the conquest of Syria in the summer of 1941, or they excluded de Gaulle entirely, as in the capture of Madagascar in May 1942. Any sign that the British were trespassing on French territory produced explosions of rage from de Gaulle, fuelled by his profound suspicion of perfidious Albion. And Churchill responded in kind: 'There is nothing hostile to England this man may not do once he gets off the chain', he told his Foreign Secretary Anthony Eden, in May 1942.[5]

The other problem was that the Anglo-French marriage of 1940 was complicated by the appearance of a third party when the United States entered the war in December 1941. De Gaulle had two reactions to Pearl Harbor. First, he told his chief of Staff, 'the war is over, because its outcome is no longer in doubt. In this industrial war, nothing can resist the power of American industry'. But he added: 'From now on, the British will do nothing without Roosevelt's agreement'.[6] It was a shrewd prophecy. Churchill wrote to Eden in November 1942: 'My whole system is based on friendship w[ith] Roosevelt'.[7] The American president, for his part, had no time for de Gaulle, and was confident he could still exert influence over Pétain and Vichy. There was a flaming row when Free French forces unilaterally occupied the Vichy-controlled islands of St Pierre and Miquelon, off the coast of Newfoundland, in December 1941. Cordell Hull, the American secretary of State, spoke caustically of 'the so-called Free French'. In November 1942, the president insisted that the initial landings in Algeria and Morocco (Operation Torch) should be a purely American affair, confident that if there were no British or Free French the Vichy forces would cooperate with their liberators. De Gaulle was awakened with news of the operation only as the troops were going ashore. 'Well, I hope the Vichy people will fling them into the sea!' was his initial, explosive reaction, standing there in his pyjamas.[8] And when FDR's hopes of no resistance proved a delusion, the Americans suddenly concluded a deal with Admiral François Darlan, Pétain's deputy, who had been captured in Algiers. Darlan was allowed to assume power in French North Africa in return for declaring a ceasefire. De Gaulle's anger was matched by waves of criticism in America and incredulity in London but, although unhappy, Churchill stayed loyal to Roosevelt.

As November wore on, however, the prime minister's mood became more positive. On 26 November, he told Eden that Darlan had 'done more for us than de G[aulle]'. Two days later, after the admiral had kept his promise and scuttled the French fleet rather than letting it fall into German hands, Eden's private secretary noted that Churchill was 'getting more and more enthusiastic over Darlan'.[9] On 10 December, in a secret speech to the Commons, the prime minister combined defence of the Darlan deal with warnings that de Gaulle was by no means 'an unfaltering friend of Britain', noting that his tour of French colonies in Africa 'left a trail of anglophobia behind him'. Churchill told MPs not to 'base all your hopes and confidence upon him' and added: 'I cannot feel that de Gaulle is France, still less that Darlan and Vichy are France. France is something greater, more complex, more formidable than any of these sectional manifestations'.[10] This uneasy balancing act was brought to an end by Darlan's murder in Algiers on Christmas Eve by Fernand Bonnier de la Chapelle. Although portrayed as a lone actor, Bonnier was in league with the Gaullists who in turn were supported by local elements of Britain's Special Operations Executive. How far the Government in London was implicated remains unclear but, as François Kersaudy nicely puts it, rarely has a political assassination been 'so unanimously condemned and so universally welcomed'.[11]

With Darlan dead and all of France now under Nazi occupation, the Vichy option was clearly closed. But the Allies still looked for alternative Frenchmen. At Casablanca in January 1943 Roosevelt and Churchill forced de Gaulle to work with their preferred figure, General Henri Giraud, in a unified administration of French North Africa. This was a 'shotgun wedding' that de Gaulle bitterly resented. The president left Casablanca convinced that de Gaulle considered himself a combination of Joan of Arc and Clemenceau but also hopeful, in his usual breezy way, that he had now fixed the French problem. It was another delusion. Over the next few months, de Gaulle, despite a much weaker hand, outplayed Giraud and enlarged his authority within the French Committee of National Liberation (FCNL). Watching the train of events, Roosevelt pressed hard for Britain to break with de Gaulle. When Churchill was in Washington in May 1943, he was fed daily stories about de Gaulle's machinations until eventually he cabled the Cabinet on 21 May 'with a diatribe about 'this vain and even malignant man', whether they 'should not now eliminate de Gaulle as a political force'. He cited as justification the General's Anglophobia and his attempts to sabotage transatlantic relations, even casting aspersions on de Gaulle's courage and integrity: 'He has never himself fought since he left France and took pains to have his wife brought out safely beforehand'. However, Eden – consistently more supportive of France and sceptical about America than Churchill – stiffened the Cabinet. As Eden privately acknowledged, it was much easier to stand up to Churchill in his absence. In person, the prime minister's belligerent loquacity usually wore the opposition into silence if not assent.[12]

In July, however, the two men clashed head on. Eden argued so vehemently for political recognition of de Gaulle that Churchill warned him, 'we might be coming to break'. Eden said he had no intention of resigning. What had so provoked Churchill was a paper from Eden arguing that it was erroneous for Britain to rely so heavily on the United States, especially given the doubts in Whitehall about whether American isolationism would reassert itself after victory was won. 'In dealing with European problems of the future', he wrote, 'we are likely to have to work more closely with France even than with the United States'.[13] This exchange revealed very clearly the two men's differing priorities. In principle both shared the goal, as Churchill put it, of 'a strong France friendly to Great Britain and the USA',[14] but they disagreed about what to do in a conflict of interest. Despite his Francophilia, when the chips were down, Churchill would side with the United States. In the last analysis, Eden went the opposite way – as Suez in 1956 would show so dramatically.

Caught between Roosevelt, Eden and the indefatigable de Gaulle, it was not surprising that Churchill frequently lost his cool. Despite all the political strains, however, his personal relationship with de Gaulle survived. According to the prime minister's private secretary Jock Colville, Churchill summoned de Gaulle to Downing Street for a formal rebuke about his summer 1941 tour of the Middle East. Before the meeting, he announced that he would speak to him only in English and that Colville should act as interpreter. Given Churchill's *franglais*, this might seem an act of courtesy to his guest, but the prime minister clearly intended it as a sign of profound disapproval. According to Colville's account, when de Gaulle arrived in the Cabinet Room, Churchill said sternly, 'General de Gaulle, I have asked you to come here this afternoon' and then paused for a translation. 'Mon Général', Colville began, 'je vous ai invité à venir cet après-midi'. Churchill interrupted: 'I didn't say *Mon Général* and I did not say that I had *invited* him'. Colville stumbled through a few more sentences, with frequent interruptions, and then it was de Gaulle's turn. After Colville had translated the first sentence, the General interjected, 'Non, non, ce n'est pas du tout le sens de ce que je disais'. Colville had no doubt that it was but Churchill said that, since he clearly could not do the job, he had better find someone who could. An embarrassed Colville quickly summoned Nicholas Lawford of the Foreign Office, whose linguistic credentials were impeccable. But within minutes Lawford came out of the Cabinet Room, red in the face and furious to have been told that, since he could not speak French properly, they would have to manage without an interpreter. After an hour, fearful that the two leaders had come to blows,

Colville was preparing to enter the room with a bogus message. Then suddenly the bell rang. He found Churchill and de Gaulle sitting side by side, conversing amicably in French, with the General smoking one of Churchill's cigars.[15]

This proved a familiar pattern for subsequent meetings. In March 1943, for instance, Churchill refused permission for de Gaulle to visit Africa and the Middle East, fearing more anti-British agitation. 'Je suis prisonnier', de Gaulle exclaimed when they met. 'Bientôt vous m'enverrez à l'Iloman.' A puzzled Churchill asked him to repeat the last word. After three attempts, he gathered that de Gaulle meant the Isle of Man – a remote island off the northwest coast of England. Whereupon, in his best French, Churchill declared: 'Non, mon Général, pour vous, très distingué, toujours la Tower of London'. But once again a sulphurous start led eventually to a happy ending. The two men entertained a deep respect for the other which survived their political differences.[16]

By late 1943 we move from the not-so-grand alliance to a final phase that, again in Churchillian terms, we might term 'triumph and tragedy'. In July 1943 the British and American governments extended grudging political recognition of the FCNL as the body 'administering those French territories which acknowledge its authority'. This was limited but it was a step. By the end of the year de Gaulle had control of the FCNL, forcing out Giraud entirely. He now dominated the French abroad, but still stood on the periphery of the Allied war effort. That became quite clear in the run-up to D-Day. As with *Torch*, FDR refused to bring de Gaulle into the planning. It was only after repeated pleas from Eden that Churchill summoned the General from Algiers on 4 June to be told of the impending landings. Roosevelt was also refusing to accept the FCNL as the provisional government of France. De Gaulle was furious that Eisenhower would be imposing a government of occupation, complete with its own 'French currency'. Churchill, equally inflamed, said that in any unbridgeable rift between de Gaulle and Roosevelt, he 'would almost certainly side with the President' and that 'no quarrel would ever arise between Britain and the United States on account of France'.[17]

When Eisenhower asked de Gaulle to broadcast a liberation message to Frenchmen, the General took umbrage at the line-up of Allied leaders speaking on the eve of D-Day, which placed him last behind even the Grand Duchess of Luxembourg. He said he would speak to his countrymen at a time and in a form of his own choosing. Understanding, erroneously, that de Gaulle had simply refused to broadcast, Churchill became incandescent with rage. All night on 5–6 June the Free French ambassador in London shuttled between the two leaders – each on his high horse but also tired and desperately worried about the morning to come. In the early hours of D-Day, with Allied paratroopers already landing in Normandy, Churchill ordered de Gaulle to be sent back to Algiers, 'in chains if necessary. He must not be allowed to enter France'. It took all Eden's finesse to have the order rescinded.[18]

De Gaulle returned to French soil on 14 June – almost exactly four years since he had departed. The rapturous reception impressed British and American observers with his popularity in France and in July, Roosevelt finally agreed that he could visit America. But the President still dragged his feet on according full political recognition of the FCNL, which did not come about until the end of October. This finally resolved Churchill's most fundamental problem in the triangle with Roosevelt and de Gaulle and it paved the way for his remarkable visit to Paris the following month. On Armistice Day, 11 November 1944, the two leaders walked down the Champs-Elysées to cheers from hundreds of thousands of Parisians. They paid their respects at Clemenceau's statue, Foch's grave and Napoleon's tomb. Deeply moved, both men were gracious and expansive in their speeches over lunch: de Gaulle toasted the fidelity of 'our old and gallant ally, England' and Churchill, close to tears, welcomed France back to the rank of 'the great nations' and praised 'the capital part' played by de Gaulle in the transformation of his country's fortunes.[19] But their business discussions over the next two days showed that sentiment could not outweigh *Realpolitik*. When de Gaulle suggested an exclusive bilateral alliance of the sort mooted in the crisis of June 1940, Churchill indicated that his priorities remained transatlantic. Although desiring no rift with France, he wished to work first with the United States, using his close personal tie with Roosevelt to persuade and guide the Americans to use their 'immense resources' to best advantage.[20] *Entente cordiale* – yes, Churchill was saying. But the only special relationship would be between Britain and America.

Given Churchill's priorities and Roosevelt's prejudices, France, even after liberation, would therefore remain on the margins. The president, in fact, was not merely Gaullophobe but frankly

Gallophobe, entertaining profound doubts about the future of France itself. In the winter of 1942–43 he had twice suggested to British Cabinet ministers that a new state called Wallonia should be carved out from the francophone part of Belgium, Luxembourg, Alsace, Lorraine and north-eastern France around Lille. Eden responded with incredulity.[21] In September 1944, FDR was predicting revolution in France. In December, as Greece descended into civil war, he told another British minister that 'no doubt we should see the Greek situation repeated elsewhere, probably in France' and that he was 'determined that American troops should not be mixed up with the French civil war'.[22] Clearly Roosevelt had no sense of France as a cohesive state, let alone a great power. His confidant Harry Hopkins told de Gaulle in January 1945 that the root problem was the shock and disappointment felt in Washington at the French collapse in 1940: America's traditional sense of the power and value of France had crumbled in a moment.[23] Churchill had a far higher estimation of France, especially after his visit in November 1944. But when Eden started pressing the idea of a 'Western European bloc' centred on France, as a contribution to continental security, the prime minister was dismissive. 'Until a really strong French Army is again in being, which may be more than five years away or even ten, there is nothing in these countries but hopeless weakness.'[24]

In December 1944, de Gaulle went to Moscow and signed a treaty of friendship. The visit sent shockwaves through London and Washington but Stalin made clear that France did not count for much in Soviet policy. This was underlined at the Yalta Conference in February 1945, from which de Gaulle was entirely excluded. It was only after repeated pressure from Churchill and Eden that France was given an occupation zone in Germany and a place on the Allied Control Commission. Roosevelt and Stalin considered this as an act of 'kindness' rather than a response to international realities.[25] So triumph still had a bitter taste for de Gaulle. And it turned sour for Churchill, too, in the spring of 1945 as he tried ineffectually to persuade the Americans to take a firmer line against Soviet expansion in Central Europe. Moreover, personal tragedy soon intervened. In July, Churchill found himself voted out of Downing Street by the British electorate. It was a total shock, bitterly resented, beginning what I call his 'second Wilderness Years'. In November, de Gaulle was elected president of the new Fourth Republic but this triumph, too, was short-lived. Petty problems, parliamentary squabbles and a weak executive dominated by a strong legislature were hardly his ideal for government. After briefly contemplating a coup, de Gaulle announced his resignation on 20 January 1946. He probably intended it as a tactical retreat: 'I thought the French would recall me very quickly', he admitted a few years later,[26] but they did not. Churchill returned to Downing Street in 1951; de Gaulle stayed in the wilderness much longer. Only in 1958 did he again become president of France, this time on his own terms.

Although out of power, Churchill and de Gaulle still kept in touch. In November 1946, Churchill requested the General's assessment of the capabilities of the Red Army. A few weeks later he drew de Gaulle's attention to his Zurich speech on a united Europe, writing: 'It is my conviction that if France could take Germany by the hand and, with full English co-operation, rally her to the West and to European civilization, this would indeed by a glorious victory and make amends for all we have gone through and perhaps save us from having to go through a lot more'.[27] When Churchill was in Antibes in September 1948, he learnt that de Gaulle was in the vicinity and sent a note of greeting and good wishes. This elicited a very cordial handwritten reply, worth quoting in the original French, in which the General expressed:

> toute l'admiration et toute l'amitié que je porte à votre personne. Si, avant que vous ne quittiez la France, votre itinéraire passait près de Colombey-les-Deux-Églises, nous serions, ma femme et moi, très heureux et très honorés, de vous y recevoir tout à fait dans l'intimité.

Churchill did not have time to accept de Gaulle's hospitality, but the invitation was a rare gesture from this intensely private man.[28] The only foreign statesman who actually visited de Gaulle at his home in Colombey was Konrad Adenauer in 1958.[29]

After losing power, Churchill soon got down to his war memoirs, which appeared in six volumes between 1948 and 1954. Although de Gaulle took longer, he published three volumes between 1954 and 1959. Roosevelt, Hitler and Mussolini, who all died in 1945, wrote no memoirs; Stalin lived to 1953 but left his legacy in blood not ink. So Churchill and de Gaulle were unique among the major war leaders in giving their accounts of the war at length. In the process, they reconstructed (or more accurately constructed) their wartime relationship on the printed page.

In Churchill's account, de Gaulle first appears in volume two, *Their Finest Hour*, after a vivid depiction of the feebleness of Gamelin and the existing French military leadership. This was a somewhat caricatured account of his meeting with them at the Quai d'Orsay on 16 May 1940.[30] De Gaulle is then brought onto the stage as the embodiment of 'Fighting France' in contrast with his defeatist superiors. He is a brooding presence at the last Anglo-French conclaves, 'impassive' and 'imperturbable'. At Tours on 13 June, Churchill glimpses him in a crowded passage: 'I said in a low tone, in French: "L'homme du destin"' – corrected by Bill Deakin, one of his research assistants, from the *franglais* in Churchill's draft, 'l'homme de la destinée'. Of a meeting three days later, Churchill says: 'I preserved the impression, in contact with this very tall, phlegmatic man, "Here is the Constable of France"'.[31]

De Gaulle's biographer Jean Lacouture has made a good deal of these episodes. Did the General hear the reference to him as 'the man of destiny'? No, said de Gaulle when asked in the 1960s. And did Churchill know that de Gaulle's longstanding nickname, a legacy of the Saint-Cyr military academy before the Great War, was 'the Constable'? (This was the title of the supreme commander of the French armies in medieval times.) The answer is 'probably not': more likely Churchill took the term from Shakespeare's history plays.[32] As with other vivid stories in Churchill's memoirs, he may well not have used these phrases at the time, but there seems little doubt that de Gaulle made an immediate impact on the prime minister in June 1940: Churchill's account in the memoirs contain poetic, if not literal, truth.

The 'man of destiny' tag also serves as an interpretative key to Churchill's treatment of de Gaulle throughout the memoirs. The reader is left in no doubt that this was a difficult, often turbulent relationship but, throughout, Churchill's account is moderated and modulated by hindsight. The first simplification was political. From the competing wartime claimants, de Gaulle had triumphantly emerged as the representative of France, so Churchill's memoirs play down Britain's understandable attempts to keep open all options and conceals the extent of his dalliance with Vichy and with alternative anti-Vichy French leaders. Responsibility for the Darlan deal is laid at the American door and Churchill makes no mention of his brief but real enthusiasm for the admiral in November 1942. The Roosevelt administration is also fingered as the main reason for Britain's slowness in extending political recognition to de Gaulle. Churchill is, in fact, misleading in volume five when stating that at Quebec in August 1943 the British and Americans announced 'formal recognition of the French National Committee', which placed the latter 'on formal terms with the Allies as the representatives of France'.[33]

The other simplification is personal. By the time Churchill started writing, de Gaulle's first presidency was over but the *Rassemblement du Peuple Français* (RPF) had been founded in April 1947 and was clearly a major force in the fractious and increasingly polarised politics of the Fourth Republic. De Gaulle's eventual return to power was likely and it therefore seemed prudent to suppress some of Churchill's more rebarbative wartime asides about the General. His old friend and adviser Lord Cherwell warned that, if de Gaulle did make a political comeback, 'cooperation with him might be even more difficult if he had read some of these comments'.[34] Some of Churchill's choicest expletives were therefore removed from his wartime documents before they appeared in print, such as 'symptoms of a budding Führer' (July 1943) or his comment in February 1945 that de Gaulle's presence at Yalta 'would have wrecked all possible progress'.[35] Readers are also deprived of what was probably Churchill's most honest verdict on the General: 'I should be sorry to live in a country governed by de Gaulle, but I should be sorry to live in a world, or with a France, in which there was not a de Gaulle'. But there remains a very fair account of his feelings about de Gaulle in a passage dictated specially for his chapter on the Casablanca Conference of January 1943. 'Always, even when he was behaving worst, he seemed to express the personality of France – a great nation, with all its pride, authority, and ambition.'[36]

Although, like Churchill, de Gaulle started writing in 1946, as soon as he left office, he was preoccupied by plans for a return to power and it was not until the failure of his political party, the RPF, in the elections of June 1951 that the General retreated to Colombey-les-Deux-Églises and worked in earnest on his memoirs. Volume one (on 1940–42) appeared in 1954 and volume two (1942–44) followed in 1956, but the last volume was not published until 1959, after the General had become president once more.

Unlike Churchill with his 'Syndicate' of research assistants, who prepared and drafted much of the material for their 'Master', de Gaulle scrawled out his text painfully by hand before having it deciphered and typed by his daughter.[37] He had only a single researcher, from the Ministry of Foreign Affairs, who helped pull together official documents,[38] and his volume was much more of a clean narrative than Churchill's, who saved time and energy by reproducing masses of telegrams and minutes he had dictated during the war – in some cases over half the wordage of a volume. Churchill had numerous copies of his draft chapters printed for comment from his assistants and former colleagues. De Gaulle consulted only a few close family and associates: even prospective publishers were only allowed to inspect the text at the home of Georges Pompidou. This, then, was a very different work from Churchill's.

Like Churchill, however, de Gaulle toned down some of his more caustic wartime comments during the process of revision. For instance, he deleted a reference to his conviction that 'in times of war policy is too serious a matter to be left to politicians' – which might have seemed to confirm suspicions of Bonapartism.[39] Yet his volumes do make clear the extent and frequency of his differences with Churchill. He provides, for instance, a colourful account of their flaming row on the night of 5–6 June 1944 – glossed over by Churchill. And for their meeting on 4 June, which Churchill does discuss, he quoted the prime minister as saying: 'each time we have to choose between Europe and the open sea, we shall always choose the open sea. Each time I must choose between you and Roosevelt, I shall always choose Roosevelt'. It is doubtful that Churchill used those words – and one wonders how many of the 'quotations' in de Gaulle's memoirs are precisely accurate – but the General was surely conveying the gist of Churchill's message.[40]

Equally, de Gaulle also makes clear his fundamental respect for his British protagonist. A long passage on their first meeting on 9 June 1940 includes this tribute to Churchill:

> The harsh and painful incidents that often arose between us, because of the friction of our two characters, of the opposition of some of the interests or our two countries, and of the unfair advantage taken by England of wounded France, have influenced my attitude towards the Prime Minister, but not my judgment.

> Winston Churchill appeared to me, from one end of the drama to the other, as the great champion of a great enterprise and the great artist of a great history.[41]

A 'great artist of a great history' – here de Gaulle was writing about Churchill the orator but these words can be applied to both men, and in at least two ways. First, with respect to the composition of their war memoirs. Unlike many memoirists, who write in tranquil (or bitter) retirement, Churchill and de Gaulle were determined to return to power. Churchill, humiliated by his massive defeat in the election of 1945, had his eye on a second spell in Ten Downing Street, which he duly achieved in October 1951 and his memoirs were constructed to show his indispensability. For instance, the practice of quoting at length from so many of his minutes and directives, while including very few replies, gave the impression – to quote Norman Brook, the Cabinet secretary, who vetted the drafts for the British Government – 'that no one but he ever took the initiative'.[42] De Gaulle's memoirs had a similar purpose. In the 1950s the historiographical paradigm in France was dominantly *résistant*, with virtually no mention of Vichy, but de Gaulle shifted attention away from resistance in France to resistance outside France – to London and Algiers, above all to himself.[43] Like Churchill's, this is very much a 'great man' version of history, with larger social and economic forces merely noises offstage.

The two men were great artists of a great history in an even larger sense. Famously, de Gaulle understood himself as incarnating 'the soul of France'. There is that sonorous opening paragraph of the memoirs, which begins, 'Toute ma vie, je me suis fait une certaine idée de la France' and ends, 'la France ne peut être la France sans la grandeur'. Even more striking is the near-mystical account of his triumphal progress down the Champs-Élysées on 26 August 1944, through a 'sea' of people. As he walks, de Gaulle evokes the glories and the tragedies of France's past, including four occasions in the space of what he calls 'two lifetimes' (1814, 1870, 1914 and 1940) when that great avenue had been forced to submit to 'odious fanfares' of victorious invaders. He presents himself as the embodiment of the nation – 'I felt I was fulfilling a function which far transcended my individuality, for I was serving as an instrument of destiny' – and that is expressed in his shift from the first person to the third person, from autobiography to metaphysics: 'Since each of all those here had chosen Charles de Gaulle in his heart as the refuge against his agony and the symbol of his hopes, we must permit the man to be seen, familiar and fraternal, in order that at this sight the national unity should shine forth'.[44]

De Gaulle's sense of himself as a man of destiny was one of the profoundest traits of his personality. As André Malraux reflected in 1958, 'this man, whose powers of memory were celebrated and whose past for eighteen years belonged to History, seemed to carry on his most private dialogue with the future and not the past'.[45] Pierre Nora has depicted him as author of the last of three great *mémoires d'état* in French historical writing, 'updating and re-enacting' those of Louis XIV and Napoleon.[46] For Nora these works personified three decisive moments in French history, when the polity was stabilised essentially by one man after the crises of the Fronde, the Revolution and 1940. What made them special was their sense that, in that moment, 'l'état, c'est moi'. Together this trio, said Nora – the great memorialist of French memory – 'constitute the superego of the French state' (*notre surmoi d'État*).[47]

Churchill's memoirs are less lucid and lyrical than de Gaulle's, with documents often crowding out purple prose. He was working more in the Victorian tradition of 'life and letters' biographies. But Churchill, unlike de Gaulle, was a popular historian by profession: he had spent much of the 1930s writing a four-volume life of his martial ancestor the First Duke of Marlborough – presented as the leader of a 'grand alliance' against an earlier continental dictator – and in drafting his *History of the English-Speaking Peoples*, which celebrated the growth of English liberties and institutions. In the peroration to volume one of his war memoirs, *The Gathering Storm*, where Churchill evoked his feelings on finally achieving the premiership on 10 May 1940, he wrote: 'I felt as if I were walking with destiny, and that all my past life had been but a preparation for this hour and for this trial'.[48] At the end of volume two, *Their Finest Hour*, he recalled the patriotic saga about the defence of freedom against continental aggressors – mentioning Philip II of Spain, Louis XIV and Napoleon – but insisted that 'nothing surpasses 1940'. Earlier in that volume, he wrote of the national mood that summer: 'There was a white glow, overpowering, sublime, which ran through our Island from end to end'.[49] All these were sentiments that de Gaulle would have readily understood.

The title *Their Finest Hour* was taken from Churchill's speech to the Commons on 18 June 1940 – also the day on which de Gaulle broadcast his historic 'Appel' to the French people. In the speech, delivered in the aftermath of the French surrender, this phrase was used as exhortation and prediction – urging his countrymen so to bear themselves that if the British Empire were to last for a thousand years, men would still say 'This was their finest hour' – but in his memoirs prediction became description, hope was turned into history. And Churchill's version of 1940 as Britain's 'finest hour' has become a fundamental part of national identity. It lies behind the country's continued sense of distance from the Continent of Europe and its fixation with an Anglo-American 'special relationship' (another Churchillism). It also engendered a powerful set of myths about wartime national unity and political consensus that would underpin British politics at least until the era of Margaret Thatcher.[50] If one wished to adopt Nora's categories, it would not be going too far to describe Churchill's 1940 as the 'superego' of Britain's collective memory.

For him, that year was a sublime moment to be celebrated and cherished; for de Gaulle, of course, 1940 was a disaster and humiliation to be overcome. (When *Their Finest Hour* was translated into French, it appeared under the title *L'Heure Tragique*.) But the essential point is that the two men who made British and French history in that decisive year also became the most celebrated historians of 1940.

And so, despite the obvious differences between the tall, phlegmatic Frenchman and the impulsive little Englishman, there were striking similarities – as proud national leaders of indomitable will, as memoirists making a pre-emptive strike on the verdict of posterity and as patriots each imbued with a profound sense of his country's history and identity. Throughout their turbulent relationship, they were also entwined by deep mutual regard. De Gaulle later told John F. Kennedy that he had quarrelled violently and bitterly with Churchill but always got on with him, whereas he had never quarrelled with Roosevelt but never got on with him.[51] In April 1960, he paid a state visit to Britain – his first trip across the Channel since the end of the war. Intent on rehabilitating France as a great power, de Gaulle obstinately spoke French throughout his visit. The schedule included a meeting with Churchill, now 85 and fading fast, but when the president arrived, he dragged himself to his feet with sudden animation: 'Ah, mon général, c'est un grand plaisir de vous rencontrer aujourd'hui'. De Gaulle smiled warmly: 'Ah, Sir Winston, how good of you to be here'.[52]

Notes

1. All students of the relationship are indebted to François Kersaudy, *Churchill and de Gaulle* (London: Collins, 1981). Since publication of that book, however, more material has become available. There are also useful essays by Douglas Johnson, 'Churchill and France', in Robert Blake and Wm. Roger Louis, eds, *Churchill* (Oxford: Oxford University Press, 1993), pp. 41–55, and by François Bédarida, 'Winston Churchill's Image of France and the French', *Historical Research*, 74 (2001), 95–105. On the wartime Anglo-French relationship see also Simon Berthon, *Allies at War* (London: Collins, 2001).
2. Roy Jenkins, 'Churchill and France', in Richard Mayne, Douglas Johnson and Robert Tombs, eds, *Cross Channel Currents: 100 Years of the Entente Cordiale* (London: Routledge, 2004), p. 91.
3. Winston S. Churchill, *The Second World War* (6 vols, London: Cassell, 1948–54), vol. 1, p. 220; Michael Wolff, ed., *The Collected Essays of Sir Winston Churchill* (4 vols, Bristol: Library of Imperial History, 1976), vol. 1, pp. 394–5. More generally see David Reynolds, *In Command of History: Churchill Fighting and Writing the Second World War* (London: Penguin, 2004), pp. 119–20.
4. Record of meeting on 30 September 1942, p. 6, prime minister's operational files, PREM 3/120/6 (The National Archives, Kew, Surrey – henceforth TNA).
5. Churchill, note, 30 May 1942, PREM 3/120/7, fo. 282.
6. Pierre Billotte, *Le temps des armes* (Paris: Plon, 1972), p. 187.
7. Churchill to Eden, 5 November 1942, prime minister's operational files, PREM 4/27/1, fo. 48 (TNA).
8. Jean Lacouture, *De Gaulle: The Rebel, 1890–1945* (New York: W.W. Norton, 1990), p. 397.
9. John Harvey, ed., *The War Diaries of Oliver Harvey* (London: Collins, 1978), pp. 192–3.
10. Text in Chartwell papers, CHAR 9/156, fos 256 8 (Churchill Archives Centre, Churchill College, Cambridge – henceforth CAC).
11. Kersaudy, *Churchill and de Gaulle*, p. 230. For further detail see Reynolds, *In Command of History*, pp. 328–31.
12. Quotation from Churchill to Attlee and Eden, 21 May 1943, copy in Churchill papers, CHUR 4/293, fos 163–4 (CAC); see also Elizabeth Barker, *Churchill and Eden at War* (London: Macmillan, 1978), pp. 72–4. Chapters two to nine of Barker's book provide a very useful survey of Anglo-French-American relations in this period.
13. Eden, memo, 13 July 1943, PREM 3/181/8, quoting fo. 35. See also Lord Avon, *The Reckoning* (London: Cassell, 1965), pp. 397–8.
14. Churchill to Duff Cooper, 14 October 1943, PREM 3/273/1, fo. 33.
15. John Colville, *Footprints in Time* (London: Collins, 1976), pp. 113–5. In his memoirs, Colville does not date the conversation precisely. Kersaudy, *Churchill and de Gaulle*, 154–60, presents it as an account of the

Churchill–de Gaulle meeting on 12 September 1941. It should be noted, however, that there is no mention of this story in the diary Colville kept at the time – see John Colville, *The Fringes of Power: Downing Street Diaries, 1939–1955* (London: Hodder and Stoughton, 1955), p. 439. The original manuscript diary in CLVL 1/5 (CAC) shows that Colville went off on leave on 12 September and was away from London for more than a week!

16. Lord Halifax, diary, 12 May 1943, Hickleton papers, A 7.8.12 (Borthwick Institute, York) – Churchill related the story later to the British ambassador in Washington. See also Kersaudy, *Churchill and de Gaulle*, pp. 267–8.
17. Record of Churchill–de Gaulle conversation, 4 June 1944, Cabinet papers, CAB 66/50, WP (44) 297 (TNA).
18. Reynolds, *In Command of History*, pp. 412–13.
19. Kersaudy, *Churchill and de Gaulle*, pp. 375–6.
20. For this we must rely on de Gaulle's recollection – *The Complete War Memoirs of Charles de Gaulle* (New York: Carroll and Graf, 1998), pp. 727–8.
21. Oliver Lyttelton, notes on meeting with Roosevelt, 24 November 1942, Foreign Office private papers FO 954/29B, US/42/260; Avon, *The Reckoning*, p. 373.
22. Robert Dallek, *Franklin Roosevelt and American Foreign Policy, 1932–1945* (New York: Oxford University Press, 1979), p. 611, note 37; Richard Law, memo of conversation with Roosevelt, 22 December 1944, Foreign Office general political correspondence, FO 371/44595, AN 154 (TNA).
23. De Gaulle, *Complete War Memoirs*, p. 760.
24. Churchill to Eden, 25 November 1944, PREM 4/30/8, fo. 488.
25. US Department of State, *Foreign Relations of the United States: The Conferences at Malta and Yalta, 1945* (Washington: Government Printing Office, DC, 1955), p. 573.
26. Jean Lacouture, *De Gaulle: The Ruler, 1945–1970* (New York: W.W. Norton, 1992), p. 124.
27. Churchill to de Gaulle, 1 November and 26 November 1946, CHUR 2/30 (CAC).
28. Churchill to de Gaulle, 12 September and 14 October 1948, and de Gaulle to Churchill, 17 September and 3 November 1948, CHUR 4/22, fos 227–44 (CAC).
29. According to Charles Williams, *The Last Great Frenchman: A Life of General de Gaulle* (London: Abacus, 1995), p. 4.
30. For fuller discussion of this point see Reynolds, *In Command of History*, pp. 166–7, 185–6.
31. Winston S. Churchill, *The Second World War*, vol. 2, p. 162; cf. CHUR 4/155, fo. 76.
32. Lacouture, *De Gaulle: The Rebel*, pp. 17, 200, 205.
33. Reynolds, *In Command of History*, pp. 329–32, 411–3, 453–4.
34. Cherwell to Churchill, 11 January 1951, Cherwell papers K69/21 (Nuffield College, Oxford). This was also the advice of his research assistant Bill Deakin and his son-in-law Christopher Soames – see CHUR 4/311, fos 107–15 and CHUR 4/338, fo. 121.

35. CHUR 4/311, fos 52, 107–8 and CHUR 4/362, fo. 267.
36. CHUR 4/300, fo. 532; Churchill, *Second World War*, 4: 611.
37. Lacouture, *De Gaulle: The Ruler*, pp. 154–8. See also the annotated Gallimard edition of all his memoirs – Charles de Gaulle, *Mémoires*, ed. Marius-François Guyard (Paris: Gallimard, 2000), pp. 1229–31. There is a brief but suggestive essay by François Kersaudy, 'Les mémoires de De Gaulle et Churchill sont-ils fiables?', in [no editor], *De Gaulle, 1940–1958* (Paris: Poche, 1998), pp. 88–101, though this needs to be updated in places because of subsequent work.
38. The assistant was René Thibault but Kersaudy says that this was an invented name, to preserve secrecy – 'Les mémoires de De Gaulle et Churchill', pp. 90–1. On Churchill's methods see Reynolds, *In Command of History*, pp. 68–74.
39. See the text and original draft in de Gaulle, *Mémoires*, ed. Guyard, pp. 292, 1270.
40. De Gaulle, *Complete War Memoirs*, p. 557; cf. Johnson, 'Churchill and de Gaulle', p. 54.
41. De Gaulle, *Complete War Memoirs*, p. 58.
42. Brook to Attlee, 26 February 1948, prime minister's papers PREM 8/1321 (TNA).
43. Henry Rousso, *The Vichy Syndrome: History and Memory in France since 1944* (Cambridge: Harvard University Press, MA, 1991), pp. 244–5.
44. De Gaulle, *Complete War Memoirs*, pp. 3, 653–6.
45. André Malraux, *Antimémoires* (Paris: Gallimard, 1967), p. 151.
46. Pierre Nora, *Rethinking France: Les Lieux de Mémoire, vol. I, The State* (Chicago: University of Chicago Press, 2001), p. 440. In the original French text Nora uses the word 're-actualisation' – see Pierra Nora, *Les Lieux de Mémoire: II/2, La Nation* (Paris: Gallimard, 1986), p. 391. It should, of course, be noted that de Gaulle – sensitive to accusations of Bonapartism and genuinely ambivalent about the Emperor – kept his distance from Napoleon: see Robert Gildea, *The Past in French History* (London: Yale University Press, 1994), pp. 108–10.
47. Nora, *Rethinking France*, p. 440; cf. *Les Lieux, II/2*, p. 391.
48. Churchill, *Second World War*, 1: 526–7.
49. Churchill, *Second World War*, 2: 88, 555.
50. See the discussion in Malcolm Smith, *Britain and 1940: History, Myth and Popular Memory* (London: Routledge, 2000).
51. Note of de Gaulle's remarks at dinner at Versailles, 1 June 1961, in Arthur M. Schlesinger papers, box W-3: Berlin notes (John F. Kennedy Library, Boston, MA).
52. As recalled by the diplomat, Sir Antony Acland, British Library, London, 8 June 2004.

7

The Singularity of Suez in post-war Anglo-French Relations: *Une Entente mal entendue*

Peter Catterall
Queen Mary, University of London

The idea of an Anglo-French *Entente Cordiale* is one that does not seem to feature particularly in contemporary reflections on *trans-manche* relations of the 1950s. There is certainly a degree of warmth on both sides felt by many but by no means all of the relevant policymakers, but in memoirs such as those of René Massigli, the long-serving French ambassador to London, it is tempered by a good deal of mutual misunderstanding, not least among his masters at the *Quai d'Orsay*. For although the recent war still served as a common experience for statesmen on both sides of the Channel, and had helped men like Harold Macmillan to forge close friendships at least with those Free French he had encountered in Algiers in 1943, dealing with its aftermath did not prove quite so unifying. Their differing responses to the challenges of the post-war world were to produce frequently divergent tactics in London and Paris. Moments when British and French foreign policy are in complete accord, such as the Austrian State Treaty of 1955, appear comparatively rare. Even during Suez, although they might be on the same page, they seem to be singing different tunes. This was a moment of co-operation for specific and limited purposes which belies the dissonance more general to Franco-British relations in these years.

This dissonance appears despite, or more probably because, of the problems both countries faced. For, at the end of the Second World War, there were significant differences in circumstances between Britain and France. Not least, the war had proved much less socially and politically divisive in the former than in occupied France. However, France had nevertheless eventually emerged as one of the victorious powers, with a permanent seat on the Security Council of the new United Nations and with its empire, courtesy not least of British assistance in Indo-China, substantially restored. Both countries, then, entered the 1950s sharing a similar international status, nominally on a par with but in practice as very much junior partners with the USA in the Western Alliance, extensive imperial burdens and the difficulty of lack to resources to maintain them. As Harold Macmillan observed in 1955:

> The French are very anxious to go on pretending to be a Great Power. They know that we are doing the same. But they tell us that it's no good. The world is bound to be dominated by the new barbarians, in the West and the East.[1]

One obvious solution to the diminution of status of Britain and France might have been to pool their resources in some way. Undoubtedly many statesmen in both countries did talk in this period of the desirability of pooling resources, but not necessarily, and certainly not exclusively with each other. This was not what advocates of a 'Third Force' on the Labour Left in the late 1940s had in mind. Nor, it seems, did the politically rather different figure of Georges Bidault, then French foreign minister, in suggesting in July 1948 the formation of an economic and customs union of Benelux, France and Italy.[2] Macmillan himself was convinced that 'There is room for a third great power, but not for a fourth',[3] but he and, in slightly different ways his Labour opponents,[4] had an even broader combination in mind.

Building this third great power, however, was not so much a matter of Franco-British co-operation as of competing visions of what it might be. Even if, particularly after the partial rehabilitation of the West Germans in 1950, the process of European integration was always at least in part about *le problème allemand*,[5] it was also felt to have a beneficial effect on both French security and status. Although some important figures, notably de Gaulle, were slow to be converted to the virtues of this process, and there remained considerable debate as to how best *faire l'Europe*, there was therefore reasonable consensus within French elites on this issue. In Britain, however, although the issue became more acute after the Tories' return to power in 1951, there was no consensus among that party's leaders. Churchill may have spoken eloquently on European unity when in opposition in the late 1940s, but quite what part he envisaged Britain playing in this process was much less apparent. His foreign secretary and successor as prime minister, Sir Anthony Eden, was contrastingly unenthusiastic about European integration. If there was common ground between Eden and the more pro-Europeans in the Cabinet, like Macmillan, Maxwell Fyfe or Eccles, it was on the undesirability of a constitutionally complex, tightly drawn and 'Little' Europe of the kind that Monnet in particular, supported in practice by Schuman, seemed so keen on. This, however, was not necessarily to prove a fruitful basis for Anglo-French co-operation. Eden's focus instead, at least in documents like the 'British Overseas Obligations' paper of June 1952, was more upon leverage with the Americans as a way of maximising British status in the world. Meanwhile, his successor as prime minister in 1957, Macmillan, had spent much of the late 1940s and early 1950s unavailingly hoping for a loose Commonwealth/European combination as an alternative to reliance upon the Americans.

What is noticeable is that none of these policy ploys, on either side of the Channel, was centred around the other. To achieve some of them, notably Macmillan's schemes, nevertheless required the willing co-operation of the other. And Robert Schuman was by no means the only French politician to state a similar desire for willing British co-operation with the schemes that he had set in train for European integration. However, in the end, British participation was not a necessity for the European Coal and Steel Community (ECSC) resulting from the 1950 Schuman Plan. And Massigli was certainly not the only person in London who felt that the whole idea was presented to the British in such a way as to maximise the chances of their non-participation. This is not to say that British participation would have been unwelcome, so much as to observe that it would have had to have been on French terms.[6] Indeed, Eden's attempts in March 1952 to square this particular circle by placing the ECSC within the broader context of the Committee of Ministers of the Council of Europe, were to be rejected by Schuman within four months.

The one possible exception to this rule is the European Defence Community (EDC) scheme that eventually foundered in 1954. Ostensibly, the cause of this was the failure, after much procrastination, of the French National Assembly in Paris to ratify the scheme. It is no doubt true that many deputies might have felt able to ratify it if

Britain had been involved. Paul Reynaud, after all, had said as much as long ago as November 1951, after Eden had first stated that Britain could only associate with the EDC. But this does not mean that Benelux, and especially the Belgians, did not share responsibility given their refusal to accept the EDC budget proposals. This problem was rather less remarked upon though. As Massigli subsequently lamented, 'Il était si commode de pouvoir abriter nos propres doutes derrière l'insularité britannique!'.[7] He went on to observe the ease with which 'L'habitude de mettre l'Angleterre en accusation était prise'.[8]

That an Anglophile ambassador should have tender sympathies for the feelings of his hosts is one thing. Sensitivity to the feelings of the other, however, does not seem to be a particularly common feature of the bilateral relations of Britain and France in these years. The British did not bother to inform the French when they devalued in 1949, an act which revived cries of 'perfide Albion'. They were not best pleased when the compliment was returned the following summer and they found themselves bounced by the Schuman Plan with little time to respond. Not that this, or a change in government in London, seems to have produced much of a shift in British behaviour towards their neighbours.

Churchill's return to power in October 1951 ushered in a more Francophile, and francophone, government. The new prime minister, more struck by the Soviet threat than by the risk of German revanchism, was however 'impatient with the French, and does not seem to understand their hesitations'.[9] Despite his efforts to do so, Macmillan could be similarly critical. Reflecting in 1955 upon the weakness of France portrayed in Louis Spears' account of its collapse in 1940, he concluded 'Nor has anything really changed yet. France is tied up in an agony of indecision, caused by her absurd and unworkable constitution'.[10] Indeed, so convinced was he of this climate of indecision, the hostility of the French *Patronat*, and the complications posed by Franco-German wrangling over Saarland that it was not until many months after the 1955 Messina negotiations that Macmillan accepted that French ratification of what became in 1957 the Treaty of Rome was, in this instance, likely to occur. A similar condescension was apparent in the British response to Guy Mollet's attempt on 10 September 1956 to revive the Anglo-French union ideas of 1940. Despite sitting next to Mollet at dinner that evening even so Francophile a figure as Macmillan did not record the proposal in his diary. And the subsequent

British consideration of it concluded that French economic and political weakness meant that it held few attractions.[11]

British frustration with the seeming hesitations of the French could meanwhile, on occasion, lead to strong-arm tactics. Churchill's protests of profound friendship towards the French people in January 1955 veiled the threat that the French chair at the Western European Union could be taken by a different state if there was not more progress towards its ratification.[12] The fact that the British did not always have a government to negotiate with, as long as the Fourth Republic lasted, also seems to have encouraged a slightly cavalier attitude towards French sensibilities. For instance, during the long hiatus in late 1957 which preceded the appointment of the Gaillard government the British responded positively to a Tunisian request for arms to cope with the spillover effects of the Algerian conflict, a response which again elicited complaints of 'perfide Albion'.[13]

The return to power of de Gaulle in 1958, of course, brought a very different situation. British governments no longer had to deal with fragile French governments of very limited lifespan. They now confronted an increasingly powerfully entrenched figure determined to restore, as far as possible, a distinctive conceit of French glory. They could no longer hope as they had under the Fourth Republic, albeit unavailingly as it often turned out, that when the French government and assembly finally made up their minds they would share the British perspective. Instead it was much more a case of trying, equally unavailingly, to persuade the General to change a mind which, however Delphic it might have proved over Algeria in 1958–60, was usually on the issues which mattered to the British already firmly made up. There remained, however, even for so Francophile a figure as Macmillan, a degree of condescension. When de Gaulle on coming to office suggested a tripartite relationship with Britain and the USA the British prime minister sniffily observed, 'His "nuclear" claim is absurd. They have not any nuclear capacity and cannot have any H-bomb capacity without a diffusion plant'.[14]

In France, on the other hand, there were certainly those who were aware of British sensitivities. *Le Monde* observed in 1949 'Si on n'effraie pas les Anglais avec des développements théoriques sur les spécialisations économiques et les limitations de souveraineté, on a quelque chance de retenir leur vaisseau sur les côtes européennes'.[15] Such advice, however, does not seem to have been taken in the framing of the Schuman or Pleven Plans the following year. Avoiding frightening the British with theoretical constitutional architecture does not seem to have been high on the French agenda. Massigli, indeed, seems at times to have been at a loss as to what the *Quai* hoped for from their British neighbours. He later complained, referring to policy at the time of the EDC negotiations: 'Pour restaurer une politique de collaboration franco-anglaise, il était en tout cas nécessaire que l'on eût à Paris une vision claire de ce que l'on souhaitait. Ce n'était pas le cas'.[16]

Although some kind of British guarantee clearly featured as a *sine qua non* for many deputies, seeking this support did not seem much of a priority for either the Faure or the Pinay governments in 1951–52. There was no response from Paris to Massigli's pleas that some gestures on their part might strengthen those, like Macmillan, within the Cabinet who favoured a more positive stance towards the EDC.[17] Pinay, understandably preoccupied with economic problems during his short but effective premiership, in fact hardly mentioned Britain in the nearest we have to an autobiography. Almost the only reference, in fact, is to a conversation with Macmillan during the Geneva conversations of 1955 when they both served as foreign minister for their respective countries. Macmillan is recorded as having told Pinay:

> Vous savez, chez nous, en Grande-Bretagne, nous sommes très longs à comprendre ce que l'on veut dire. Il faut nous mettre les points sur les i. Si vous m'expliquez ce qu'est un éléphant, je ne comprendrai pas, mais si vous me le montrez, alors là je comprendrai.[18]

During the EDC negotiations, however, it was quite apparent to Macmillan, and more importantly to Eden, just what kind of elephant the French were asking for. It was not so much, as Pinay's anecdote misleadingly implies, that Franco-British relations were a dialogue of the deaf, with neither side comprehending the other's wishes. Instead the miscommunication lay in an inability to accept the legitimacy of the other's unwillingness to comply. A bilateral meeting of April 1953 achieved little other than the spectacle of Maurice Schumann declaiming that the EDC was a unique lightning conductor to guard against the German reunification that France did not want. It was not, however, deemed sufficient. Anthony Nutting, a Foreign Office junior minister, complained to Massigli that in addition France demanded guarantee after guarantee from Britain, culminating in the brusque request of 12 March 1953 that Britain declared its willingness to send troops to Europe equal in numbers to those to be deployed eventually by re-armed Germany. The French, as well as the British, could be insensitive to the considerations and requirements of the other.

At least the governments of the Fourth Republic seem to have felt that they wanted something from Britain, however undiplomatically or unrealistically they pursued their ends. De Gaulle, on the other hand, notwithstanding his fine words in Westminster Hall in 1960, did not. He had been bequeathed by the politicians he despised a Europe which, regardless of his earlier doubts, could be used to pursue his purposes. It was Macmillan who, responding to the European realities established in 1957–58 of which de Gaulle was now the beneficiary, had to come to him as a supplicant. All de Gaulle had to do was close the door firmly in his face, firstly over the Free Trade Area in 1958, and then even more brutally, over the European entry negotiations in 1963. This is not to say that there were not matters that the British could have potentially brought to the table which might have been of interest to de Gaulle, notably in the nuclear arena. The idea of Anglo-French co-operation in nuclear weapons as a check against Franco-German neutralism and insurance against US withdrawal from Europe had, after all, been broached in a Cabinet memorandum in 1957.[19] Little progress was however made when Macmillan subsequently raised this with the Americans, as de Gaulle no doubt suspected would be the case. Even if Macmillan had succeeded, it is a moot point whether it would have made much difference. As the case of Concorde makes clear, it was quite possible to cherry-pick areas for fruitful Anglo-French technological collaboration. Ministers on the British side, such as Aubrey Jones, might have seen this as a kind of Trojan horse, softening up the French and preparing the way for European entry.[20] There seems little evidence that de Gaulle saw it in the same way. The hopes Harold Wilson later invested in the seductive qualities of his European technological community idea at the time of the second bid in 1967 therefore seem to have been doomed to failure. De Gaulle did not need such things from the British, at least as the price for allowing them to join his

Europe, though he was quite happy to take the technology transfer that the Concorde project brought with it. Nor did he need, as Fourth Republic governments had felt they needed, British guarantees against German rearmament. By the time he returned to power in 1958, German rearmament was slowly occurring and all the British (and American) guarantees that the French might require were already in place. Therefore all the British could bring to his European party was their presence as an unwelcome guest. As the French Minister of Agriculture M. Pisani remarked during the latter stages of the Brussels negotiations to his British opposite, Christopher Soames,

> Mon cher. C'est très simple. Maintenant, avec les six, il y a cinq poules et un coq. Si vous vous joignez, (avec des autres pays) il y aura peut-être sept ou huit poules. Mais il y aura deux coqs. Alors – c'est pas aussi agréable.[21]

In a rather less colourful way de Gaulle seems to have made much the same point to Macmillan during their talks at Chateau des Champs in June 1962. While the generally well-connected former British ambassador to France, Lord Gladwyn, seems to have felt, at least from hints later dropped by the French, that these discussions were promising,[22] Macmillan clearly concluded at the time that de Gaulle opposed British entry because:

> (1) It will alter the character of the Community, both in the economic and the political field. Now it is a nice little club, not too big, not too small, under French hegemony. With us, and the Norwegians, and the Danes etc it will change its character. Is this to France's advantage?
> (2) He thinks that, apart from our loyalty to the Commonwealth, we shall always be too intimately tied up with the Americans. De G regards American alliance as essential, but he feels that America wants to make Europe into a number of satellite states.

Against such views Macmillan tried to conjure up the idea of the benefits that might flow from an effective *Entente Cordiale*, something which he implies had never in fact fully existed at any earlier point in the century, pleading that

> a close Anglo-French alliance, really effectively managed from day to day, would have avoided both wars and all that has flowed from them. Nevertheless, I am not at all sure how far de Gaulle and the French really feel it to be in France's interest to have us in. It cannot be done without much discussion and negotiation and without disturbing some of the agreements so painfully arrived at by very hard bargaining between the Six. Moreover, it means the end of the French hegemony.[23]

In the decades immediately following the Second World War postings to the embassies in each other's countries nevertheless remained among the most prestigious available to French and British diplomats. Massigli also, clearly, was extremely well-connected among the London political elites, not least because of his length of service as ambassador, though it has to be admitted that this was not as true of his immediate successor, Jean Chauvel. The problem is whether this provides much of an index of how important their bilateral relations were to the two countries. Macmillan at the Château des Champs seems to have been almost the only statesman on either side of the Channel who in these years invoked an Anglo-French alliance as a positive end in itself. Even then he clearly had ulterior motives in view. But this was very characteristic of Anglo-French relations at that time.

Sabine Lee has argued that Anglo-German relations in the 1950s were largely instrumental, a means of addressing other, more important relationships, one of which in her view was that between Britain and France.[24] In a sense she is right, in that the British seemed throughout the 1950s and 1960s repeatedly to hope, contrary to mounting evidence, that the Germans might somehow prove a means of leveraging influence upon the French. But this is to skate over the point that Anglo-French differences were not least over policy towards Germany. Consider the disagreements, for instance, over policy towards Saarland in the early 1950s. What was for the French essential to their security was, for the British much more a thorn in the process of rehabilitating West Germany, itself crucial within a broader Cold War context. The Anglo-French relationship was thus not important in and of itself in the way that Macmillan implied it should be. It was not even the shared enlightened self-interest in the multitude of arenas in which those interests overlapped that, for

David Bruce, characterised Anglo-American relations in this period.[25] Anglo-French interests certainly overlapped in almost as many arenas. But the outcome was competitive. The relationship was marked, on the whole, not by similarities in approach, but by pronounced differences.

At first sight the 1956 Suez Crisis appears to be an exception to this rule. But the fact that a joint Anglo-French expedition to Egypt was mounted simply obscures the extent to which both the diagnosis of the problem and the approach to possible solutions differed on either side of the Channel. This is not to deny that there are interesting similarities in their demonising of Nasser and their anxieties about the effect of his nationalisation of the Suez Canal shared by Eden and his French opposite number, Guy Mollet. And within two days of Nasser's decision, Anglo-French military talks were convened in London, resulting by 11 August in the first Musketeer plan. The French, who conceded primacy in the operation to their allies because of superior British knowledge in the area and their own embroilment in Algeria, were however struck by the differences in approach. General Ely noted the British astonishment at 'notre fermeté et l'ampleur de l'effort que nous sommes prêts à consentir'.[26] The British, in contrast, seemed to his compatriots constantly to be trying to put back the operation day, as well as changing the nature of the operation. And while bellicose members of the British government were prepared to contemplate some kind of Israeli involvement in the action – Macmillan writing a memorandum to that effect at the start of August – this seems to have been in part because of anxieties that the Israelis might otherwise attack Jordan.[27] This seems to reflect deeper differences of emphasis. As late as 23 October the Foreign Secretary Selwyn Lloyd was still telling the Cabinet of his hopes for a settlement, while noting that the French 'would not give their full co-operation in such a policy'.[28] The French, of course, had instead been leading instigators of the collusion with the Israelis that eventually provided the pretext for the ill-fated military intervention.

Some of these differences in approach might have been amplified by the pro-Israeli complexion of the Socialist government then in power in France. On becoming foreign minister, Christian Pineau had told the *Quai* of his intention not simply not to follow their advice, but to err in a pro-Israeli direction.[29] A re-thinking of British relations with Israel was however not to occur at any fundamental level until the Jordan crisis of 1958, by which time, ironically, the close alignment France had often had with the state of Israel since its foundation in 1948 was effectively over.[30] As the Algerian Crisis moved simultaneously towards its final stages, British and French policy in the Middle East thus moved in different directions. Their policies in the region had hardly been close before, witness the way in which the French put pressure on the Syrians not to support the British-sponsored Baghdad Pact in 1955.[31] Any alignment of Anglo-French policies in 1956 was thus temporary and adventitious.

This was not the only irony to flow from Suez. It is worth noting that, although the British had military primacy, it was the French who were, in the main, the more belligerent. The British instead were cautious, considering and then dropping the idea of an assault on Alexandria and subsequently proving unwilling to go further than Port Said, or to contemplate operations before the US presidential elections were safely out of the way. Their failure to achieve this latter end was, of course, to have significant consequences. Moreover, the French were also the suppliers of the *casus belli*. When presented with the straw of collusion, Eden nevertheless grasped it. But this is arguably simply because the British prime minister had become so fixated on toppling Nasser that he was ready by then to grab any straw which offered the chance of doing so.

There was, however, more common ground between the French and the British during the Suez Crisis than this implies. Common on both sides was, for instance, a broad agreement that some sort of action alone could, as Mollet put it 'prévenir la dégradation rapide de la situation et empêcher que l'Union soviétique exerce prochainement une influence déterminante dans la zone intéressée'.[32] Conscious both of the fragile state of Britain's finances, and of the general dependence of Western Europe upon Middle Eastern oil, Macmillan saw the crisis as a means of shaking continental allies out of their Maginot Line mentality and awakening them not only to the Soviet threat on their Eastern borders but on their flanks as well. This did not prevent him, however, being among the first to call for a halt to operations, without showing particular consideration for the wishes of his French ally, once the currency reserves began to seriously drain away in November. That national considerations, and in the eyes of the French, considerations regarding Anglo-American relations, remained more important to the British was accordingly one of the principal lessons drawn from Suez. It provided a temporary and limited ground for an Anglo-French drawing together, and its dénovement left them afterwards if anything even further apart.

One of the realities this reveals is that Anglo-French relations were never an end in and of themselves, but always a means to something else. Suez merely proved a brief moment of coincidence of view. The relationship instead operated primarily in a distinctive series of contexts: of policy towards European integration; towards Germany; towards the Cold War. In the first two of these, as already discussed, it was characterised by competing visions. But this was also true of the Cold War context. Suez may have, again, provided a brief moment of commonality on the subject of attitudes towards the Soviet Union. The period when the more than usually hawkish Pinay was French foreign minister, during the Geneva four-power talks of 1955, also appears as one of relative harmony. Pinay was, however, rather patronisingly described by his British opposite number, Macmillan, as 'charming manners, honourable and straight – rather naïve'.[33] In the latter's account the French contribution to the talks was as much gastronomic as anything else. For instance, on 22 July 1955:

> At the luncheon adjournment, poor Pinay (whose first experience this is of Russian stonewalling tactics) got very cross. M[olotov] teasingly proposed that we shd meet again at 2.30. P indignantly cried out 'What about lunch!'. He proposed 3.30. I admitted that I was going to lunch with the French, and was looking forward to it; but I thought perhaps 3pm might do. M said 'Mr Macmillan always makes compromises – and good ones. Let it be 3pm'. So it was agreed. The French luncheon was certainly superb.

The only substantive matter Macmillan records discussing with the French in this period in fact had nothing to do with East-West relations but was instead the French indignation at the inscription of the Algerian conflict at the UN. Macmillan went out of his way to be supportive, even persuading the Norwegian Foreign Minister Halvard Lange, to change his tactics in New York to spare French embarrassment, prompted in part by his awareness that contemporary British difficulties in Cyprus were as vulnerable to criticism.[34]

Much of the time, however, there was not so much agreement, either over East-West relations or other issues, between Britain and

France. At the start of 1951, Massigli claimed that the two countries saw eye to eye for the first time for many years over their approach to the Soviet Union,[35] but if so it did not last. Ironically, the source of tension was often the same as in European affairs. When Molotov said to the French diplomat Hervé Alphand in 1955, 'France and Russia should really be friends. We have much between us', Alphand replied, 'Yes, all Germany'.[36] This simple territorial fact was indeed to be the origin of a number of Russian charm offensives aimed at the French in the early 1950s. While the British broadly accepted the need for German rearmament in the face of the Soviet forces retrenched in Eastern Europe, both the Russians and the French had their differing reasons for fearing such a development.

Britain and France thus each saw the Cold War through different prisms. The British, indeed, tended to think that they saw it through a broader prism. In 1961 Macmillan complained at his first meeting with the Kennedy administration in Washington that 'The European powers were not interested in problems elsewhere in the world'.[37] This applied as much to the French as the other continental countries. Their attitude towards Germany was seen as determined by concerns about their own security. And insofar as the French were interested in other parts of the world, to British eyes it was because of colonial legacies which perennially distracted them from matters of greater moment, or indeed exacerbated the global Cold War. For instance, when Edgar Faure threatened in 1955 to withdraw France's 90,000 troops from Indo-China, Macmillan records Dulles hoping that this would in fact turn out to be a promise, which presumably was the British foreign secretary's view as well.[38]

After 1955, however, the creation of Western European Union, the rehabilitation of West Germany and the advent of the H-Bomb meant that Anglo-French attitudes towards the Cold War operated in a different context. The result was a shift in both cases, but not in a direction which produced greater coincidence of view. It was the British who now found Germany a problem. Nuclear weapons were felt to have rendered redundant the large forces that Adenauer still demanded that his allies maintained in Germany. The costs associated with stationing a large number of British troops in Germany also contributed to the perennial weakness of sterling. Macmillan was incensed in late 1958 by what he felt was a German betrayal of his plans for a Free Trade Area (FTA) in Europe. And, not least, there was alarm that American military plans designed to reassure the Federal Republic were foolishly provocative. This became particularly apparent during the crisis that began on 27 November 1958, with the Soviet note declaring all existing arrangements for Berlin null and void, and arguing that West Berlin should be demilitarised as a free city within six months or all Soviet powers there would be handed over to the East German authorities. Throughout the crisis Macmillan was sceptical about treating this as a *casus belli,* though it was not until 2 June 1959 that he could record with relief that 'All the old nonsense about "occupying the road and rail communications" or "sending the tanks through" is . . . abandoned'.

Some of these difficulties were exacerbated by the French. In the case of the FTA, for instance, the British had hoped to use the Germans to put pressure on the French, but instead found themselves outmanoeuvred by de Gaulle. It is therefore ironic that it seems that it was Macmillan who urged the German chancellor, who had regarded the de Gaulle's return to power with deep misgivings, to seek a rapprochement with the General.[39] Although de Gaulle seems initially to have regarded a meeting with Adenauer with equal reluctance, when the two men met for the first time on German soil in November 1958 it was a great success, and led directly to German agreement to ending the FTA negotiations.

Cold War, as well as economic, considerations may have played a part in Adenauer's decision. De Gaulle had begun his return to office by going out of his way, much to Macmillan's irritation, to be more emollient to the Russians, without consulting his British or American allies in the process. He had then equally annoyed the chancellor by an ineptly handled request in September 1958 for some kind of tripartite world directorate of France, Britain and America. When Soviet threats emerged however, such as the threat to Berlin, de Gaulle was ready to reassure the Germans that he was their best friend:[40] that Britain was not was meanwhile confirmed in Adenauer's eyes by Macmillan's willingness to go to Moscow in February 1959. It did not particularly matter that Macmillan's trip was prompted as much by concern about the stalling of the test ban talks in Geneva as by the concurrent Berlin Crisis. Indeed, if Adenauer had known that Macmillan was at this time prepared at least to contemplate some moves towards German neutrality if it would help to reduce East-West tensions (and British costs),[41] he would have been even more suspicious.

As Anglo-German relations deteriorated, Franco-German relations improved. In Macmillan's view this was because 'quite cynically, it suits France to support West Germany politically in return for absolute freedom for France to pursue her economic protectionism'.[42] His first port of call on his return from Moscow was Paris. There he found

> De Gaulle rather put out of countenance his team, by admitting right away that one cd not have a nuclear war in Europe on the question of who signed the pass to go along the autobahn or the railway to W Berlin – a USSR sergeant or a DDR sergeant. In his view the only question which wd justify war wd be an actual physical blockade. I asked 'did he say this to Adenauer?' He admitted that he had not. It wd depress him. He also thought the Russians shd be kept guessing. On the 2 Germanies, de Gaulle also said that reunion was impossible without war, and that France and Britain cd not fight such a war. But the 'idea' of reunification shd be kept alive in order to give some comfort to the German people. This is 'the light at the end of the tunnel' idea, about wh much has already been said. 'La chose-Allemande' – that must be kept alive. Meanwhile there shd be practical cooperation on economic, supply, and cultural matters between the two Germanies. What Dulles had called 'confederation' shd be pressed. Again, I asked 'Had he said this to Adenauer?' He said 'Non'. It was clear that the French (who are getting money and support from Germany on a big scale) expect Britain or America to put this forward.[43]

There was thus clearly more coincidence between the French and British views of the German question than the declaratory policies of each suggested. However, from this point onwards the French, in British eyes, frequently talked tough on East-West relations for the sake of wooing their German audience, secure in the knowledge that they would never be called upon, or allowed, to back up their words with actions. Indeed, from their continuing tendency to aim charm offensives at the French, the Russians seem to have been well aware of this.

De Gaulle was well aware of fundamental common interests with the British and Americans when it came to East-West relations, but it suited his purposes to play an independent hand. And it suited

Macmillan's purposes to play up an image of de Gaulle as a trouble-maker on occasion. He may have sought to assure Eisenhower of the General's good intentions before the president's first reunion with the French leader in 1959. But he was also quite prepared to cast de Gaulle in the role of villain, at least in American eyes, as the European entry negotiations dragged to their conclusion in 1962–63.[44]

In practice there thus may have been more common ground between them than appearances suggest. For instance, Macmillan had been unenthusiastic about NATO at the start of the 1950s, and regarded de Gaulle's objections to its military structures with a certain amount of sympathy, even noting that such a reorganisation 'might let us out of our 50 year treaty and our £50m a year paid across the exchanges to keep our troops in Germany'.[45] In the end, however, their divergent policies towards Germany were at the root of many of the differences in Anglo-French relations in these years. At bottom, the British saw Germany as an object within a wider Cold War context, while the French instead saw it primarily in terms of their own security.

There was one other allied partner who brought out divergences between the British and the French. This was, of course, the United States of America. This was not always the case. The three countries eventually worked together in, for instance, the tripartite guarantee of the borders of Israel in 1950. And the French seem to have hoped that such tripartism could become more embedded. Maurice Schumann told the National Assembly after Pleven's successful trip to Washington in 1952 that the Franco-British-American relationship was 'un irremplaçable trait d'union'.[46] However, Pleven's suggestion of a three-person consultative organisation for the world seems to have been met with polite silence by his American hosts. French wooing made little headway. Pinay found that his appeals to John Foster Dulles invariably met with the response 'Nous avons nos informations, nous n'avons besoin ni de conseil, ni d'avis'.[47] Nor were de Gaulle's tripartite suggestions of 1958 met with greater enthusiasm. Macmillan's slightly disingenuous response was that there was nothing for the French to join, which is certainly not how de Gaulle saw it. Even if there was, the Americans did not seem to want the French in. A change of administration in Washington made seemingly no difference to this position. One of the briefing papers for Macmillan's first visit to the Kennedy administration made the point that there was no interest in institutionalising tripartitism with the French. The American view of what the French brought to the table seemed to have changed little since 1952: 'They listen to and comment on what we have to say but generally do not have concrete ideas of their own to put forward'. Not ideas about the Cold War anyway, although the memorandum did recognise that the French had very clear ideas about what was in their own interest, commenting that de Gaulle wanted to be the strongman of Europe.[48]

Macmillan's view of de Gaulle's tripartite proposals in 1958 was that they were designed 'to claim for France "as a coming nuclear power" a special position, with Britain and America'.[49] In other words, they were about appearances, not substance, a view with which the Americans for their own reasons seem to have concurred. Something which was more substantial would have constrained de Gaulle's ability to play a lone hand in Europe, and his approach towards NATO made it clear that he was not prepared to pay that price. Britain, on the other hand, notwithstanding the benefits which might flow from disengagement in Germany, almost invariably was. There was nevertheless a broad agreement between Britain and France over fundamentals, including the Atlantic alliance. However, in practice, differences in approach, particularly towards Germany, ensured that there was frequently little agreement over policy. Macmillan's 1962 appeal for a close Franco-British alliance remains simply that, a rhetorical flourish which in no way describes the reality of these years. Like Mollet's 1956 proposal, it was concocted primarily for the benefit of the country from whence it emanated. Not appealing to the interests or objectives of its recipient on the other side of the Channel, it suffered a similar fate.

Notes

1. Peter Catterall (ed.), *The Macmillan Diaries: The Cabinet Years 1950–1957* (London: Macmillan, 2003), p. 456 (22 July 1955).
2. René Massigli, *Une Comédie des erreurs 1943–1956: Souvenirs et réflexions sur une étape de la construction européenne* (Paris: Plon, 1978), p. 145.
3. Harold Macmillan, *Ruin or Recovery?*, speech delivered on 29 September 1949 at Central Hall, Westminster organised by the Empire Industries Association and the British Empire League, p. 6.
4. P.M.H. Bell, *France and Britain 1940–1994* (Harlow: Longman, 1997), p. 91.

5. See Massigli, p. 223.
6. Some have therefore seen it as a more or less deliberate abandonment of the *Entente Cordiale*; see François Duchêne, *Jean Monnet: The First Statesman of Interdependence* (London: Norton, 1994), p. 204.
7. Massigli, p. 293.
8. *Ibid*, p. 299.
9. Catterall, p. 144 (18 February 1952).
10. *Ibid*, p. 407 (17 March 1955).
11. Bell, pp. 156–7.
12. Christiane Rimbaud, *Pinay* (Paris: Perrin, 1990), p. 293.
13. Department of Western Manuscripts, Bodleian Library, Oxford: Harold Macmillan's Diaries (henceforward HMD): 1 December 1957.
14. HMD: 8 October 1958.
15. Quoted in Massigli, p. 168.
16. Massigli, p. 293.
17. *Ibid*, p. 315.
18. Antoine Pinay, *Un Français comme les autres (entretiens avec Antoine Veil)* (Paris: Pierre Belfond, 1984), p. 109.
19. National Archives, London: CAB 129/84, CP(57)6, Foreign Secretary, 'The Grand Design', 5 January 1957.
20. Comments at a conference on Concorde at the Science Museum, London, 19 November 1998, published in Kenneth Owen, *Concorde* (London: ICBH, 2002).
21. HMD: 12 January 1963.
22. Gladwyn Jebb, *De Gaulle's Europe: Or Why the General says No* (London: Secker & Warburg, 1969), p. 74.
23. HMD: 3 June 1962.
24. Sabine Lee, *An Uneasy Relationship: British-German Relations between 1951 and 1961* (Bochum: Universitätsverlag Dr. N. Brockmeyer, 1996).
25. John F. Kennedy Presidential Library, Boston (henceforward JFK): NSF 170, folder 5, Bruce to Rusk, 17 July 1961.
26. Denis Lefebvre, *Guy Mollet: le mal aimé* (Paris: Plon, 1992), p. 248.
27. Catterall, p. 583 (3 August 1956).
28. Anthony Gorst and Lewis Johnman (eds), *The Suez Crisis* (London: Routledge, 1997), p. 95.
29. Lefebvre, p. 252.
30. Orna Almog, *Britain, Israel and the United States 1955–1958: Beyond Suez* (London: Cass, 2003).
31. Matthew Elliot, 'Defeat and Revival: Britain in the Middle East', in Wolfram Kaiser and Gillian Staerck (eds), *British Foreign Policy 1955–64: Contracting Options* (Basingstoke: Macmillan, 2000), p. 246.
32. Lefebvre, p. 246.
33. HMD, 30 October 1955.
34. HMD, 26 October 1955. This did not stop the British from following the American lead in voting against the French tactics in Algeria in 1958: Bell, p. 176.
35. Catterall, p. 43 (3 January 1951).

36. *Ibid*, p. 484 (28 September 1955).
37. JFK: NSF 174A, 'The president's meeting with Prime Minister Macmillan: International economic problems', 5 April 1961.
38. Catterall, p. 423 (7 May 1955).
39. Lee, pp. 78–9.
40. Bell, p. 177.
41. HMD, 4 February 1958.
42. HMD, 27 June 1959.
43. HMD, 10 March 1959.
44. Oliver Bange, *The EEC Crisis of 1963: Kennedy, Macmillan, de Gaulle and Adenauer in Conflict* (Basingstoke: Macmillan, 2000).
45. HMD, 13 March 1960.
46. Massigli, p. 269.
47. Pinay, p. 89.
48. JFK: NSF 174A, 'Background and objects of visit', 21 March 1961.
49. HMD, 8 October 1958.

8
De Gaulle and Anglo-French *Mésentente*, 1958–67

James Ellison
Queen Mary, University of London

On 12 May 1964, the Foreign Secretary R.A. Butler submitted to the Cabinet a memorandum entitled 'Gaullism'. For busy ministers with little time to read through this lengthy analysis, Butler summarised its implications for Anglo-French relations:

> What it boils down to is that in dealing with President de Gaulle we have to weather a storm which should gradually subside after he disappears. We must go on treating him as a tricky kind of ally, but we can no longer think in terms of an *Entente Cordiale*. This is a relationship which we must hope to restore gradually with his successors. Meanwhile we must prevent him having his way with the Western alliance while avoiding, if at all possible, a head-on clash with him.[1]

To British governments in the 1960s General Charles de Gaulle was close to being enemy number one. The diplomat Nicholas Henderson recounted in a memoir of his time as private secretary to post-war foreign ministers that when he assessed the 'outstanding features of the international scene as viewed from the British standpoint' at the beginning of 1965, it was not 'the change of government in London . . . nor the substitution of Brezhnev for Khrushchev in Moscow, nor the crisis in the Congo, not Vietnam, not the uncertainties over Sukarno's health, not the revolution in the Sudan, not even the appalling weakness of sterling' that stood out. What did was 'the dominance of de Gaulle'.[2] The French president's 'looming presence' and his ability to affect global events had a direct impact on

Britain's interests and painfully underscored declining British influence on the world stage. Such was his threat to British interests that in March 1964 the Foreign Office produced 'A Check-List of General De Gaulle's Unco-operative Policies' to which one official added that '[t]he check-list has been kept pretty strictly to cases of disloyalty or hostility. If it were extended to cover all cases where General de Gaulle has been uncooperative, it would become very long indeed'.[3]

Perhaps the most famous occasion on which de Gaulle's power was wielded over British fortunes was his press conference of 14 January 1963 when he said *non* to Britain's application for membership of the European Economic Community (EEC). Indeed, this episode, and the run-up to it after de Gaulle's return to power in June 1958, has received the most historical attention in the study of Anglo-French relations during his presidency.[4] What happened afterwards has not been credited with the same importance given the assumption that de Gaulle simply played out positions established by 1963.[5] Certainly, de Gaulle's attitudes towards the British were consistent before and after that date. Despite his regard for their martial valour and for Churchill's leadership, he consistently criticised their post-1945 attachment to the Americans. For de Gaulle, and many leading French governmental figures of the 1950s and 1960s, British entry to the EEC would hold threats to French leadership of the Community and to the European identity and future orientation of that institution.[6] Hence the veto of 1963 was repeated in 1967 as de Gaulle confirmed that *non* meant *non*. To date, historians have not depicted the rejection of 1967 as having the same significance as its predecessor. Yet it is possible to see the events of 1967 as equally and arguably more important in the longer-term development of Anglo-French relations. While it is true that the motives of the British in making the second application were fundamentally little changed from the first (although the necessity of gaining membership had been heightened by economic imperatives and Britain's declining international status), the timing and tactics of the second application ensured that de Gaulle's veto did not have the effect of 1963. As this chapter will show, the British used the hesitancy in Europe surrounding de Gaulle's nationalistic foreign policies in the EEC and the North Atlantic Treaty Organisation (NATO) in the mid-1960s to strengthen their standing on the continent. As de Gaulle's stock declined, so Britain's rose and the result was that the British were in a stronger position in Europe at the end of the decade than they had been at the start. De Gaulle may have succeeded in blocking British membership of the EEC during his presidency but as he left office, the power balance in Anglo-French relations began to change as his successor accepted British entry.

The threat of the General, 1958–63

It was as de Gaulle returned to the presidency of France in June 1958 that profound differences in outlook between the British and the French towards the leadership of the Atlantic Alliance and the shape of Western European unity began to unsettle Anglo-French relations. The clash between the two countries which would become a fact of life in their relationship after 1963 had its origins in choices made in the late 1940s. Since then, Britain had pursued a foreign policy which had a global outlook, rather than first and foremost a European one, and had as its basis strong relations with the Commonwealth and the United States.[7] In contrast, the French saw Western Europe as the centre of their foreign policy and European integration as a means of restoring French economic and political strength and of controlling the development of the Federal Republic of Germany. For the French, the EEC thus became synonymous with paramount national interests and for de Gaulle it was the institutional foundation for his policy of a European Europe free from American influence. Through leadership of this new Europe in which Franco-German rapprochement would ensure stable relations with the Federal Republic, France would play an independent, leading role in negotiations with the Soviet Union and its Eastern European satellites to create East-West détente.

De Gaulle recognised that divorce between the United States and Western Europe was not in the interests of France or its European allies as only American military power could provide for the defence of the West. He also believed that American military influence in Europe did not mean that the Americans should enjoy influence in other European matters. It was this principle which led de Gaulle into confrontation with the British. Although it may seem clichéd and simplistic to refer to de Gaulle's antipathy towards those he described as the Anglo-Saxons when it has been clearly established that the Anglo-American relationship was a mixture of competition as well as co-operation, it is nevertheless true that he saw Britain's attachment to the United States as a threat to the independence of Western Europe.[8] In his memoirs he wrote that his aim in supporting the EEC was to set up 'a concert of European States' and in so doing prevent 'certain others, in particular Great Britain, from dragging the West into an Atlantic system which would be totally incompatible with a European Europe'.[9] Military logic made the Atlantic Alliance a necessity and thus NATO became something that had to be lived with until de Gaulle could strike an independent course for France outside of that institution's integration. What could not be lived with was the idea of an economic NATO and thus Britain had to be kept out of the EEC.

The conflict in foreign policies between Britain and de Gaulle's France began in 1958 when two events exposed fundamentally contrary positions. The first was Britain's attempt to adapt to the progress of European integration by proposing in 1956–7 the idea of a European Free Trade Area (FTA) as a limited, confederal trade arrangement which would encompass the EEC. Stopping short of membership of the EEC but going far enough to bring the necessary economic dividends and political influence, the FTA was designed perfectly for British interests and was of great significance to the government of Harold Macmillan. Its major failing, however, was that it was not perfectly designed for those it intended to attract as member states, especially the French who saw it at best as a British plan to gain much by giving little and at worst as a takeover bid. Thus in December 1958, de Gaulle rejected the FTA in the first of what would become a hat trick of vetoes of British initiatives towards the EEC.[10]

The second event which produced Anglo-French disagreement was instigated by de Gaulle when on 17 September 1958 he sent memorandums to Macmillan and the US President Dwight D. Eisenhower proposing an Anglo-American-French tripartite directorate for the defence of the free world. Newly returned to office, de Gaulle lost no time to 'hoist . . . [his] colours', calling into question not only France's membership of NATO, but the leadership and purpose of the Atlantic Alliance itself. His proposal was clearly an assertion of his belief in the right of France to sit with the Americans and the British at the highest tables in the West, not least because the French would soon have a national nuclear deterrent. The denial that he received from Eisenhower and Macmillan, who had in 1957 signed agreements on nuclear defence cementing their unique collaboration and preventing co-operation with other states, was perhaps what de Gaulle had hoped for anyway. It gave him the grounds to readjust France's relationship with NATO that he sought as part of his greater foreign policy agenda. What it also did, however, was put yet further distance between de Gaulle and the British and confirmed in his mind where their priorities lay.[11]

The collision in ambitions apparent in 1958 was only aggravated by Britain's first application for membership of the EEC in 1961. Given the political and economic investment made by the Macmillan government in Britain's new European policy and its significance for a country whose future was uncertain, so much greater was the fall that came with de Gaulle's veto on 14 January 1963.[12] Although Harold Macmillan was no stranger to the theatrical, there was none in his often-quoted diary entry of 28 January 1963 when he wrote that '[a]ll our policies at home and abroad are in ruins . . .'.[13] It was after the veto that de Gaulle and France became the focus of much of the frustration felt in the governments of Macmillan, Alec Douglas-Home and Harold Wilson about Britain's weakening international situation. The Foreign Office was, in particular, consistent in its indignation and it maintained a policy of opposition to de Gaulle over 1964–5. Britain's Ambassador to Paris at that time, Sir Pierson Dixon, reported regularly and forcefully of de Gaulle's hostility towards Britain.[14] On 22 April, this led him to urge London to inform France's EEC partners and the Americans of French duplicity, especially in their policy towards the United States, a recommendation which by early summer became policy.[15] The British government would seek to avoid giving the impression that it was 'conducting a vendetta against de Gaulle or the French' but the Foreign Office noted that there was no reason why diplomats 'should be too mealy-mouthed about saying what we think to our friends about French policy whenever we find it, or its manner, objectionable'.[16]

By spring 1965, the Foreign Office was moved to apply pressure directly to the prime minister by convincing the Foreign Secretary, Michael Stewart, of the growing threat presented by de Gaulle to British interests. On 9 February, Michael Palliser, head of the Planning Staff, produced a bleak assessment which equated de Gaulle's successful exploitation of the leadership crisis in the Atlantic

Alliance (linked to the vexed question of nuclear defence in NATO) with the danger of Britain's 'growing irrelevance' to its American and European allies. The bluntness of Palliser's conclusion was no doubt intended to spur action but it also reflected established concerns: 'unless [the British government] can soon evolve a more effective relationship with Western Europe and the United States within the Atlantic framework Britain will cease to be a world power'. To stop the rot, Palliser called for 'a more robust approach to de Gaulle'.[17] Convinced of the necessity of doing something, Stewart submitted a minute to the prime minister on 3 March which argued for a rejuvenated policy towards 'the right sort of Europe' within an Atlantic framework to halt Britain's marginalisation. Although the minute became the basis of a Cabinet memorandum, at this stage the Foreign Office was ahead of Wilson's thinking and a new policy towards Europe would not emerge until autumn 1966.[18]

While the threat posed by de Gaulle to Britain's interests and the need to do something about it had become well established in Whitehall during 1964 and 1965, the opportunity to do so had not presented itself. Despite the adverse reaction in the Community to de Gaulle's instigation of the empty chair crisis in 1965, the Wilson government had decided that this was not a moment to exploit in favour of Britain's position in Western Europe.[19] Moreover, even though Britain was ready to act in defence of NATO given de Gaulle's anticipated move against it, there was a consensus of opinion shared with the Americans that nothing precipitate should be done to goad de Gaulle into action. A waiting policy was safer than a baiting policy as de Gaulle's tactical adroitness would ensure that he would take any chance to accuse France's allies of initiating a crisis.[20] What the British required was an opening to meet the challenge posed by the French president and gain support and influence among allies by doing so. De Gaulle gave them just that in spring 1966.

Turning the tables: Britain's diplomacy in NATO and its 1967 EEC application

On 21 February 1966, de Gaulle put an end to speculation and surpassed the comments he made on 9 September 1965 about his intent to adjust France's status in NATO by announcing in a further press conference that France would seek to restore her sovereignty 'as regards soil, sky, sea and forces, and any foreign element that would be in France, will in the future be under French command alone'.[21] In a letter to Johnson on 7 March, de Gaulle then proceeded to confirm his intent and in effect give notice on his country's involvement in NATO's integrated military command structures as well as demanding that all NATO men and materials leave France.[22] While the consequent crisis has been described as 'the most traumatic moment in NATO's history', it has also been recently portrayed as an opportunity which was taken principally by the Johnson administration to repel the Gaullist challenge and preserve NATO by transforming it in an era of détente.[23] It was certainly seen as such by the British who from the outset of the crisis suggested to the Americans that order could be the product of disorder. On 29 March 1966 Wilson wrote a substantial letter to Johnson outlining British policy towards the crisis which had as its keynote the judgment that 'the General's action' ought to be seen 'both as a threat and as an opportunity'.[24] If NATO could solve its internal problems related to security issues and adopt a new agenda which matched the priority of Western defence with a positive approach towards détente with the Soviet Union and Eastern Europe, the crisis created by de Gaulle would not only be quietened without any loss to the organisation but in fact would produce positive outcomes for its strength and purpose. This evaluation was not unique to the British as it became the leitmotif of the allied response to France over 1966 and 1967 but it did have particular resonance for them. The NATO crisis offered Britain opportunities beyond the settlement of differences in the Atlantic Alliance. It was of wider consequence to the pursuit of Britain's foreign policy objectives in Europe and the Cold War and it was also the long-awaited occasion to respond to the Gaullist challenge.

It is likely that de Gaulle knew that he risked mobilising British diplomacy against his actions by striking against NATO military integration. Evidence for this can be found in the tenor of the letter he sent to Wilson on 9 March 1966 explaining his motives and in the speech of the French State Secretary for Foreign Affairs, Jean de Broglie, at the Western European Union (WEU) on 15 March. In his letter to Wilson de Gaulle described Britain in terms which contradicted those he used in the veto of 1963 and would use in the veto of 1967. Britain, he wrote, was a 'great European state which is, *par excellence*, aware of the world situation'.[25] In Washington, the State

Department analysed and compared de Gaulle's letters to Johnson, Wilson, Ludwig Erhard, the Chancellor of the Federal Republic of Germany and Giuseppe Saragat, the President of Italy. The State Department concluded that 'Great Britain receives the most fulsome praise both as a tested and traditional ally and as a great and wise European power'; US officials also speculated that de Gaulle's 'effusive tone . . . may reflect [his] hopes that, in due course, Britain will cast in its lot with French schemes for reorganizing the continent'.[26] A more likely explanation is that de Gaulle expected a robust response from the British to his NATO actions and thus indulged in a little timely flattery. If he had any expectation that Britain would join with France in directing the future of Europe, this would most certainly have been one set very much in the long term. Tactics, rather than an invitation to begin talks about the EEC, can also be the only reason why in a WEU debate on the NATO crisis on 15 March 1966, de Broglie 'intervened unexpectedly' 'to say that France was involved in the construction of the Common Market which she earnestly hoped that Britain would join'.[27] This enigmatic declaration was quickly dampened by the French government which depicted it as nothing more than a restatement of policy and in doing so strengthened suggestions that it had been made to deflect attention from events in NATO.[28]

If it had been de Gaulle's intent to deflect a forthright British reaction to his diplomacy in NATO then it met with failure. Very quickly, the British involved themselves in the coordination of France's fourteen NATO allies to respond to the problems thrown up by the crisis. Moreover, the British sought from the Johnson administration its sanction to play a leading role among European countries in the response to de Gaulle. This they received from the Americans, who were highly sensitive to the possibility that should they themselves champion the fourteen, de Gaulle would attempt to win propaganda points by accusing them of converting the crisis into a bilateral Franco-American dispute. British diplomacy in the opening stages of the crisis, according to the US Ambassador to London, David Bruce, was both 'militant and energetic'.[29] The reason for this was that the Wilson government utilised the NATO crisis to hit many targets. This strategy resulted from the chief conclusions of a comprehensive report written by officials for ministers on the international consequences of the crisis.[30] It argued that in seeking its resolution Britain could secure three objectives: the stability and military security of Western Europe; influence over American and German policies; and '[s]atisfactory economic relationships with our allies including the option for Britain to join the Common Market on acceptable terms'. In essence, what the British hoped to get out of the NATO crisis of 1966 was a chance to take the lead in the Atlantic Alliance, enhance Britain's status in Washington and Western European capitals and, for the first time since January 1963, take on de Gaulle from a position of relative authority.

There was a correlation between Britain's dynamism in taking such a principal place in the diplomacy of the NATO crisis and a downturn in relations between the British and the French. Britain's Ambassador to Paris from 1965, Sir Patrick Reilly, warned in June that Britain's diplomacy had seen its reputation damaged in France: 'At the start [of the NATO crisis] the French Government were at pains to present the differences in NATO as an argument between France and the United States. They now talk of the Americans' reasonableness and the intransigence of the British, whom they regard as more tied to the Americans as ever'.[31] French anger was exposed more forcefully in the run up to, and during the visit of the Prime Minister Georges Pompidou and the Foreign Minister Maurice Couve de Murville, to London from 6 to 8 July 1966. Intended as a gathering to discuss the array of issues which affected current Anglo-French relations, the meetings were foreshadowed by Couve's briefing to British correspondents in Paris in the days before his arrival. Reilly reported that Couve 'evidently spoke of current British policy towards France, especially over NATO, with a sustained hostility which must surely be unparalleled in a Foreign Minister about to pay a friendly visit to the capital of an ally'.[32] With this in mind, the Foreign Office informed embassies ahead of Pompidou's and Couve's arrival that in 'several respects the visit is bound to be something less than a love-feast'.[33]

The visit did prove a low point. In his preliminary meeting with Pompidou, Wilson suggested that it would 'be best to concentrate on topics where our direct common interest made it likely that we might agree; rather than on those where disagreement was inevitable. He was sure that they both wished these talks to be as fruitful as possible'.[34] Given that there was active disagreement on most important topics, this suggested a rather hollow Anglo-French encounter. The British were concerned at what they saw as the rather awkward connection that had developed between matters in NATO and the prospects for a future British application for EEC membership. One of the effects of the NATO crisis had been to raise the issue of Britain's relationship with the EEC to prominence again. It was widely known that the question was under consideration in Whitehall and the government had indicated movement in its position by adding the EEC to the remit of George Thomson, the chancellor of the Duchy of Lancaster, in his tour of NATO capitals to discuss the crisis caused by the French.[35] It would take until the autumn for the British to begin the process leading to the May 1967 announcement of a second application to the EEC, but in July 1966 the issue was clearly back on the agenda. What the British suspected was that the French ministers would use the visit to try to link Britain's position in NATO with its entry into the EEC; a more liberal British approach in dealing with France in NATO might equate to a more liberal French approach to dealing with Britain in the EEC.[36] Should this sort of tactic be deployed, the British were ready to reject it. The protection of NATO was the primary objective; a future EEC application was not yet policy.

The record does not show that either Pompidou or Couve made such an attempt to link Britain, NATO and the EEC. Instead, on NATO there was simply a restatement of respective positions, which was the best that could be hoped for. On the EEC, there was a fuller discussion with Wilson pressing Pompidou and Couve on the question of whether there remained a fundamental political French objection to British entry: '*The Prime Minister* said that he wished to press this point. The basic issue was whether we should at the end of a further negotiation be told that, because of our foreign policy, we were back in a Rambouillet/Nassau situation. *M. Pompidou* and *M. Couve* both said that this would not be the case.'[37] Instead, the French ministers concentrated on the economic obstacles, particularly the weakness of sterling which was revealed in stark light in July by financial crisis. The British thus took it that the French would not want to veto a British application, not least because of the wider support for it in Europe and in parts of France. Nonetheless, they still believed that de Gaulle's position had changed little since 1963, hence his requirement, reiterated by Couve, that the price of entry for Britain was acceptance of the Treaty of Rome and all agreements made between the Six EEC powers after 1957.[38]

De Gaulle set this price purposefully high. Whether he set it so high that Britain would not be able to reach it, or whether he would have acquiesced if the British did meet his criteria, is a highly debatable point. What is more certain is that de Gaulle's opposition to Britain's membership of the EEC was related to a fundamental difference of international outlook. This was apparent during the meeting between Wilson, his Foreign Secretary George Brown, and de Gaulle and Couve in Paris on 24 January 1967 amid the British probe of the EEC powers to determine the prospects for an application.[39] Wilson's tactics were to depict Britain and France as sharing the goal of bringing détente to Europe: 'The task of the great European Powers – of France and of Britain – was not to be mere messenger boys between the two Great Powers. They had a bigger role to play . . . than merely waiting in the ante-rooms while the two Great Powers settled everything direct between themselves'. Wilson's implication, that Britain would wish to act alongside France independently of the superpowers, 'greatly struck' de Gaulle although it is doubtful that he was convinced by it. Indeed, after a discussion on Britain and the EEC which saw no movement in de Gaulle's position, the French president made his views clear: 'whether or not [Britain and France] achieved economic unity within Western Europe, nothing could be expected to come of this unless they could achieve the complete unity of Europe and the total independence that he sought from the United States'.[40] '[T]otal independence' was not something that the Wilson government would accept, a fact that was underlined by its support for interdependence between Western Europe and the United States in the resolution of the NATO crisis and its defence of multilateralism during the Harmel Exercise of 1967.[41] It was nevertheless a condition of entry that de Gaulle maintained when he met Wilson at Trianon on 19 June 1967 after the British had announced their application and he had indicated his reservations in May.[42] Wilson recounted this meeting to President Johnson, noting that de Gaulle's 'general theme' was that

> the United States which was now the greatest power in the world behaved (as France and Britain had done in their hey-day) exclusively in her own interests. The only way for a medium-sized power like France, (or, in his view Britain), to conduct their affairs in such a situation was to disengage and to make it clear that

> America's quarrels are not our quarrels and their wars will not be our wars. [. . .] [T]here was no hope of a Middle East settlement while the war in Vietnam continued to poison the world scene, and he gave as the main reason for France's withdrawal from NATO his determination to keep his hands free in this cataclysmic situation.[43]

The two leaders went on to discuss Britain's EEC application and once again de Gaulle's 'constant theme', as Wilson described it to Johnson, 'was our involvement with yourselves and the danger that if we came in, all the weaker brethren in the Six . . . would follow our lead and the whole thing would become an American-dominated Atlantic arrangement. It was to prevent this that France was in the Community'. Exhibiting surprising confidence, the prime minister remained optimistic about entry even after de Gaulle's intransigence was patent during five and a half hours of talks. Wilson claimed to be 'moderately encouraged' because he doubted whether de Gaulle 'any longer has the strength finally to keep us out'. He admitted that this was 'a dangerous prophecy, as prophecy always is with the General'.[44] It was not only dangerous but wrong. After initially indicating his opposition in May, de Gaulle made a final statement in November and the EEC Council of Ministers decreed in December that it was not possible to proceed with Britain's application.[45]

The prospects for Britain's second bid at membership were never good and it had always been more probable that it would face another *non* from de Gaulle rather than a *oui*. Nevertheless, the significance of the Wilson government's application was that it was made despite this prognosis. Once any expectation had passed that de Gaulle could be won over or that France's Five EEC partners would fight Britain's corner to the point of crisis with the French president, success was for the Wilson government to present itself and its bid in a manner which achieved the related goals of displaying Britain's commitment to European unity, isolating de Gaulle in his obstruction of British entry and laying the foundations for British accession in due course. Measured by these objectives, the highest accomplishment that the British could expect was for them to be in a position at the point of veto when they could show that they had done all that was possible to present Britain ready and willing to join the Community and that if there was a barrier, it was put up by others. The Wilson government would have thus been gratified by the Central Intelligence Agency's (CIA's) judgment that 'the British have prosecuted with vigor and ingenuity their second bid' and that 'given France's opposition, the UK application has proceeded about as well as London had any reason to expect'.[46] Although the prophecy that Wilson made after his meeting with de Gaulle at Trianon had been wrong as de Gaulle did have the strength to keep Britain out, Wilson had drawn the right lesson: that Britain should 'keep firmly beating at the door'.[47] That was the way to accede to the EEC as it showed Britain's determination and commitment, in contrast with the vacillation and half-heartedness of the past. This did not move de Gaulle while he was still in office, just as it did it did not convince the Five to make Britain's application a breaking point with France, but there was widespread support among them for it and for Britain's future membership. As such, the diplomacy of 1967 became part of the greater progress in the Community which saw de Gaulle's challenge finally defeated at The Hague Summit in 1969.[48] Although it would take until January 1972 for the British to sign the Treaty of Accession to the Community, the route to entry had begun in 1966 when Britain used the NATO crisis to commence a new movement towards Western Europe, in turn preparing the way for the 1967 application.

Conclusion

The decade or so in which de Gaulle held the presidency of the Fifth French Republic was one in which Anglo-French relations were characterised far more by *mésentente* than *entente*. Of the many international affairs which were of mutual relevance to the British and French governments at that time, the future of Western Europe and its relationship with the United States in the evolving Cold War were the most prominent. These subjects had since the end of the 1940s separated the two countries as the British pursued foreign policies that allied them closely with the United States, encouraging strong US-Western European relations, while the French followed contrasting foreign policies which accepted the necessity of an American military shield to protect Western Europe but nevertheless promoted a particularly French view of a unified Europe which was not subordinate to Washington. This fundamental difference in outlook set Britain and France on a collision course as the 1950s progressed.

Once British governments had concluded that EEC membership was vital to Britain's long-term interests, an Anglo-French clash was inevitable. It was a stroke of the greatest historical irony that this event should take place as the personification of French nationalism and the foreign policies of independence should return to the Elysée Palace. The result was the now infamous veto of 14 January 1963 and the Gaullist phenomenon that unsettled Anglo-French relations throughout the 1960s.

14 January 1963 was not the only the occasion when de Gaulle issued a unilateral veto of a British attempt to gain entry to the EEC. He did so again in two acts in 1967, the first on 16 May and the second on 27 November. In the grand scheme of things, historians have not awarded these events the same magnitude as their predecessor. It is true that sequels are often disappointing. However, in the case of Anglo-French relations and the question of Britain's EEC membership, this is not so. The first application and veto were undoubtedly events of great importance, yet the second application and its veto were also of comparable importance. While in 1963 the British were certainly outmanoeuvred by de Gaulle and left without a European policy on 14 January, in 1967 they had learnt how to deal with him and their European policy endured. Such a verdict may seem easily despatched by the fact that the Wilson government made an application to join the EEC in May 1967 and had it turned down in December. In this light, the incontrovertible failure of 1967 does suggest that it was simply a postscript to 1963. Yet to adopt this view is to ignore the advances made by the British in their diplomacy during the NATO crisis of 1966 and in the form and presentation of the second application to the EEC in 1967. As this chapter has shown, in 1966 the British used the opportunity provided by de Gaulle's widely unpopular actions in NATO to bring stability where France had brought instability and to promote multilateralism and interdependence as a leading Western European power in the Atlantic Alliance while France upheld bilateralism and independence. In 1967, the shape of Britain's second EEC application and the manner in which the British presented themselves contrasted so distinctly with the application and diplomacy of 1961–63 that despite de Gaulle's veto, Britain had begun the process of entry to the Community with prevalent support among its member states. In the longer-term development of post-war Anglo-French relations, these events,

coming as they did in parallel with Britain's momentous retrenchment from East of Suez, were as least as important as those of 1963 and perhaps more so given the realignment in the Anglo-French relationship that they brought.

The case in favour of 1967 being attributed such significance is strengthened when Britain's diplomatic successes are given their full context. It would be wrong to assume that the British achieved what they did without the assistance of allies and circumstances. The Wilson government played a leading part in the rejection of de Gaulle's challenge to NATO in 1966, but this achievement was a multilateral business. In the resolution of the crisis and the success of the Harmel Exercise which redirected NATO's agenda in 1967, multilateralism overwhelmed de Gaulle's unilateralism. Without the assistance of the Johnson administration in particular, the British would not have been able to play as prominent a role as they did. Similarly, the solution to the problems of the Alliance was only achieved by the flexibility of the Federal Republic of Germany. In addition to these NATO factors, there were developments in the EEC which also assisted the British. Although France's Five EEC partners did not ultimately challenge de Gaulle over Britain's second application, their commitment to enlargement meant that British membership would remain on the agenda regardless of whether de Gaulle intervened or not. The Gaullist challenge and its promotion of the nation-state over the Community, at its height during the empty chair crisis, strengthened the ambition of France's partners to protect EEC institutions and to extend the Community programme further. British entry was thus supported as a means of diluting French influence and became embroiled in the wider revival of integration that was signalled by the Hague Summit of December 1969. This outcome was one which was predicted by the Johnson administration. Representing a view broadly held in Washington, the CIA judged in January 1967 that a British application was 'more crucial now than in 1963' because '[i]n the present situation in which Europe is having increasing difficulty in advancing its further unification and in which its future ties with the US are in a state of considerable uncertainty, the renewed possibility of the UK's taking its place in a European system is one of the few positive prospects'.[49]

Ironically, Britain's policies also received help from de Gaulle himself. 1966 was in many ways the zenith of his influence on the world stage. Thereafter, his ability to wield independent influence in international affairs and gain support in doing so declined. This was most apparent in his failure to lead the way in bringing détente to Europe through interventions with the Soviets in 1966 and with the Eastern Europeans in 1967. By the time of his September 1967 visit to Poland, this was all too clear. Perhaps foreknowledge of this depressing turn of events explains why de Gaulle gave Wilson the impression during his meeting with him at Trianon in June 1967 that he was a 'lonely old man obsessed in his fatalistic way by a sense of real impotence (a word he used twice with me)'?[50] Impotence in international affairs was something that British prime ministers had been seeking to ward off since the mid-1950s. Their way out, membership of the EEC and adjustments in their international commitments, had led them into an Anglo-French quarrel in which their French allies, especially under de Gaulle's leadership up to the mid-1960s, held the ascendancy. After 1966, however, that began to change.

Acknowledgement

The author would like to express his gratitude to the Arts and Humanities Research Council and the British Academy for their generosity in supporting the research upon which this article is based.

Notes

1. The National Archives (Public Record Office), Kew, London (hereafter TNA) CAB129/118, CP(64)102, 12 May 1964.
2. Nicholas Henderson, *Inside the Private Office: Memoirs of the Secretary to British Foreign Ministers* (Chicago: Academy Chicago Publishers, 1987), pp. 94–5.
3. TNA, FO371/177865/RF1022/34, Barnes to Hood, 17 March 1964 and Hood minute, 20 March 1964.
4. The extensive literature is well summarised in John W. Young, *Britain and European Unity 1945–1999* (Basingstoke: Macmillan, 2000), pp. 53–82.
5. For example, Simon Serfaty, *France, de Gaulle and Europe: The Policy of the Fourth and Fifth Republics toward the Continent* (Baltimore: Johns Hopkins University Press, 1968) and Jeffrey G. Giauque, 'Offers of partnership or bids for hegemony? The Atlantic Community, 1961–1963', *International History Review*, XXII/1 (March 2000), pp. 86–112, p. 111.
6. On de Gaulle's view of Churchill, see the contribution by David Reynolds to this book. In general, John Newhouse, *De Gaulle and the Anglo-Saxons* (London: André Deutsch, 1970).

7. For example, Alan S. Milward, *The UK and the European Community. Vol. I: The Rise and Fall of a National Strategy 1945–1963* (London: Frank Cass, 2002) in general; David Reynolds, *Britannia Overruled: British Policy & World Power in the 20th Century* (London: Longman, 1991), pp. 173–202; John W. Young, *Britain and the World in the Twentieth Century* (London: Arnold, 1997), pp. 141–68.
8. On the Anglo-American relationship see Nigel Ashton, *Kennedy, Macmillan and the Cold War: The Irony of Interdependence* (Basingstoke: Palgrave Macmillan, 2002).
9. Charles de Gaulle, *Memoirs of Hope: Renewal and Endeavour* (trans. Terence Kilmartin) (New York: Simon & Schuster, 1971), pp. 171–2. On de Gaulle's foreign policies, Frédéric Bozo, *Two Strategies for Europe: De Gaulle, the United States and the Atlantic Alliance* (trans. Susan Emanuel) (Oxford: Rowman & Littlefield, 2001); Georges-Henri Soutou, 'French Policy towards European Integration, 1950–1966' in Michael Dockrill (ed.), *Europe within the Global System, 1938–1960: Great Britain, France, Italy and Germany: From Great Powers to Regional Powers* (Bochum: Universitätsverlag Brockmeyer, 1995), pp. 119–33. In general, Maurice Vaïsse, *La Grandeur: Politique étrangère du général de Gaulle 1958–1969* (Paris: Fayard, 1997).
10. James Ellison, *Threatening Europe: Britain and the Creation of the European Community, 1955–58* (Basingstoke: Macmillan, 2000), in general.
11. De Gaulle, *Memoirs of Hope*, pp. 202–3; *Foreign Relations of the United States, 1958–1960. Vol. VII: Western Europe* (Washington: United States Government Printing Office, 1993), document 45, 17 September 1958; Bozo, *Two Strategies*, pp. 18–9. On the 1957 agreements, Jan Melissen, *The Struggle for Nuclear Partnership: Britain, the United States and the Making of an Ambiguous Alliance, 1952–1959* (Groningen: Styx, 1993), p. 39.
12. Milward, *The UK and the European Community*, vol. I, pp. 310–442 and 463–84.
13. Quoted in Alistair Horne, *Macmillan 1957–1986* (London: Macmillan, 1989), p. 447.
14. TNA, FO371/177865/RF1022/31, Dixon to Butler, 12 March 1964.
15. TNA, FO371/177865/RF1022/44, Mason, 'Policy Towards France', 30 April 1964. Also see TNA, FO371/177864/RF1022/18, Dixon to Butler, 14 February 1964; TNA, FO371/177865/RF1022/59, Dixon to Caccia, 22 June 1964; TNA, FO371/177866/RF1022/81, Dixon to Butler, 2 October 1964.
16. TNA, FO371/177865/RF1022/44, Hood to Ambassadors, 2 June 1964; TNA, FO371/177867/RF1022/115, FO to Certain of Her Majesty's Representatives, 3 July 1964.
17. TNA, FO371/184288/W6/12, Palliser to Nicholls, 9 February 1965.
18. TNA, PREM13/306, Stewart to Wilson, PM/65/38, 3 March 1965; TNA, CAB129/121, C.(65)51, 26 March 1965; TNA, FO371/184288/W6/12, Palliser to Nicholls, 9 February 1965.
19. Helen Parr, *Britain's Policy towards the European Community: Harold Wilson and Britain's World Role, 1964–1967* (London: Routledge, 2006), pp. 41–70. Also, John W. Young, *The Labour Governments 1964–70*. Vol. 2: *International Policy* (Manchester: University Press, 2003), pp.142–66.

20. *Foreign Relations of the United States, 1964–1968. Vol. XIII: Western Europe Region* (Washington: United States Government Printing Office, 1995) (hereafter *FRUS* 1964-1968 XIII), document 90, 16 June 1965 and document 97, 13 July 1965.
21. Charles de Gaulle, *Discours et messages: Janvier 1966 – avril 1969* (Paris: Plon, 1970), p. 19. On the 9 September press conference, Bozo, *Two Strategies*, p. 155.
22. *FRUS* 1964–1968 XIII, document 137, 7 March 1966.
23. Lawrence S. Kaplan, *NATO and the United States: The Enduring Alliance* (Boston: Twayne, 1988), p. 96. Andreas Wenger, 'Crisis and opportunity: NATO's transformation and the multilateralization of détente, 1966–1968', *Journal of Cold War Studies*, 6, 1, Winter 2004, 22–74. Also see Thomas Alan Schwartz, *Lyndon Johnson and Europe: In the Shadow of Vietnam* (Cambridge, MA: Harvard University Press, 2003), in general.
24. Lyndon Baines Johnson Library, Austin, Texas (hereafter LBJL), Papers of Lyndon Baines Johnson, National Security Files (hereafter Johnson Papers, NSF), Head of State Correspondence.
25. For de Gaulle's letter, TNA, PREM13/1042, Le Cheminant to Wilson, 9 March 1966.
26. National Archives and Records Administration, College Park, Maryland, USA (hereafter NARA), RG59 Lot File 67D516 NATO-French Relations Box 6, REU-19, 11 March 1966.
27. TNA, PREM13/1043, FO to Paris 695, 15 March 1966.
28. LBJL, Johnson Papers, NSF, Country File, Box 209, Intelligence Note 173, 19 March 1966.
29. LBJL, Johnson Papers, NSF, Country File, France, Box 177, Bruce to Rusk 4437, 21 March 1966.
30. TNA, CAB148/27, OPD (66)44, 1 April 1966; TNA, CAB148/25, OPD (66) 18th meeting, 6 April 1966.
31. TNA, PREM13/1509, Reilly to FO 42, 22 June 1966.
32. TNA, PREM13/1509, Reilly to FO 46, 14 July 1966. Also see the Sir Patrick Reilly Papers, Bodleian Library, Oxford, MSS. Eng. c. 6925, Sir Patrick Reilly Memoirs, 1964–6, pp. 194–204.
33. TNA, PREM13/1509, FO to Certain Missions, 4 July 1966.
34. TNA, PREM13/1509, Record of a conversation, 6 July 1966.
35. TNA, CAB148/25, OPD(66)22nd meeting, 27 April 1966.
36. TNA, PREM13/1509, FO to Certain Missions, 4 July 1966.
37. TNA, PREM13/1509, Record of a conversation, 8 July 1966.
38. TNA, PREM13/1509, Reilly to FO 46, 14 July 1966.
39. For the decision on the probe, TNA, CAB134/2705, E(66)3rd meeting, 22 October 1966.
40. TNA, CAB129/128, C(67)33, 16 March 1967.
41. On the Harmel Exercise, Helga Haftendorn, *NATO and the Nuclear Revolution: A Crisis of Credibility, 1966–67* (Oxford: Clarendon Press, 1996), pp. 320–85; Wenger, 'Crisis and Opportunity', pp. 22–74.

42. For the application and de Gaulle's May press conference, Uwe Kitzinger, *The Second Try: Labour and the EEC* (Oxford: Pergamon Press, 1968), pp. 177–9, 179–89.
43. LBJL, Johnson Papers, NSF, Head of State Correspondence, Box 10, Wilson to Johnson, 22 June 1967.
44. LBJL, Johnson Papers, Head of State Correspondence, Box 10, Wilson to Johnson, 22 June 1967.
45. For de Gaulle's November veto and the Council communiqué, Uwe Kitzinger, *The Second Try*, pp. 311–17, 317–21.
46. LBJL, Johnson Papers, NSF, Country File, UK, Box 211, CIA Memorandum, 1 August 1967.
47. LBJL, Johnson Papers, Head of State Correspondence, Box 10, Wilson to Johnson, 22 June 1967.
48. N. Piers Ludlow, *The European Community and the Crises of the 1960s: Negotiating the Gaullist Challenge* (London: Routledge, 2006), pp. 174–98.
49. LBJL, Johnson Papers, NSF, Country File, UK, Box 210, CIA Memorandum, 16 January 1967.
50. LBJL, Johnson Papers, Head of State Correspondence, Box 10, Wilson to Johnson, 22 June 1967. On the decline in de Gaulle's influence, see Garret Martin, 'Untying the Gaullian knot: France and the struggle to overcome the Cold War order, 1963–1968' (unpublished Ph.D. thesis, London School of Economics, 2006). The author is grateful to Mr Martin for allowing him to read drafts of his thesis.

9
Franco-British Relations during the Wilson Years, 1964–70

John W. Young
University of Notingham

From the outset, relations with France were viewed as central to the foreign policy of the Labour governments of Harold Wilson, who came to office in October 1964 after thirteen years of Conservative government.[1] Instructions to British delegates at the December 1964 NATO Council, the first major multilateral meeting after the election, warned officials to 'avoid confrontations with France'.[2] Shortly afterwards Nicholas Henderson, the private secretary to the foreign secretary, argued that the behaviour of President de Gaulle was more significant than the Vietnam situation or the activities of the Soviet Union, because he impacted on so many areas such as relations with the European Economic Community (EEC), the cohesion of NATO and the pursuit of détente.[3] The following years saw not only the dramatic withdrawal of France from NATO, de Gaulle's spearheading of détente and his veto of a second attempt to open talks on EEC enlargement, but also his resignation as president, a growing British focus on European concerns and the eventual agreement to discuss the country's entry to the EEC. The Wilson years have been unjustly neglected in the history of the *Entente Cordiale*. They witnessed some deep divisions between Britain and France, but they were important for seeing a drawing together of the two in terms of outlook on world affairs, paving the way for the close relationship enjoyed by de Gaulle's successor, Georges Pompidou, and Wilson's successor, Edward Heath.

Historiography

Several publications already touch on Franco-British relations between de Gaulle's veto of the first British application to join the EEC, in 1963, and the start of successful negotiations on entry in 1970. Most were written before the opening of government archives and tend to concentrate on policy towards the EEC to the detriment of other issues. None deal with the Wilson governments in a way that is both focused on the years 1964–70 and broad in its treatment of Franco-British interactions. But some are valuable for hinting at a tendency of British and French outlooks to draw closer together, even if serious differences remained. The earliest general study of Franco-British relations to cover the 1960s was that edited by Neville Waites in 1971. Here Guy de Carmoy provided a closing essay on events since 1958, concentrating on the EEC and defence issues. He pointed out that the foundation of the Fifth Republic created a presidential system very different to Britain's parliamentary democracy; that de Gaulle's pursuit of a genuinely independent nuclear deterrent and his withdrawal from NATO in 1966 had set France on a divergent course to Britain in defence terms; that, while the Macmillan and Wilson administrations became more open to membership of the EEC, the General was pursuing a particular vision of the Community's future which excluded British membership; and that, while both countries had to respond to post-imperial realities, de Gaulle's policy initiatives seemed far bolder and less defensive than those of Wilson. De Carmoy did note that, in 1968, faced by social discontent at home, the strength of the deutschmark and the Soviet invasion of Czechoslovakia, the General was forced to recognise limits to his détente policy, rely on economic support from other Western powers and consider an opening to Britain on the EEC. However, when his proposals for a joint initiative to create a 'Europe of nations' went awry in the Soames Affair, the main result was renewed friction with London. The essay therefore concluded that there had been a 'negative balance-sheet' in the 1960s, pessimistically referring to 'the political confrontations of the sixties, certainly sterile if not exactly hostile . . .'.[4]

Given how close he was to the events he discussed, de Carmoy's pessimistic conclusion is unsurprising. But the 1960s were also briefly touched upon in the same collection by Ann Williams, in a review of relations in the Mediterranean since the First World War. Here she highlighted a convergence in this particular theatre in two areas: first, the declining ability of either London or Paris to influence events in the Mediterranean and Middle East, following the collapse of the French Empire in North Africa and Britain's decision to withdraw from its bases 'East of Suez'; and second, the interest both countries had in reducing Arab-Israeli tensions, with both participating (alongside the US and USSR) in the process of Four-Power talks following the 1967 Six Day War.[5] A longer perspective could be taken by Philip Bell a generation later, when he produced his two-volume study of Franco-British relations in the twentieth century, though he was still without access to official archives for this period. He concentrated very much on decisions concerning the EEC, an approach that allowed detailed treatment of Wilson's bid to enter the Community, at the cost of omitting other issues of importance to London and Paris. Significantly, he chose to divide two of his chapters, not with the launch of the 'second try' at EEC entry in 1967 or the advent of the Heath government in 1970, but with the nadir of Franco-British relations during the Soames Affair and the ensuing – some would say fortuitous – departure of de Gaulle.[6] This, of course, was the point at which de Carmoy's account broke off and in retrospect, if any time could be described as 'a turning point' for the relationship, this was it. 1969, a year which had begun so badly, was to end with de Gaulle's successor, Georges Pompidou, agreeing to open talks on the enlargement of the Community. It will be argued below that the last year or so of the Wilson government also evidenced a broader convergence of views between Britain and France.

In 2000, in the collection of essays edited by Glyn Stone and Alan Sharp a single essay covered the four decades since 1958. Inevitably the discussion of the 1960s was sparse and, once again, the principal focus was the relationship in the context of the EEC.[7] Since then Anthony Adamthwaite has produced a more detailed essay on this same subject. His essay benefits from access to archival sources and is highly critical of the tactics of both the British and French leaders during the 'second try': while de Gaulle overestimated his country's ability to pursue an independent policy, Wilson overestimated his ability to win the General over to enlargement and then, when the inevitable veto came, followed a sterile policy of awaiting de Gaulle's departure. A better course for both countries, Adamthwaite argues, would have been to try to build a 'firm partnership at the heart of the EEC . . .'.[8] Meanwhile, yet another study of Franco-British relations in the twentieth century appeared in 2002, edited by Philippe Chassaigne and Mike Dockrill. While it lacked any comprehensive attempt to cover the 1960s, it did include three essays of relevance. In a short discussion of the 'problem of de Gaulle' in 1958–67, Richard Davis made use of archival materials to argue that the British were unable to deal effectively with de Gaulle because of a precipitate decline in their own power, coinciding with his creation of a more resilient French political system, linked to a more forthright foreign policy. Yet British officials also recognised that, whatever the differences with the obstinate, idiosyncratic de Gaulle, a certain community of interests existed between the two countries as liberal-democratic, European, Western powers. Thus a Foreign Office memorandum of 1962 felt that 'French and British interests in the world of today are becoming more and more similar'.[9] The two other essays in the volume concerned economic questions but were suggestive of the extent to which the similarities were growing. In a general study of the post-war period, Isabelle Lescent-Giles showed the ways in which the countries became closer in terms of the balance between industry and agriculture, the scale of their mutual trade, the pursuit of joint ventures, even if some key differences (for example, the role of the stock exchange in the British economy) remain marked. In looking more specifically at the 1960s, Jacques Leruez pointed out how, partly through a misinterpretation of French practices, the British tried to adopt a greater element of planning into their economy, including the abortive Brown Plan of 1965.[10]

The negative image: Wilson and de Gaulle, 1964–69

It would be easy to paint an entirely negative picture of Anglo-French relations in the Wilson–de Gaulle years. Wilson himself wrote that, just before the General left office, 'Anglo-French relations fell back to the low level at which they had been after [his] veto in 1963'.[11] In terms of European integration, which has been the focus of most academic study in the period, these years not only stand between the first veto and the successful entry talks of 1970–72, but also saw the General's second veto of entry talks in November 1967, without even allowing any negotiations to begin. He seemed determined to keep the EEC a select group, with France the predominant power. In 1964 there was general agreement that a second application was impossible. Even the Conservative manifesto said so. And in 1965–66 the Community itself was embroiled in the 'empty chair' crisis, when de Gaulle tried to prevent the strengthening of supranational elements, eventually securing the Luxembourg compromise, which suggested that he could veto decisions that he disliked in future. Some figures in the Labour government seem to have been coming round to a renewed attempt at entry and Wilson himself never categorically ruled it out, but only after he secured a healthy majority in the March 1966 election did he study entry seriously and he may only have decided to proceed after a major balance of payments crisis in July forced swingeing spending cuts. This suggested that some radical step was needed to set Britain on a course to economic health. It also brought an outspoken 'pro-European', George Brown, to the Foreign Office. True, Wilson insisted on a lengthy series of visits around European capitals in early 1967, followed by an equally exhausting series of Cabinet meetings, before he agreed to launch an application. But this tortuous process was probably designed to neutralise 'anti-Europeans' in the Cabinet and, once the application went ahead it had far more support, across the political board in Britain, than had Macmillan's. By vetoing it, de Gaulle arguably lost the chance to let Britain into the Community when support for that option was overwhelming. As it is, by the time Heath took the country in, most of Labour had turned against the option. But the bad behaviour was not all on the General's side. To add to the pessimistic image, the veto was preceded and followed by some elements of 'bullying' in British policy as London tried to work with the so-called 'Friendly Five' (the EEC members other than France, all of whom favoured British entry) against de Gaulle.[12]

While most studies focus on EEC issues, the doldrums in Franco-British relations in the sixties extended beyond those particularly troubled waters. On the transatlantic front this was the time when the General, after years of criticising the organisation, finally quit NATO. On becoming French president in 1958 he had wanted to work with London and Washington in a kind of 'tripartite directorate' of the West, but the rejection of this concept by Eisenhower and Macmillan led to an alternative approach for maximising French influence. Believing that the Cold War served to limit the independence of all countries other than the superpowers, he sought greater independence from the US, set out to dominate EEC and built up an independent nuclear arsenal. Simultaneously, he ran down the French formal empire remarkably rapidly, recognising it as an outdated basis of power, which had cost France dear during the wars in Indochina (1946–54) and Algeria (which he settled in 1962). His March 1966 announcement that France was leaving NATO was not unexpected, but it triggered a crisis that forced the alliance to move its headquarters from Paris to Brussels. Furthermore, this distancing of France from the US was accompanied by unilateral moves towards détente with the Eastern bloc. De Gaulle – who had already upset the Americans by recognising Communist China in January 1964 – visited Moscow in June–July 1966, a matter of months after leaving NATO. He also continued his criticisms of US policy in Vietnam, at a time when Wilson gave rhetorical backing to American policy in Southeast Asia.

As the British appreciated, the pursuit of détente and the withdrawal from NATO were two elements in a single policy. De Gaulle believed it easier to pursue improved relations with the USSR outside the American-dominated Atlantic alliance. He would both break free of US hegemony and pursue détente in such a way as to limit Soviet domination of the Eastern bloc, by establishing separate ties to China and independent-minded East European leaders like Romania's Nicolae Ceausescu. Meanwhile France would also maintain close relations with West Germany, remain predominant in the EEC and foster improved relations with the less-developed world. The result would be a more independent and influential France.[13] From a Franco-British perspective this was a significant reflection not merely of specific differences on policy, but of a broader separation of visions on world affairs. For the British remained loyal to NATO and close to the US throughout these years. Under a 1962 deal, the Americans provided Polaris missiles to deliver the British strategic nuclear deterrent. Anglo-American intelligence co-operation, going back to the Second World War was close and, while Wilson refused to become involved in the Vietnam War, Britain provided the Americans with intelligence material, weapons and training facilities. There were also intimate links between London and Washington, too, on monetary questions, with the US providing support for the beleaguered pound which, in many ways, was a first line of defence for the dollar.[14] De Gaulle was critical of the sterling-dollar link and French actions contributed to instability of the pound in the mid-sixties, culminating in its devaluation in November 1967. The devaluation provided de Gaulle with just the proof he needed that Britain was economically unfit for Community membership and provided the occasion for his veto of the 'second try'. He was therefore very much involved in bringing Wilson to the nadir of his political fortunes in late 1967.

If Britain and France did not seem close on key political strategies concerning transatlantic relations, the Cold War and European integration, they were also divided over various minor irritants. On taking office, Labour tired to pull out of the project to build the Concorde supersonic airliner, which the Conservatives had signed up for a few years before. The prospect of seeing the French continue the scheme and present London with half the bill kept the Wilson government involved, but it did distance itself from other projects for European scientific and technological co-operation.[15] For their part the French irritated Britain with aspects of their policy towards Africa, where de Gaulle was keen to maintain influence despite the formal end of the Empire. In particular, the British were disappointed that Paris would not fully support measures to bring down the White supremacist regime of Ian Smith in Rhodesia (now Zimbabwe) after it illegally declared independence in 1965. Overt support for Smith would have been unthinkable when de Gaulle was trying to maximise French influence in Black Africa, but foot-dragging over UN sanctions against Rhodesia was possible. It is significant that, when it became evident Smith was obtaining plentiful oil supplies, Wilson's reaction was that the guilty parties must be the French oil companies. It was doubly embarrassing when the culprits turned out to be British suppliers, BP and Shell, sparking a political scandal.[16] De Gaulle also supported the region of Biafra when it tried to break away from Nigeria in 1967, provoking three years of bitter civil war in the former British colony. While Britain, despite a growing chorus of criticism at home and abroad, became the key supplier of arms to the Nigerian federal government, France induced some of its former colonies to recognise the independence of Biafra and supplied arms that largely kept the secession alive after 1968.[17] Two other examples from the British archives will serve to illustrate the scale of the cross-Channel rifts could be in the Wilson years. One is rather pitiful: in

1965 British officials found the French to be highly sensitive about British celebrations of the 150th anniversary of the Battle of Waterloo.[18] The second suggests a more chronic ailment: in 1966 the Joint Intelligence Committee (JIC) learnt in August 1966 that Britain was de Gaulle's second most important intelligence target. After the USA that is, but before the USSR.[19]

How great a divide?

Despite the many negative elements in the relationship, the picture was not unremittingly bleak. Indeed, the fact that one key change – the resignation of de Gaulle as French president in 1969 – could herald a rapid improvement in relations suggests that the foundations for co-operation must already have existed. It may even be the case that, despite the bitterness he felt over the Soames Affair, the General himself considered a closer relationship with London. For one thing, even after the French withdrawal from NATO, the two countries remained allies. De Gaulle may have pulled out of the military structure of the Atlantic alliance, but he remained a signatory of the North Atlantic Treaty: besides, there were always challenges other than France even within NATO. While Nicholas Henderson might have deemed France to be the most complicating factor in world affairs, his colleague Oliver Wright, private secretary to the prime minister, argued that it was Germany that was the real challenge. Germany's power was growing alongside its influence in NATO, its future was still of central importance to the Cold War and a close alliance with Bonn was deemed essential by the US. 'How to promote movement in East-West relations and to make sense of . . . NATO . . . in modern conditions without alienating the Germans . . . is . . . the question of questions for our diplomacy'.[20] When Michael Stewart set out Britain's aims within the Western alliance for the Cabinet in September 1965 they included not only the need to preserve NATO in the face of Gaullist criticism, but also to influence American policy and to prevent German access to nuclear weapons while coming to terms with Germany's rising influence.[21] In 1966–67 London, Bonn and Washington became embroiled in a complex wrangle over the cost of deploying British and US troops in Germany which, even if it did not prove as grave a threat to NATO as French withdrawal, showed that there were divisions within the alliance that had nothing to do with de Gaulle.[22]

French withdrawal from NATO did not spark any crisis in the actual defence of the West, perhaps because the Cold War was no longer so intense as it had been in the 1950s, but also because French forces remained on the Western 'side' and such debates as there were about military strategy, primarily with the development of 'flexible response', were largely unaffected by de Gaulle's decision. The shift of the NATO headquarters to Brussels went smoothly and Lyndon Johnson deliberately avoided a clash with de Gaulle, remarking that 'when a man asks you to leave his home . . . you just pick up your hat and go'. British Foreign Secretary Michael Stewart took a similar view, telling the Cabinet's Overseas Policy and Defence Committee that an angry response to the withdrawal would simply make matters worse and that one beneficial result of French departure would be to raise Britain's profile in the alliance. John Barnes, head of the Western Organisations Department of the Foreign Office recognised 'our policy had to be that we should no nothing to drive France further apart from her allies . . . Thus I believe we kept the way open for a return to fuller cooperation later on'.[23] It is also worth recalling that, in 1964–66, de Gaulle and Wilson shared one important aim in NATO: they both opposed the US project to create a Multilateral Force (MLF), which would have created a surface fleet of nuclear-armed ships. This would have allowed Germany a share in the control of nuclear weapons, a proposal that was condemned by the Soviet Union and risked setting back hopes for détente. But it was also aimed at restricting the nuclear independence of France and the UK. The reaction from the two was different. De Gaulle stood completely aside from it; Britain, keen to retain American goodwill, helped to undermine it more subtly, launching an alternative proposal for an Atlantic Nuclear Force in December 1964. But French opposition to the project was quite convenient for the British. When the British embassy in West Germany reported in late 1964 that de Gaulle's opposition to the MLF was leading the Erhard government to slow down on the project, Oliver Wright considered it, 'The best news out of Bonn for a long time . . .'.[24] Too much was at stake on the European front for the Bonn regime to risk the French partnership over MLF and eventually it accepted a process of nuclear consultation in NATO short of a shared ownership of weapons.

In other areas, too, Britain and France found that a difference of approach did not prevent a measure of co-operation. In particular, technological co-operation went on with both countries convinced that Europe had to prevent itself falling under US domination in this field. In France the publication of Jean-Jacques Servan-Schreiber's *Le Défi Américain* symbolised the near-panic created by the prospect of American technological hegemony while, as Leader of the Opposition in 1963, Wilson had talked of the 'White Heat' of technology transforming Britain's economic prospects. True, once in power the revolution proved difficult to realise and, in one of its most celebrated early decisions, the incoming Labour government cancelled production of the TSR-2 strike and reconnaissance aircraft, alongside other projects, replacing them with American 'planes such as the Phantom and Hercules'.[25] But there was a certain logic to this policy, linked to their doubts about Concorde and a European space programme: the British planned to restrict spending on 'prestige projects' and focus on more marketable products. In 1966–67, when trying to win de Gaulle over to British membership of the EEC, Wilson felt one of his strongest cards was to hold out the prospect of a 'European Technological Community'. This did not impress de Gaulle, but that was partly because he was well aware that technological co-operation was possible without joint membership of the EEC. Indeed, these years saw a number of projects being launched by Britain and France. Not only Concorde but military aircraft projects like the swing-wing AFGVA 'Jaguar' fighter.[26]

While de Gaulle was undoubtedly troublesome to the British on a number of fronts in the mid-sixties, their differences should not be exaggerated. On détente, for example, it is true that the General linked his departure from NATO to a bolder pursuit of talks with the Soviet Union. But partly because of his actions, NATO began more earnestly to look at détente, publishing the Harmel Report in December 1967. This added the political aim of East–West negotiations to the alliance's military aim of preparing the West's defences against Soviet attack. Besides, Wilson had long been known as a proponent of improved relations with Moscow, especially in the trade field. He visited Moscow more frequently than de Gaulle did, if with less dramatic effect, in February and July 1966, and again in January 1968.[27] French policy on currency questions was an irritant but the devaluation of the pound in November 1967 owed more, in the long term, to structural problems in the British economy and, in the short term, to the after-effects of the Six Day War, which had closed the

Suez Canal and damaged international trade.[28] And, as to the Vietnam War, it may be true that de Gaulle was vocal in his criticisms of American policy while Wilson outwardly showed sympathy to Lyndon Johnson's predicament. But the most significant point is that, to Johnson's annoyance, Wilson would not commit troops to Vietnam. In private the prime minister could be critical of the US and British officials were favourable to the kind of 'neutralised' Indochina that de Gaulle advocated as a solution to the conflict.[29]

It also has to be said that, but for a few occasions, such as the celebrated Soames Affair – which in any case came only a few months before de Gaulle's resignation – personal relationship between British and French representatives were generally good under Labour. Not all were as personally enthusiastic perhaps as George Brown, who became foreign secretary in 1966–68 and who, however unlikely it sounds, is reputed to have put his arm around President de Gaulle and called him 'Charlie'.[30] But the General got on well with British Ambassador Patrick Reilly, even telling him in September 1968, at their last meeting, that Britain and France were closer than ever. Reilly did not agree: he felt relations were much worse than they had been when he arrived. Yet he remembered de Gaulle with respect, as someone with whom you could talk frankly and who was ready to meet you at short notice.[31] The appointment of Christopher Soames, a son-in-law of Winston Churchill and former Conservative Cabinet minister, confirmed France's importance to Britain and de Gaulle would not have talked to him as he did in February 1969 if he had not respected him. At least until the veto of the 'second try', Wilson and de Gaulle met quite regularly and amicably. The first, brief occasion was during Churchill's funeral in January 1965[32] but fuller summits followed in April 1965, February 1967 and June 1967, and there was a visit by Premier Georges Pompidou to London in July 1967. Wilson's first visit to Paris, in April 1965, showed that both sides were determined to maintain a civil relationship and to develop co-operative ventures where possible (especially in the technological field), while accepting that they differed on such substantial questions as Vietnam, the future of NATO and the world monetary system. Indeed, both leaders made a virtue of this situation in the last plenary meeting of the summit, with Wilson remarking that 'each had stated the differences frankly, as between friends . . . The *entente* had now become much more *cordiale*'.[33]

Patrick Reilly recognised that one reason the French were so keen to create an amicable relationship was that this made it seem that London had accepted its exclusion from the EEC. This in turn blunted criticism of the General's 1963 veto from the 'Friendly Five' and his own people.[34] For a time, as seen above, the British were content not to offend de Gaulle on the EEC. They stayed out of the 'empty chair' crisis in 1965–66 and Wilson abandoned schemes to tie together the EEC and the British-led European Free Trade Association. Certainly, with the launch of the 'second try' the situation became more difficult. But it is worth underlining two points. First, whatever difficulties it caused for Wilson in November 1967, de Gaulle did give plenty of warning of the likelihood of a veto if Britain pressed its case. At the two summits with Wilson, in Paris in February and at Versailles in June, he held out no real hope that he would let Britain in the EEC. And in a press conference in May he all but said that he would veto an application. Reilly warned London that a proper veto would occur if the application was pushed too urgently, but that did not stop Wilson and Brown pressing on against the odds.[35] The second point is that, in their vision of the future EEC, de Gaulle and Wilson may not have been that far apart. In fact Wilson, admittedly in contrast to the Foreign Office, was interested in working with the General to minimise supranational elements in the EEC. In 1965, the prime minister told newspaper chairman, Cecil King: 'the French are intent on maintaining a separate foreign and defence policy, which fits in best with British interests' and when the Foreign Office criticised de Gaulle for disrupting the EEC, Wilson asked, 'Why should we find the acceptance of French conditions "dangerous" since they reject supranationality?'.[36] Such ideas may even have helped lead to the Soames Affair, when de Gaulle suggested over dinner with the new ambassador that the two countries might indeed work together to try to create a 'Europe des Patries'. But, with the Foreign Office wedded to the idea of joining the existing EEC, with the British fearful of upsetting the 'Friendly Five' if news of the conversation leaked, and with Wilson just about to meet German Chancellor Kurt Kiesinger, the British hastily decided to publish details of the General's ideas. His anger at this embarrassing step was entirely predictable, as was the disappointment felt by Soames, and it was fortunate that an unexpected setback in a referendum led him to resign so soon afterwards.[37]

Growing together

If Franco-British relations as a whole in 1964–69 were far from a completely negative image, it was also the case that underlying developments were drawing them closer together in certain ways, and that one-off incidents like the Soames Affair could not alter the fact that the potential for co-operation was improving. Key differences might remain in their economic models but, as noted above, there were now elements of economic planning in British policy and the 1960s saw profound changes in London's global position. Most strikingly, the retreat from bases East of Suez, first announced in the Defence White Paper of July 1967, left the country with no alternative to a European future – not if it wished to have any effective influence in world affairs which, as an island power that depended on a stable trading environment, was a necessity rather than a luxury. Small wonder that, in 1969–70, Britain took a lead in forming a 'Eurogroup' in NATO.[38] Yet a meaningful relationship with Europe required good relations with France as Wilson already knew only too well. During the 'second try' not only did he try to tempt de Gaulle with the European Technological Community, he even distanced Britain from the US in final stage of 'Kennedy Round' of trade talks, which led to a new set of tariff reductions under the General Agreement on Tariffs and Trade.[39]

The declining importance of the 'special relationship' at this time was another key development, linked to the retreat from East of Suez and the devaluation of the pound, and one that reinforced the need to focus on a European future. Even if personal relations between Washington and London remained good, even if the nuclear and intelligence alliance went on and even if their cultural-linguistic ties continued to haunt the Gaullist mind, the simple fact was that Britain, in terms of material power and political significance, was no more important to the US than a large number of other countries, such as Germany, Japan or Israel. The British withdrew from East of Suez in the face of US protests and Wilson only ever had a lukewarm relationship with Lyndon Johnson.[40] In any case, some senior British figures did question the wisdom of relying on America and falling out with France. When, in January 1966, Michael Stewart put a paper critical of French policy before the Cabinet, another minister, Richard Crossman objected: the FO paper 'argued . . . that we must regard General de Gaulle as the worst enemy in the world because of his wicked plan for knocking the supranational elements out of the Common Market and for working with the Soviet Union to get an understanding over Germany's head. As I thought these were pretty sensible policies I [tried to] scotch the paper'.[41] Another leftist minister, Barbara Castle, was prepared to admit during the Soames Affair that 'we have made a mess of it'. Both Crossman and Castle were critics of the Vietnam War.[42]

The decline in fortunes for Britain at this point seemed quite precipitate, while France might be said to have been bouncing back from the rapid evaporation of its Empire. Yet, even for de Gaulle painful lessons had to be learnt about the realities of power, especially as his term in office drew to its close. This should not really have been a surprise. When drawing up a memorandum entitled 'Haute Politique' in early 1965, Wilson's Private Secretary for foreign affairs Oliver Wright had written that while the French president, like China's Mao Zedong, was one of the few leaders of vision 'they are men who . . . have only a nuisance value, since they do not dispose of real power'. For, Wright reasoned, if the General made progress on détente this would inevitably lead to German reunification, and a reunited Germany could only be controlled if Paris and London worked closely together. The private secretary went too far, perhaps, when he foresaw 'An All-Europe des Patries, led by Britain and France' but his analysis was not far off the mark in perceiving that whereas, in the short term, the General's potency was limited, in the long-term France would see the value of working with Britain.[43] For a time de Gaulle could, through sheer *tour de force*, appear to hold back reality. Ending the war in Algeria, recognising China, condemning the war in Vietnam, quitting NATO, visiting Moscow, these cumulatively suggested someone who controlled world affairs, not vice versa, just as his creation of the Fifth Republic suggested that French internal politics might escape the upheavals of the previous regime.

But in 1967–69 de Gaulle looked suddenly human. The frailty was all too obvious at the time of the riots of May 1968, whose causes he seemed at a complete loss to understand. Among other results, the riots weakened the franc on the money markets, so that it followed sterling on the road to devaluation. It may have been in order to avoid taking responsibility for that distasteful step that the General took the opportunity to resign. But the frailty was clear in foreign affairs too. In particular he was forced to accept that improved East–West relations could not be pushed forward outside the context of the Western alliance. The fact was that the USSR still treated the US as more important than France, not least because it was the key to any nuclear arms control measures. While de Gaulle stood aside from the 1963 Test Ban Treaty and the 1968 Non-Proliferation Treaty, the USSR signed both and actively worked for bilateral talks with the US on strategic arms. The Nixon years would show that China, too, saw Washington as far more significant than Paris. Most dramatically of all, the Soviet-led invasion of Czechoslovakia in August 1968, only months after the Paris riots, showed the limits to European détente and to any hopes de Gaulle had that the Warsaw Pact might be broken up. It is noteworthy that Patrick Reilly had recognised the many tensions inherent in the General's pursuit of détente as early as 1965: moving too close to the USSR could both upset Germany and weaken Western interests; getting too close to China and Ceausescu could offend the Soviets; and Moscow was bound to realise that 'he has no real position of economic or military power, and at 74, can have only a limited period of active life ahead of him . . .'.[44] The perceptiveness of this analysis was now all too clear and made it unthinkable for de Gaulle to carry out any plans he may have had to withdraw from the North Atlantic Treaty itself, as signatories were allowed to do after its first twenty years expired. By April 1969, when that anniversary arrived, de Gaulle's position was a shadow of what it had been when he quit the alliance's military structures three years before. At the end of the month he resigned.

On the Franco-British front, not only did the weakening of French internal stability, economic fortunes and power overseas hold out the prospect of a more amenable government in Paris, it can be said that the Wilson government had helped to force de Gaulle on to the back foot in the EEC, weakening the French position there too. Despite Anthony Adamthwaite's view that British policy was bankrupt during the 'second try' in fact it ultimately proved remarkably successful. This was perhaps more due to fortuitous circumstances than careful judgment. Logically, the 'second try' should not have been made at all because, as many even in government predicted, it was always likely to end in a veto from de Gaulle. But British policy was in a quandary. With the withdrawal from East of Suez being planned and the 'special relationship' in decline, London simply had no alternative to knocking at the European door. Hence, when the veto came, the Labour government pointedly left the application 'on the table' ready to be taken up at any time. By then, the very process of applying had isolated France, highlighted the support for enlargement of the EEC from all its other members, and created the impression that some day, sooner or later, Britain would enter the Community. The British decision to apply had made sense after all, even if none of Wilson's ministers or officials had expected it to work out quite this way. British tactics cannot be described as consistent: there was always a tension between their attempts to isolate France, by working with the 'Friendly Five', and their attempts to win de Gaulle over to British membership, as Wilson tried to do (at least down to June 1967) and as Edward Heath would do in 1970–72. Yet, they had put de Gaulle in a difficult position, forcing him to issue a veto he would rather have avoided and wounding his standing with his EEC partners. Thus, Piers Ludlow has written that in 1968 in the EEC, 'Paris came increasingly to recognise that no significant forward movement would be possible until the impasse over enlargement had been resolved'. And James Ellison argues that, by making the second application the British helped frustrate de Gaulle's 'power play in the EEC and NATO' in the mid-1960s, helping to show that he could not have things his own way.[45] Furthermore, all this occurred when Britain's commitment to the EEC could not easily be doubted. All three major British political parties backed entry second time around, as seen in the government's overwhelming majority of more than 400 in the parliamentary debate of May 1967. Indeed, if the Soames Affair showed anything it was that Britain was prepared to be a better 'European' than de Gaulle was, in that his offer of a partnership that would undermine the EC was rejected. London wanted membership of the existing Community or nothing. Wilson and Michael Stewart, back as foreign secretary in 1968–70, were clear their strategy was one of breaking down French resistance so that entry occurred when de Gaulle was gone.[46]

Entente renewed: Wilson and Pompidou in 1969–70

When Georges Pompidou became president of France in June 1969[47] the potential for a Franco-British partnership was already there.

Britain, while still a member of NATO and a close ally of America, was no longer a country with global pretensions. It needed to secure its future in Europe and Wilson agreed with Stewart that they should 'let it be seen that we are ready to start a fresh page in Anglo-French relations'.[48] France, while it wished to maximise its own influence in world affairs and would not return to the NATO fold, needed to restore its leadership of the EC, control West German power and come to terms with the devaluation of the franc (an operation finally carried out in August 1969). Pompidou and Wilson only overlapped in office by a year in 1969–70 and did not meet face-to-face, but the period was noteworthy for a further drawing together of the foreign policy interests of their countries. Both, as seen above, were involved in Four-Power talks on the Middle East in this period, which vainly sought an Arab-Israeli settlement. Limits to the influence of both London and Paris were highlighted by the beginning of Strategic Arms Limitation Talks between the US and USSR in November 1969. The end of the Nigerian civil war, with the crushing of Biafran secession in January 1970, removed Franco-British differences on that score, while Nixon's determination to reduce US troop levels in Vietnam, with the first cuts announced in March 1970, ended another reason for disagreement. As a further indication of their declining ambitions, the British decided not to purchase Poseidon missiles from the US as a successor to Polaris. Willy Brandt's victory in the German elections of October 1969 opened the way to a more independent foreign policy towards the Soviet bloc. With the German economy continuing to grow and the deutschmark one of the strongest currencies on the world markets, this revival of German power caused special concern to Pompidou and does much to explain his readiness to consider EEC enlargement.

While formal talks on Britain's eventual entry to the EEC only took place under the Conservative government after June 1970, it is easy to forget that the process was planned under Wilson and marked an acceptance of the application put by George Brown back in 1967. This application had, of course, remained 'on the table' after de Gaulle's veto, it was viewed favourably by the 'Friendly Five' and all that was needed to bring it to fruition was a shift in French policy. In an early indication that he was open to British entry, Pompidou made Maurice Schumann his foreign minister, bringing someone to the Quai d'Orsay who, while he might not be described as an

Anglophile, was much better disposed to Britain than de Gaulle's long-serving foreign minister, Maurice Couve de Murville. The British were determined to do all possible to keep Schumann friendly, even to the extent of having Michael Stewart accompanied by as few officials as possible during their bilateral meetings – so that Schumann had a ready-made excuse to exclude any 'anti-British' officials from his own negotiating team.[49] The key breakthrough came at the Hague Summit of EEC leaders in December 1969 where Pompidou agreed to open talks on enlargement in return for other leaders agreeing to settle the financing of the Common Agricultural Policy, which was important to France because of the support it would provide for the country's agricultural sector. With the veto removed, preparations for talks on enlargement went forward and a date in late June was set for them to open. Wilson was cautious in public about the prospect, but this may have been in order to create a strong bargaining position because he had already promised to appoint a leading 'pro-European', Roy Jenkins, as foreign secretary if Labour won the general election and Labour's manifesto was favourable to entry.[50]

Conclusion

In the months following Wilson's election defeat the Foreign and Commonwealth Office (FCO) drew up a substantial study of relations with France that took a balanced view of the current situation. It recognised that, while the 'departure of General de Gaulle has led to a substantial improvement in the climate of Anglo-French relations', with closer views on Africa, the Middle East and Southeast Asia, there were still disagreements over relations with the US, the process of détente and the future shape of the EEC, while the two were also rivals as industrial and trading powers. London and Paris, it was noted, even disagreed regularly over their joint administration of the sparsely populated and remote New Hebrides. Centuries of rivalry and suspicion were not to be wiped out with the passing of one particularly difficult individual and officials feared that, if France's gross national product continued to grow faster than Britain's, then the problems of managing French power might actually grow worse. On the positive side, however, there were undoubtedly common interests that could be built upon, such as developing European security, increasing Western European influence in the world, avoiding technological dependency on the US, balancing the power of West Germany, creating a stable monetary system, expanding world trade and aiding less developed countries.[51] This was a balanced appraisal, reflecting the ingrained caution of the civil servant, but it was realistic enough. Relations had undoubtedly been improving under Wilson's last year, but this improvement built on a growing together of British and French outlooks that long predated the resignation of de Gaulle. Had Wilson been re-elected prime minister in 1970 there seems little reason to doubt that he would have led Britain into the EC instead of Heath; not with the same scale of enthusiasm perhaps, but with a less vaulted view of what the Community could offer.

It is also tempting to ask whether, if de Gaulle had remained in power, British entry to the EEC would have become possible. The official report drawn up in the FCO on EEC entry described him as an 'irremovable obstacle', but he had been a bugbear for British officials too often for them to have any belief in him.[52] Yet, Pompidou had long been close to the General and it is possible to see that enlargement *could* have fitted de Gaulle's programme by around 1970: with Britain's world role ended, the special relationship meaningless but the British economy healthier than it had been in 1966–67, might it not have made sense to draw the country into the Community where it could help to control Germany, pay for the costly Common Agricultural Policy and temper any moves towards greater supranationalism? Perhaps not: de Gaulle may in a sense have got the British where he had long wanted them, but he was an old man, suffering from arteriosclerosis, too set in his ways to abandon ingrained policies like the veto on enlargement and exploit the new reality. But the very fact that one event – de Gaulle's resignation from the presidency – could herald both enlargement and a revived *entente*, shows that not all was wrong between Britain and France in the 1960s. It was not necessary to quit NATO, break with America, abandon Polaris and remould (or destroy) the EEC for Britain to work with France in the long term. All that was necessary was to wait for one increasingly beleaguered old man to leave office, while preparing on other fronts for a European future: maintaining good relations with the 'Friendly Five', emphasising Britain's value to Western Europe, making an EEC application and leaving it on the table. By continuing to knock on the door the British became a rather embarrassing presence that could only be removed by letting them in. And, given the ups and downs of the *Entente Cordiale* over the century, it was perhaps inevitable that a convergence of interests would, at some point, make it in France's interest to open the lock. But it would be pointless to claim that the convergence that occurred as the 1960s drew on removed all the differences between them. The continued existence of NATO, the persistence of the Anglo-American alliance and popular British doubts about EEC institutions, as well as more deep-seated cultural and philosophical differences, would continue to trouble Franco-British relations in future.

Notes

1. I am grateful to the British Academy for helping to finance the research in The National Archive, Kew, on which this essay is partly based.
2. The National Archives (TNA), PREM 13/72, Steering Brief for meeting of 15–17 December 1964.
3. Nicholas Henderson, *Inside the Foreign Office* (Chicago: Academy, 1987), pp. 94–5.
4. Guy de Carmoy, 'Defence and unity of Western Europe since 1958', in Neville Waites (ed.), *Troubled Neighbours: Franco-British Relations in the Twentieth Century* (London: Weidenfeld and Nicolson, 1971), pp. 344–74, quote from p. 374.
5. Ann Williams, 'Security and settlement in the Mediterranean since 1914', in Waites (ed.), *Troubled Neighbours*, pp. 333–5.
6. P.M.H. Bell, *France and Britain, 1940–94: The Long Separation* (London: Longman, 1997), pp. 204–20.
7. Joanne Wright, 'The Cold War, European community and Anglo-French relations, 1958–98', in Alan Sharp and Glyn Stone (eds), *Anglo-French Relations in the Twentieth Century* (London: Routledge, 2000), pp. 329–31.
8. Anthony Adamthwaite, 'John Bull versus Marianne, round two: Anglo-French relations and Britain's second EEC membership bid', in Oliver Daddow (ed.), *Harold Wilson and European Integration* (London: Cass, 2003), pp. 151–71, quote from p. 168.
9. Richard Davis, 'The "problem of de Gaulle", 1958–67', in Philippe Chassaigne and Michael Dockrill (eds), *Anglo-French Relations, 1898–1998* (Basingstoke: Palgrave, 2002), pp. 161–73, quote from p. 161, citing NTA, FO 371/163494/1, Note by Rumbold (9 January 1962).
10. Isabelle Lescent-Giles, 'The "Mésentente Cordiale": Economic relations between France and Great Britain since 1945' and Jacques Leruez, 'Britain, France and economic planning in the 1960s' in Philippe Chassaigne and Michael Dockrill (eds), *Anglo-French Relations*, pp. 138–60 and 174–88.
11. Harold Wilson, *The Labour Government, 1964–70: A Personal Record* (London: Weidenfeld and Nicolson, 1971), 618.

12. But stories that Britain would itself withdraw from the defence of Europe were exaggerated: Alun Chalfont, *The Shadow of My Hand: A Memoir* (London: Weidenfeld and Nicolson, 2000), pp. 121–5. For discussions of the 'second try' based on archival evidence: Daddow (ed.), *Harold Wilson*; Helen Parr, *British Policy towards the European Community: Harold Wilson and Britain's World Role* (London: Routledge, 2005); and John W. Young, *The Labour Governments, 1964–70*, vol. 2: *International Policy* (Manchester: University Press, 2003), chapter 6.
13. PREM 13/324, Reilly to Stewart (18 March 1965). For a more recent analysis of de Gaulle's policy see Frédéric Bozo, *Deux Stratégies pour l'Europe: De Gaulle, les États-Unis et l'Alliance Atlantique* (Paris: Plon, 1996).
14. For archivally based discussions of these issues: Jonathan Colman, *Special Relationship: Harold Wilson, Lyndon Johnson and Anglo-American Relations* (Manchester: University Press, 2005); and Sylvia Ellis, *Britain, America and the Vietnam War* (Westport: Praeger, 2004).
15. John W. Young, 'Technological co-operation in Wilson's strategy for EEC entry', in Daddow (ed.), *Harold Wilson*, pp. 96–9.
16. PREM 13/3437, Wilson minute on Maitland to Palliser (9 April 1968) and Wright to Wilson (22 April); and see Clive Ponting, *Breach of Promise: Labour in Power 1964–70* (London: Hamish Hamilton, 1989), pp. 249–55.
17. Suzanne Cronje, *The World and Nigeria: The Diplomatic History of the Biafran War, 1967–70* (London: Sidgwick & Jackson, 1972), 194–209.
18. PREM 13/326, passim.
19. TNA, CAB 159/46, JIC(66) 35th (25 August, 1966).
20. PREM 13/343, Wright to Wilson (24 October, 1964).
21. CAB 128/39, CC49(65) (23 September, 1965).
22. For a discussion of the 'offset crisis' see Hubert Zimmermann, *Money and Security: Troops, Monetary Policy and West Germany's Relations with the US and Britain* (Cambridge: University Press, 2003).
23. Lyndon Johnson Library, Austin, Texas, John Leddy oral history interview; NTA, CAB 148/25, OPD(66) 18th (5 April); John Barnes, *Footsteps on the Backstairs* (Wilby: Michael Russell, 1992), p. 96. Some officials felt that, while London may have avoided an angry public reaction to de Gaulle, it did appear to be 'leading the pack in NATO against the French': see PREM 15/2586, Palliser to Wilson (22 November 1968).
24. PREM 13/343, Wright to Wilson, handwritten on Bonn to FO (12 November 1964); and see John W. Young, 'Killing the MLF? The Wilson government and nuclear sharing in Europe, 1964–66', in Erik Goldstein and B.J.C. McKercher (eds), *Power and Stability: British Foreign Policy, 1865–1965* (London: Frank Cass, 2003), p. 295–324.
25. Sean Straw and John W. Young, 'The Wilson government and the demise of TSR-2', *Journal of Strategic Studies*, 20, 4, 1997, pp. 18–44.
26. Young, 'Technological cooperation', pp. 99–108.
27. See Geraint Hughes, 'Harold Wilson, the USSR and British foreign and defence policy in the context of East-West détente' (unpublished Ph.D. thesis, London: King's College, 2002).

28. Jim Tomlinson, *The Labour Governments*, 1964–70: *Vol. 3, Economic Policy* (Manchester: Manchester University Press, 2004).
29. John W. Young, 'Britain and LBJ's War, 1964–68', *Cold War History*, 2, 3, April 2002, pp. 63–92.
30. Peter Patterson, *Tired and Emotional: The Life of Lord George Brown* (London: Chatto & Windus, 1993), pp. 212–3.
31. PREM 13/2113, Reilly to Stewart (12 September 1968); Bodleian Library, Oxford, MSS. Eng. c. 6925, Patrick Reilly, unpublished memoir, 24 and 68.
32. PREM 13/317, record of meeting (29 January 1965).
33. PREM 13/324, record of meeting (3 April 1965).
34. PREM 13/324, Reilly to Stewart (18 March 1965).
35. PREM 13/1483, Reilly to Gore-Booth (28 June 1967).
36. Cecil King, *The Cecil King Diary, 1965–70* (London: Jonathan Cape, 1972), pp. 57–8 and see 67; PREM 13/904, Wilson minute on Stewart to Wilson (10 December 1965).
37. Details of the Soames Affair have been known for a long time: Uwe Kitzinger, *Diplomacy and Persuasion: How Britain Joined the Common Market* (London: Thames & Hudson, 1973), pp. 45–58.
38. On the defence decisions see Young, *International Policy*, pp. 42–52 and 122.
39. Donna Lee, 'Endgame at the Kennedy round', *Diplomacy and Statecraft*, 12, 3, 2001, pp. 115–38.
40. Young, *International Policy*, pp. 19–23.
41. CAB 129/124, C(66)16 (28 January 1966); Richard Crossman, *Diaries of a Cabinet Minister, vol. 1: Minister of Housing, 1964–66* (London: Hamish Hamilton & Jonathan Cape, 1975), pp. 442 and 445.
42. Barbara Castle, *The Castle Diaries, 1964–70* (London: Weidenfeld and Nicolson, 1984), p. 606.
43. PREM 13/316, Wright to Wilson (12 February 1965).
44. PREM 13/324, Reilly to Stewart (18 March 1965).
45. Piers Ludlow, 'Community institutions and the second British Application', in Daddow (ed.), *Harold Wilson*, p. 148; and James Ellison, 'Anglo-American relations, NATO and the second application', *ibid.*, pp. 172–87, quote from p. 184.
46. For example, PREM 15/2113, Palliser to Maitland (12 September 1968).
47. Alain Poher had been 'interim' President since de Gaulle's resignation in April.
48. PREM 13/2645, Stewart to Wilson (13 June 1969) and Wilson's handwritten approval.
49. NTA, FO 73/37, Palliser to Graham (29 September 1969).
50. For an archive-based study see Melissa Pine, 'Application on the table: The second British application to the European communities, 1967–70' (unpublished D.Phil. thesis, University of Oxford, 2003).
51. NTA, PREM 15/1560, Douglas-Home to Barber (16 December).
52. Con O'Neill, *British Entry into the European Community: Report on the Negotiations of 1970–72* (London: Whitehall History Publishing, 2000), p. 341.

10
From Heath to Thatcher, 1970–90

John Campbell
Freelance Political Historian and Biographer

During the later decades of the twentieth century it becomes impossible to write sensibly about the *Entente Cordiale* in isolation. Since the 1960s, the Anglo-French relationship has been largely subsumed in relations with the European Community as a whole. Of course France has usually been the leading power in the Community – certainly in the eyes of the British press and public opinion. Ever since General de Gaulle's famous '*Non*' blocked Harold Macmillan's first belated attempt to join the Common Market in 1963, it had been of overriding importance for British prime ministers to forge a good relationship with successive French presidents. By comparison the other members of the Community, even Germany, are usually seen to be of lesser importance. Nevertheless relations with France cannot be treated except in the wider European context.

Britain's relations with the EEC were transformed between 1970 and 1990, a period that falls into three phases. First there was the successful negotiation under Edward Heath which led to Britain finally joining the Community in 1973. Then British membership was confirmed by the 1975 referendum, skilfully managed by Harold Wilson to produce the right result; but the Labour Party remained deeply divided over Europe and James Callaghan's Government was at best half-hearted in its dealings with the Community. With the election of Margaret Thatcher in 1979, Britain again had a Government committed in principle to Europe, and over the next decade Britain became – institutionally if not emotionally – inextricably bound into the developing European Union. But Mrs Thatcher's personal reservations led to an increasingly embattled relationship, with Britain frequently isolated and regarded by the other members as a drag on progress.

The two key phases were the first and third, reflecting the differing approaches of two Conservative prime ministers with sharply different attitudes to Europe. Ted Heath and Mrs Thatcher were actually very similar in many ways. They came from similar backgrounds in the lower middle class from which they escaped via the classic ladder of grammar school and Oxford; they were both intensely ambitious from an early age, chillingly single-minded and a touch humourless. But their attitudes to Europe reflect different early experiences, which in turn mirror fundamentally opposed attitudes among the British people as a whole.

Both were to an unusual degree wholly English, with no trace of Celtic ancestry and no family connection with either Europe or the Empire: neither spoke any European language beyond the usual minimal school French. But Ted Heath was brought up in Broadstairs on the Kent coast, practically within sight of France on a clear day; he visited Paris as a schoolboy and travelled around Europe every year in his summer vacations from Oxford in the late 1930s. He visited Spain during the civil war, attended the Nuremberg rally in 1937 and almost got caught in Poland on the outbreak of war in 1939. As an artillery officer he took part in the liberation of France in 1944 and finished up in occupied Germany in 1945–46 among the ruins of some of the very cities he had visited seven years earlier. These experiences gave him a lifelong commitment to European unity, first declared in his maiden speech after his election to Parliament in 1950, supporting Britain joining the Schuman Plan, and cemented when Macmillan put him in charge of Britain's first application to join the EEC in 1961–63; from then on his overriding political ambition was to overcome French resistance and domestic scepticism to lead Britain into the Community.

Margaret Thatcher, by contrast, was brought up in Grantham in the East Midlands and never went abroad until her honeymoon at the age of 24; she experienced the war only at second hand as a schoolgirl and then as an Oxford undergraduate, first under German bombing – Grantham was a major target due to its important arms factories – then hearing American planes flying out from Lincolnshire airbases every night to bomb Germany. From this she drew the lifelong lesson that continental Europeans were either

Fascist enemies to be defeated or feeble dependents who had to be saved from their own weakness by British and American military strength and love of freedom. As a rising young minister under Macmillan and Heath she toed the party line on Europe – if only because Labour was against it – but she was never enthusiastic. Her true feelings came out increasingly clearly after her retirement in 1990 when she asserted that during her lifetime 'most of the problems the world has faced have come, in one fashion or another, from mainland Europe, and the solutions from outside it'.[1] She was thinking primarily of Nazism in the 1930s and Soviet Communism since 1945, both of which were defeated by American military power with British support. As prime minister in the 1980s she never ceased to believe that the Europeans should be eternally grateful to Britain – 'who either defeated or rescued half Europe, who kept half Europe free when otherwise it would have been in chains'[2] – and was outraged when they were not. 'The mainland Europeans benefited from an outcome which, by and large, they had not themselves secured; some have resented it ever since'.[3] Her geopolitical thinking, like Heath's, was fundamentally formed by the Second World War – but in the opposite sense.

When Heath became prime minister in 1970, it fell to him to pick up the pieces after the diplomatic *debâcle* of 1963, which was followed by de Gaulle's second veto of another half-hearted application by Wilson in 1967. He was fortunate to come to power at just the right moment. Of course his personal belief that Britain's destiny lay in Europe counted for a lot; but he was also – for once in his career – extraordinarily lucky. Despite de Gaulle's rebuff, the momentum within British government and business circles towards joining the Community had been building steadily since 1961, to the extent that it even forced Labour in office to embrace the cause. Then the withdrawal of de Gaulle in 1969 removed the biggest obstacle.

The crucial event was Heath's one-to-one meeting with President Pompidou in Paris in May 1971. Heath realised that it was no good trying to isolate France, as Wilson and his Foreign Secretary George Brown had done in 1967, relying on the other five founder members to persuade the French to lift their veto. He understood that he needed to overcome French opposition directly; and he succeeded. This was by no means a foregone conclusion; but Pompidou was persuaded by the force of Heath's personal conviction. There were still difficult issues to be resolved; but all those involved in the negotiations agree that it was the personal rapport between the two leaders, and Heath's meticulous preparation and passionate commitment, which ensured success. 'We didn't want a good meeting', one British diplomat said, 'We needed a very, very good meeting between the two men'.[4] They got it. After that all the other detailed problems about sugar, sterling and the British budget contribution were quickly settled. British accession followed from this breakthrough.

After the orchestrated razzmatazz of entry on 1 January 1973, Britain's first year of membership was disappointing. There was little progress on adapting internal arrangements like the Common Agricultural Policy and the Regional Fund which had been fixed before Britain joined; still less towards the ambitious target set by Heath, Pompidou and Willy Brandt in 1972 of achieving monetary union (EMU) by 1980. On the contrary Britain was forced to leave the European monetary 'snake' after just a few months. Then the new enlarged Community was rent by division over the Arab–Israeli war, the consequent threat to oil supplies and the quadrupling of the oil price. In the general election of February 1974 Heath was defeated. Pompidou died in office two months later. With their passing the opportunity for an enduring partnership between France and Britain at the heart of Europe was lost for good. To this day Heath remains the only prime minister who has tried seriously to place a commitment to Europe above Britain's traditional link with the United States. From Churchill and Eden to Thatcher and Blair, the others have all been instinctive Atlanticists. Heath was in a sense an aberration; yet his legacy has continued to bind his successors.

The incoming Labour Government conducted an essentially cosmetic 'renegotiation' of Heath's entry terms to allow Wilson – who had cynically opposed Heath's terms – to perform another somersault and recommend a 'Yes' vote in the 1975 referendum which endorsed Britain's continued membership. Thereafter the Government was grudgingly committed to staying in, but the party was still hostile and, out of office after 1979, quickly reverted to a promise to withdraw. Mrs Thatcher, by contrast, taking over the leadership of the Tory party just before the referendum, was committed to making a success of membership despite her private doubts. When Callaghan declined to join the newly formed

European Monetary System (EMS) – the precursor of the single currency – she condemned his decision as 'a sad day for Europe'. 'It would be more to Britain's advantage', she charged in impeccably Europhile language, 'if he and his colleagues dropped their abrasive and critical attitude towards our Common Market partners and behaved genuinely as partners, in which case we might get some of our problems solved'.[5] But this was not at all how she herself behaved in office a few months later.

In reality Mrs Thatcher was instinctively unsympathetic to Europe. Her antipathy derived partly from her memories of the war, partly from simple chauvinism reinforced by insularity: she believed without question that Britain was different from other nations and the British way of doing things naturally the best. There was an element of self-parody in her mockery of lesser nationalities. She once ticked off the head of her Policy Unit, John Hoskyns, for instance, for daring to like 'all those terrible EEC cheeses like Brie and Camembert'.[6] But she was only half joking. More seriously she disliked the whole ethos and *modus operandi* of the Community, with its culture of horse-trading and compromise, based on most member countries' experience of coalition governments, which she contrasted unfavourably with what she regarded as the honest cut-and-thrust of British politics. In her memoirs, published three years after she left office, she complained without irony of 'the quintessentially un-English outlook displayed by the Community', and in an accompanying television interview added that 'There's not a strand of equity or fairness in Europe. They're out to get as much as they can. That's one of those enormous differences'.[7] She believed unapologetically in getting the best possible deal for Britain, but regarded it as monstrous for others to do the same for their countries.

Moreover as a new prime minister, relatively inexperienced in foreign affairs, she felt patronized by the lordly French President Valéry Giscard d'Estaing and the German Chancellor Helmut Schmidt. Giscard in particular showed her no courtesy as a woman. The first European summit she attended was at Strasbourg in June 1979, where he was the host; but he pointedly failed to seat her next to himself at either lunch or dinner and then – pulling rank as head of state rather than a mere head of government – had himself served first. Mrs Thatcher thought his behaviour 'petulant, vain and . . . ill-mannered'.[8] When he came to Downing Street a few months later she took a childish delight in seating him directly opposite the portraits of Wellington and Nelson. At a personal level this got her *entente* with France off to a singularly uncordial start.

Her first term (1979–83) was dominated by her determination to secure a rebate on Britain's contribution to the EEC budget, which had been fixed in 1972 and not substantially modified by Callaghan's renegotiation. This dispute, which became known in Brussels at the 'Bloody British Question', thoroughly disrupted business at every European summit for five years since she refused to allow progress on anything else until she got what she wanted. She refused to compromise her demand, but played shamelessly to the gallery at home by gleeful Europe-bashing. At a time when her harsh economic policies had made her deeply unpopular, the image of 'Battling Maggie' swinging her handbag in Brussels played well with the British press and set the pattern for her relations with the Community for the whole of her time in office. Eventually – in 1984 – Britain's partners were so wearied by her intransigence that they gave her most of what she wanted: her success only confirmed her view that intransigence was the only language foreigners understood.

In fact Mrs Thatcher's relations with her European partners, and particularly with France, improved in her second term (1983–87). This was primarily because she got on so much better with the new French President François Mitterrand, elected in 1981, than with his predecessor Giscard. Mitterrand was supposed to be a Socialist, but in practice he quickly reversed his initially left-wing economic policies and adopted a more market-oriented approach. In addition Mrs Thatcher regarded him a 'patriotic' Socialist untainted by the fellow-travelling and pacifist tendencies she so despised in the British left. She respected his somewhat mysterious record in the wartime Resistance: the first time he came to London after his election the Foreign Office managed to reunite him with the pilot who had flown him to England during the war. She admired his unwavering support for the French nuclear *force de frappe*, which mirrored her own conviction that Britain must have a nuclear weapon in order to maintain her place at the top table. Finally she was deeply grateful for his prompt support during the Falklands crisis, when he overruled his Foreign Minister Claude Cheysson, and most of the Quai d'Orsay, who were much less sympathetic to Britain's case. Mitterrand not only supported Britain diplomatically but blocked the supply of spare parts for the Argentines' French-built Exocet missiles. She never forgot this timely help in her hour of need.

Above all, there was a sexual chemistry of the sort that had been lacking with Giscard. Mitterrand treated her as a woman and – even when they differed – always showed her the slightly exaggerated gallantry the British expect of a Frenchman. It was Mitterrand who famously declared that Madame Thatcher had '*les yeux de Caligula et la bouche de Marilyn Monroe*', which delighted her as much as it bewildered British critics who could see nothing sexy about her at all. In politics personal rapport often counts for more than supposed identity of outlook. By contrast Mrs Thatcher never got on at with Chancellor Helmut Kohl, whom she thought boorish, boring and – worst of all – quintessentially German.

It was at another French-chaired European Council, at Fontainebleau in 1984, that she finally accepted a deal on the British budget contribution. It was somewhat less than she had wanted and only marginally more than the last offer she had rejected at Brussels six months earlier. But on the one hand Mitterrand and Kohl knew that they would have no peace until they settled; while on the other Mrs Thatcher knew that her best opportunity was to reach agreement on French soil.

With this bugbear out of the way Mrs Thatcher entered into her most harmonious period of relations with Europe. She positively approved the drive to create a single market in the Community – a true common market at last – which she saw as a good free-market policy promoting enterprise and competition on what was coming to be called the 'Thatcherite' model, without initially grasping that a single market required the progressive harmonisation of regulations and taxes. She appointed the Tories' long-time tax expert, Arthur Cockfield – at that time one of her favourite ministers – as one of Britain's two Commissioners to drive the completion of the single market by 1992. But she soon became alarmed when Cockfield pursued his brief with what seemed to her excessive zeal, and pointedly declined to reappoint him for a second term in 1988, even though he was universally thought to be doing an outstanding job.

Likewise she initially approved the appointment of Jacques Delors as president of the Commission in 1984. She vetoed Mitterrand's first choice, Claude Cheysson, but she had approved Delors' rapid abandonment of Socialist policies when serving as French finance minister after 1981. Mrs Thatcher actually proposed Delors' re-appointment for a second term in 1988, before she became alarmed at his determination to press on from the single market towards a single currency: she then hurriedly redefined him as the embodiment of everything she abhorred in Europe, the architect of a federalist 'European superstate'. Her antagonism crystallised when Delors addressed the Trades Union Congress in Bournemouth in July 1988 and won a standing ovation from the previously Eurosceptic British unions, confirming her suspicion that the European project was a form of Socialism by the back door. 'The French socialist', she reflected grimly in her memoirs, 'is an extremely formidable animal. He is likely to be highly educated, entirely self-assured, a *dirigiste* by conviction from a political culture which is *dirigiste* by tradition. Such was M. Delors'.[9]

The high point of Mrs Thatcher's engagement with Europe – and specifically with France – was her surprising support for the building of the Channel Tunnel. She was initially opposed to the idea, saying that it would cost too much, ruin the cross-Channel ferries and destroy Kent; but she was converted when she was persuaded that it could be built not as a government project but as a showcase for free enterprise. She was also keen to make some gesture of goodwill to Mitterrand after the settling of the budget question. As a result, during an extraordinary whisky-fuelled discussion at the British Embassy in Paris in December 1984 she talked herself round into supporting the idea. According to the British Ambassador Sir Nicholas Henderson – himself a leading advocate of the project – 'She finished the evening declaring that, if accomplished, it would be the most exciting project of the century, which left everyone in the room more or less dumbfounded'.[10] The next day she agreed it in principle with Mitterrand.

She originally wanted a drive-through tunnel. She always preferred cars to railways, regarding the latter as the archetypal nationalised industry – dirty, expensive and dominated by the unions – whereas cars were a symbol of capitalist freedom: she once spoke glowingly of Britain's 'great car economy'.[11] She was eventually persuaded, however, that this was impractical (Mitterrand had favoured the even less practical idea of a bridge). The two leaders announced their agreement to build a rail tunnel at Lille in January 1986, when Mrs Thatcher made an untypically humorous speech recalling previous attempts to build a tunnel, going back to Napoleon: she claimed that Churchill had supported a Channel bridge only on condition that the last span was a drawbridge which could be raised in case of French attack! As a rare gesture to fraternity she actually delivered part of her speech in French. Doubtless remembering Ted Heath's appalling accent when he had tried to do the same thing in 1972 she made a great effort to learn her lines phonetically, and managed pretty creditably. But speaking in her constituency five days later she made a point of saying what a relief it was to be able to speak in English!

For a time she was very proud of the tunnel: she liked the idea of it as a concrete legacy of her rule and even referred to it as 'my tunnel'.[12] Four years after leaving office she attended the opening ceremony. But as she became more and more hostile to everything European she turned against it, and she did not mention it at all in her memoirs. Not only was she now less keen on the symbolism of Anglo-French partnership: since it made only losses for the shareholders who had invested in it, and still required large amounts of public money to complete the rail link to London, it could not even be held up as a triumph of free enterprise. Nevertheless the physical link with the continent stands, ironically, as one of her most enduring achievements.

Mrs Thatcher's temporary honeymoon with Europe ended in September 1988, when she made a famous speech at the College of Europe in Bruges declaring her determined opposition to any further political or monetary integration. 'We have not successfully rolled back the frontiers of the State in Britain', she declared, 'only to see them re-imposed at a European level with a European superstate exercising a new dominance from Brussels'.[13] Thereafter she never missed an opportunity to voice her visceral distaste and scorn for all things European. The change of tone in her latter years in office is partly attributable to the fact that Sir Michael Butler, Britain's ambassador to the EU and her principal European adviser, had retired in 1985. He had played a vital role in moderating her instinctive hostility to Europe and encouraging her to be constructive; after his retirement she was increasingly influenced by her foreign affairs private secretary Charles Powell, who correspondingly encouraged her Euroscepticism. As she lost faith in Geoffrey Howe, her foreign secretary since 1983, who seemed to her to embody the Foreign

Office instinct to sell out British interests in the cause of good relations, the ubiquitous Powell became effectively her real foreign secretary. Likewise as her domestic popularity declined sharply in 1989–90 with the bursting of the Lawson boom and the return of double-digit inflation, she became convinced – as in 1980–81 at the previous low point of her popularity – that patriotic Europe-bashing was a good way of shoring up her public support.

A relatively trivial but characteristic example of this untrammelled chauvinism occurred in 1989 when Mitterrand hosted a G7 Summit in Paris to coincide with the bicentenary of the French Revolution. In an interview for *Le Monde* Mrs Thatcher could not resist making a string of undiplomatic references to the Bastille and the guillotine, provocatively contrasting the violent utopianism of 1789 with the legality and moderation of the English Revolution of 1688 and pointing out that 'Human rights did not begin with the French revolution'.[14] In a BBC interview a few days later she elaborated:

> Human rights may have started two hundred years ago in France and that is a cause for celebration for France . . . but there were many many things before that, including . . . the great Magna Carta where the barons seized power from the king, including in 1688–89 when we had a Bill of Rights and a quiet revolution.[15]

In fact she did not think the French Revolution was something to be celebrated at all. 'It took us a long time to get rid of the effects of the French revolution 200 years ago', she told a Labour MP who asked why she was not supporting the new European revolution, 'and we don't want another'.[16] She denied that her comments had upset the French or spoiled Mitterrand's party; but she took an undisguised delight in the fracas they caused.

Although she believed that he was basically sound, despite being nominally a Socialist, Mrs Thatcher was disappointed in the latter part of the decade that Mitterrand failed to support her on a number of international issues – notably South Africa and German reunification – where she felt he should have done. On South Africa he adhered to the prevailing left-liberal consensus in favour of sanctions as a means of pressuring the white *apartheid* regime to release Nelson Mandela and recognize the African National Congress. Mrs Thatcher by contrast regarded sanctions as hypocritical and counterproductive, and did her best to block or dilute them, while working behind the scenes to persuade Presidents Botha and De Klerk to change their ways. Her approach arguably did more to end *apartheid* than sanctions did: but her ill-disguised contempt for the conventional wisdom left her isolated within the EU as well as in the Commonwealth.

Likewise she believed that Mitterrand privately shared her atavistic alarm at the prospect of a reunited Germany and hoped that he would support her efforts to slow the rush towards unity; she felt let down when he concluded that unification was unstoppable and was not prepared to make common cause with her if it meant blocking the cherished project of his more important ally, Helmut Kohl. 'He made the wrong decision for France', Lady Thatcher wrote in her memoirs. 'Moreover his failure to match private words with public deeds also increased my difficulties'. In her next sentence, however, she admitted that 'his judgment that there was nothing we could do to halt German reunification turned out to be right'.[17]

On both these issues Mrs Thatcher operated alone and failed to build alliances with France or any other country in Europe. This was typical of her approach to all foreign relationships except the transatlantic alliance, which she regarded as paramount. Very early in her premiership Roy Jenkins, then president of the European Commission, commented that she tended to confuse the EEC with NATO as 'two bodies which ought to be amalgamated'.[18] The Europe she approved of was a strong military bulwark against the Warsaw Pact countries to the east, a loyal partner of the United States in the defence of freedom and democracy. She had little truck with the other aspirations – social, political and economic – which sought to pool the national sovereignty of independent member countries. It was often noted – ironically – that her view of Britain's national interest was essentially Gaullist. Indeed in retirement she concluded that de Gaulle had been right to veto Britain's membership back in 1963. At the time, of course, she had been a loyal junior member of Macmillan's government; but with the experience of hindsight she believed that the General had understood better than the British themselves that Britain's fundamental allegiance would always be to America rather than to Europe.

It was also ironic that she should have been in France, attending the CSCE summit at Versailles which formally marked the ending of the Cold War, on the day that Tory MPs were voting in London in the leadership contest which precipitated her downfall. She was at the British Embassy in Paris, preparing to go out to a state banquet with Mitterrand, Reagan, Gorbachev and Kohl, when she heard that nearly half her MPs had withdrawn their support. They did so for a mixture of reasons, including the unpopularity of the poll tax, weariness of her abrasive personality and a sense that she had simply been prime minister too long. But throughout her premiership it was her hostility to Europe which had caused the greatest friction with her senior colleagues, provoking the resignations of Michael Heseltine in 1986 and Nigel Lawson in 1989; and now it was her vehement rejection of further integration following the Rome Summit of October 1990 that prompted Geoffrey Howe's departure, which in turn encouraged Heseltine to challenge her. Her unexpected successor, John Major took office with the ambition to restore Britain's relations with the Community. But out of office Lady Thatcher's instincts were off the leash. She poured all her frustration at losing power into undermining Major's attempt to forge a positive European policy. Within a few years of her resignation, helped by an increasingly xenophobic press – largely Australian-, American- or Canadian-owned – she had converted practically the whole of the Conservative party to her 'Eurosceptic' – but in reality Europhobic – line.

Behind the headline-grabbing rhetoric of conflict and contempt, however, Mrs Thatcher's decade in office nevertheless saw a steady continuation of the deepening involvement of Britain in Europe initiated by Macmillan and consummated by Ted Heath. Despite her personal scepticism and strong preference for the Atlantic connection, the institutional momentum towards 'ever-closer union' was too strong to be held back. By signing the Single European Act in 1985, which removed most of the barriers to creating the single market by 1992, she actually took Britain further and more irrevocably into Europe than Heath's original signature of accession. Though she campaigned bitterly against the Maastricht Treaty of 1991, there can be little doubt that had she remained in power she would have signed up to that too – if not, as Douglas Hurd observed, at Maastricht then the following year in Birmingham or Edinburgh. The great failure of her policy towards Europe was that it was entirely negative: she made no effort to develop a positive alternative or persuade other countries to support it. She was so scornful and superior, confident that European integration was all airy talk which would never come to anything, that she was always two steps behind the game, failing to contribute (except on the single market) and then trying furiously to wield a veto when it was too late. She talked of 'leading' Europe, but in practice only antagonised her partners, gaining no support for her view and ensuring that Britain was always left outside the key decisions – just as it had been from the very beginning, when the Eden government had declined to attend the founding Messina Conference in 1955.

Yet all the time the increasing inter-penetration of Britain and Europe, and specifically of Britain and France, went on apace – though the process has been decidedly unbalanced. While on one side there has been an invasion of bright and economically active young French people coming to work in London, the traffic the other way has seen a virtual occupation of parts of southern and south-western France by retired and semi-retired British people who often continue to work by computer from their French farmhouses. In this as in other respects, Thatcherism left a paradoxical legacy of economic internationalism coexisting with and helping to fuel an increasingly strident nationalism. Despite the virulent Francophobia of much of the British press – epitomised by two of the *Sun*'s famously cheeky headlines from the Thatcher era, 'Up Yours, Delors' and 'Hop off, you Frogs' – the *entente* remained in practice reasonably *cordiale* at both the government and popular level. Ted Heath's legacy may yet turn out to be more enduring than Margaret Thatcher's.

Notes

1. Margaret Thatcher, *Statecraft: Strategies for a Changing World* (London: HarperCollins, 2002), p. 320.
2. BBC television interview, 27 April 1979.
3. Thatcher, *Statecraft*, p. 320.
4. Uwe Kitzinger, *Diplomacy and Persuasion: How Britain Joined the Common Market* (London: Thames & Hudson, 1973), p. 119.
5. House of Commons, 13 March 1979.
6. John Hoskyns, *Just in Time: Inside the Thatcher Revolution* (London: Aurum Press, 2000), p. 121.
7. *Thatcher: The Downing Street Years* (BBC TV, 1993).
8. Roy Jenkins, *European Diary, 1977–1981* (London: Collins, 1989), p. 479 (14 July 1979).
9. Margaret Thatcher, *The Downing Street Years* (London: HarperCollins, 1993), p. 547.

10. BBC interview, 18 January 1998.
11. Speech in London, presenting 'better environment' awards to industry, 16 March 1990.
12. *The Journals of Woodrow Wyatt*, vol. 1 (London: Macmillan, 1998), p. 344 (12 May 1989).
13. Speech to the College of Europe, Bruges, 20 September 1988.
14. *Le Monde*, 11 July 1989.
15. BBC interview, 16 July1989.
16. House of Commons, 29 June 1989.
17. Thatcher, *The Downing Street Years*, p. 798.
18. Jenkins, p. 450 (21 May 1979).

11

A Complex Alliance: The Explosive Chemistry of Franco-British Relations in the Post-Cold War World

Klaus W. Larres
University of Ulster

In the post-Cold War world Britain and France share many characteristics and have a considerable number of common interests. Both countries are medium-sized powers and are strongly attached to their sovereignty. They are accustomed to punching greatly above their actual weight in world politics, a habit they wish to prolong as long as possible. Britain and France are nuclear powers and they are members of the UN Security Council. The two countries are also members of the G8 and both have largely robust though by no means particularly dynamic economies. Both Paris and London can also draw on their political, administrative and not least military experiences as former colonial powers which have provided them not only with a pool of immigrants in their midst but also with a certain martial outlook on foreign policy not shared by the majority of the other European countries.[1]

There is one additional factor which props up Britain's and France's role on the world stage. They can both draw on an external support framework for the realisation of their mutual ambition to remain among the world's leading powers. While France tends to punch above its weight with the help of its long-standing leadership position within the European Union and its close relationship with Germany which, on the whole, is still largely content to leave a considerable degree of political and military leadership to Paris,[2] Britain relies on the USA. London employs the enduring 'special relationship' with the United States to obtain economic and political advantages in order to remain among the world's most influential powers.[3]

It is imperative for both Britain and France to retain their respective support frameworks if they wish to continue punching above their weight in global politics; this necessity, however, has led to a certain competitive rivalry with the other country's support framework. Thus, France views with a good deal of disdain and suspicion Britain's continuing close relationship with Washington and resents New Labour's repeated attempts to act as mediator between the United States and continental Europe. Britain, on the other hand, cannot entirely hide its displeasure at the still very close Franco-German relationship which appears to exclude Britain to a large extent. Attempts to reverse Britain's exclusion have come to nothing – despite some signs to the contrary in the aftermath of the EU enlargement of 2004 and many rhetorical declarations regarding the importance of turning the EU's 'big two' leadership tandem into a *ménage à trois* or an EU troika. It is thus no wonder that among the most highly contested areas between France and Britain in the post-Cold War world are the contentious issues of European co-operation and transatlantic relations.

This is made even more complicated by a certain overlap between these areas. The overlap is particularly obvious with regard to both countries' defence policies. In particular since the late 1990s both France and Britain have an interest in bringing the European countries more closely together with respect to military co-operation and a more cohesive European defence policy. Yet, this immediately raises the spectre of competition with the United States and the prospect of a united European foreign and defence policy as a rival to US-dominated NATO.[4] This is viewed with some concern in both countries. Still, while the notion of a competitive defence policy with the United States is tolerated, if not on occasion appreciated and welcomed by France, it tends to be viewed with distaste in London. Moreover, forging a more common European defence policy raises the question of what to do with British and French nuclear weapons and whether or not they ought to be turned into a European nuclear deterrent.[5] In particular in the years since the events of 9/11 and the United States imposed 'war on global terror', Britain and France have differed and argued to a considerable extent about the future role of European co-operation, transatlantic relations and by implication Europe's military role.

Jean Guéginou, French ambassador to the UK in the mid- to late 1990s, referred to a commonplace when he wrote that Franco-British relations were 'somewhat complex' and had their many 'ups and downs' over the centuries. Yet, in January 1997 he believed that seven years after the end of the Cold War it was time to ask the question: 'Why are our relations so good?'. At first sight, hardly anyone would find it appropriate to ask this question ten years later, in the post-9/11 world. However, this is misleading. As this article intends to demonstrate, despite many squabbles, heated arguments and temporary conflicts, on the whole Franco-British relations in the post-Cold War world have proved to be resilient. Indeed it can be said that with only a few exceptions, such as the Iraq War in early 2003, in times of serious crisis in the post-Cold War world, Britain and France have mostly managed to avoid becoming divided for any prolonged period of time and have succeeded in co-operating reasonably well with each other, at least with regard to the really large questions and issues of the day.

Franco-British crisis collaboration

In the British and French press, recent Franco-British relations are commonly characterised as a long saga of 'figurative pub brawls'. The Anglo-French media tend to focus on the two leading personalities, the French president and the British prime minister, who are frequently portrayed as being involved in constant trench warfare with each other. The BBC, for example, wrote that 'Tony finds Jacques imperious, dismissive and infuriating, while Jacques believes Tony is an upstart who fails to show him the respect he believes he is due'. This dire state of affairs is frequently contrasted with Chirac's chummy relationship with the German chancellor and Blair's close contacts with the US president.[6]

Still, it is often overlooked that despite many long-running Franco-British squabbles about issues such as the common European agricultural policy (CAP) with its huge farm subsidies, Europe's asylum policies, difficulties in agreeing on the selection of the European Commission president and other European office holders as well as clashes over monetary and enlargement issues, the European constitution and many other conflicts, this is only part of the story. With regard to many of the crucial questions, the positions of the French and British government are often much closer than the general public in both countries are aware of. At least, the two countries are frequently able to narrow their difficulties after an initial period of dissent that is often exaggerated by the media. While the Iraq War of early 2003 is an obvious exception, a quick survey of the major international foreign policy crises since the end of the Cold War in 1989 demonstrates the essential correctness of this statement.

France and Britain were initially strongly opposed to the unification of Germany in 1990 and Prime Minister Thatcher viewed President Mitterand's gradual change of course with great suspicion. It took the persuasive powers of US President George W.H. Bush to overcome British and French opposition to the unification of Germany. Eventually both countries agreed that it was counterproductive to oppose German unification any longer.[7] Subsequently, French President Mitterrand even managed to persuade German Chancellor Kohl as well as British Prime Minister Major and the other EC leaders that anchoring a unified Germany in a common European monetary system (and eventually common currency) was the price which the Germans ought to pay for French and British agreement to German unification and the seamless acceptance of Eastern Germany as a new EC member state.

Mitterand's proposal was meant to provide added security guarantees against a resurgent and enlarged Germany, the dissolution of the deutschmark and the anchoring of Germany's independent monetary and economic system into a thoroughly integrated European economic system would prevent the newly unified state becoming too powerful. After all, it was generally assumed that unification had turned Germany into an even larger and stronger economic power house. Hardly anyone foresaw that for the next twenty years the burdens of unification would weaken Germany rather than give rise to a new German super state as had been feared by Major's predecessor Margaret Thatcher and others.[8]

During the first crisis of the post-Cold War era – Saddam Hussein's invasion of Kuwait in August 1990 – France and Britain co-operated well with the United States and Hussein's annexation of Kuwait was eventually reversed by a US-led coalition of 32 states. Both London and Paris supported the UN-authorised first Gulf War and contributed massively to the ensuing air war in January and February 1991 to destroy Saddam Hussein's anti-air defences. Subsequently in late February a ground invasion, which included British and French troops, drove the Iraqi forces out of Iraq within four days.[9]

For many years Britain and France were also in agreement regarding the European policy towards the civil wars in the former

Yugoslavia. Both complained bitterly over Germany's recognition of Slovenia and Croatia in November 1991, which they held at least partially responsible for the outbreak of the wars of succession in Yugoslavia. London and Paris were also in agreement in opposing the American 'lift-and-strike' strategy in Bosnia for fear of endangering their contingents to the UN peacekeeping forces on the ground. Moreover, they had little confidence that the American approach to the crisis in Bosnia would succeed; instead they feared that it would only prolong the suffering of the Bosnians while not preventing the ultimate Serbian victory which they expected and were largely prepared to tolerate. Both countries were suspicious that Washington might embark on an anti-Serbian bombing policy and in general dreaded becoming enmeshed in complicated and long-drawn out peacekeeping operations.[10]

Although in the view of many commentators, the British and French policy in the Bosnian war was questionable, based on dubious self-centred considerations and executed in a less than competent way, the Anglo-French strategy of passivity, which was interspersed with occasional bouts of diplomatic activity, was well co-ordinated between the two capitals. While differences over the role the West ought to play in the Bosnian war may have come close to developing into the 'greatest strain since Suez' between the leading European powers and the USA,[11] Britain and France managed to work closely with each other at a time of great international turbulence and crisis.

A similar scenario could be observed in the Kosovo War of 1999. Both countries found themselves at loggerheads with the American Clinton administration over the issue of air strikes and the use of ground troops. The bombing war against the Serb positions in Kosovo was mainly conducted by the American and British air forces, while the French showed a much greater sympathy for Russian attempts at last-minute mediation with Serbian president Milosevic. Still, disagreements between the French and British allies could be contained.[12] Again, it proved to be correct that in times of crisis, the Franco-British *Entente Cordiale* was still alive and kicking. In fact, the dire military performance of the European powers during the civil wars in the former Yugoslavia led Paris and London to meet at St Malo in December 1998 and agree on a joint declaration to re-organise European defence and make more resources available for defence purposes. Thus, the St Malo declaration essentially represented both countries' long-term commitment to the build-up of a serious European defence and security pillar, including the expansion of Europe's military strength. They agreed to develop a European Rapid Reaction Force (ERRF) which was meant to be operational by 2001 and be able to deploy a force of 60,000 within 60 days.[13]

Similarly, British and French reaction to the events of 9/11 were almost identical. Chirac announced that 'we are all Americans now' and in London Britain's 'God save the Queen' was replaced by the playing of the American national anthem outside Buckingham Palace; a symbolically very meaningful gesture. NATO invoked Article 5 of the North Atlantic Treaty, the self-defence clause, though subsequently the Bush administration decided not to rely on military aid from NATO. There was no dissension in Paris and London when the Bush administration decided to begin air strikes against Afghanistan in October 2001. After all, the Afghan government had essentially been taken over by the fundamentalist Taliban who refused to extradite Osama Bin Laden, the brain behind the 9/11 attacks.[14] However, in the aftermath of 9/11 there gradually developed some disquiet in Europe about the sweeping rhetoric of Bush's pursuit of the 'war on terror' and the hastily passed anti-terror legislation such as the *Patriot Act.* Yet, it was only in the summer and autumn of 2002 that the increasing transatlantic friction exploded in a major crisis. It was possibly the worst crisis the western alliance had ever been exposed to.

While still fighting the Taliban in Afghanistan, Washington's surprising decision to focus on Saddam Hussein and drive him out of power for allegedly possessing weapons of mass destruction (WMD) encountered major opposition in France and many other continental European countries. As early as shortly after 9/11 the Bush administration had in fact decided to topple Saddam Hussein but only towards late 2002 did world public opinion and America's allies (with the exception of the British government) begin to realise that this was indeed the intention of the American administration.[15] Paris, together with its German ally, made known in the UN Security Council its strong reservations about Bush's unilateral policy and his pre-emptive attack plans. France, as well as Germany, the Benelux countries, Russia, China and many other countries, not least those in the developing world, were strongly opposed to the US invasion of a sovereign country without UN authorisation and in the absence of unambiguous evidence that Saddam Hussein was indeed a danger to the West and to his immediate neighbours in the Middle East. In particular the Blair government blamed France for the likely failure and thus withdrawal of the second UN vote.[16]

Despite its many claims to the contrary, the Bush administration was unable to demonstrate convincingly that the Iraqi dictator did have weapons of mass destruction. When in the following years no WMD were ever found in Iraq, it became clear that the Iraqi dictator had indeed destroyed his WMD after the first Gulf War and that the sanctions and UN weapons inspections imposed on him in the early 1990s had made it impossible for him to commence a new weapons programme.[17] The Bush administration had been entirely mistaken and had perhaps even deliberately misled its allies and public opinion at large. Yet, in late 2002 and early 2003 this was still unclear and many analysts took Bush at his word and believed that Saddam Hussein might well be in possession of at least a certain number of dangerous WMD. The general public in almost all European countries, including those whose governments supported Bush, however, was not convinced and remained strongly opposed to invading Iraq. Even public opinion in the United States was more or less evenly divided.

Yet, Bush as well as British Prime Minister Blair remained undisturbed by the growing conflict among the western allies. The British intelligence services were as much in the dark as their American counterparts regarding Saddam Hussein's alleged WMD. However, Blair still claimed in what turned out to be an embarrassing speech in the House of Commons on 18 March 2003 that the Iraqi military would be able to launch biological and chemical weapons within 45 minutes of an order from presumably Saddam Hussein.[18] The British prime minister was not ready to oppose Bush's policies. Within the framework of the Bush administration's mantra that you are either 'with us or against us' in the war on terror,[19] Blair had no desire to find himself on the wrong side of the arch-conservative US president who easily took offence at political opposition and perceived slights and lack of respect. Moreover, Bush's desperate need for allies in his crusade against Saddam Hussein had made him catapult Blair onto the world stage as a true world leader and reliable ally. While French President Chirac kept arguing in favour of a multi-polar world as opposed to American unilateralism and pre-emptive warfare, Blair did his best to support Bush's position in the UN Security Council. He also attempted to mediate between France, Germany, Russia, the Benelux countries and the USA, though without much success.[20]

When US Secretary of Defence Donald Rumsfeld divided Europe into 'old Europe' that opposed the coming war, and 'new Europe' consisting of countries such as Poland, the Czech Republic and the Baltic countries which largely supported Bush's Iraq policy, Britain as well as Berlusconi's Italy and Aznar's Spain were clearly not seen as part of 'old Europe'.[21] Soon, France's neo-Gaullist attempt to oppose everything Bush's foreign policy stood for not only led to a nasty showdown with Secretary of State Colin Powell in the UN Security Council. It also led to great tension, suspicion and mistrust between France and Bush's British ally.[22] The close collaboration with Britain in many international crises during the 1990s was largely forgotten. In fact, it became clear that the Franco-American/British conflict, with the Germans playing a supporting role in favour of Paris, was about much more than Saddam Hussein's alleged WMD.

From the French point of view, the conflict was above all about the future role and standing of the American superpower in the world and by implication about Europe's and France's position as a regional great power. From the British point of view this was not a crucial aspect of the crisis; after all, London was not too worried about a further increase in American power. It could be expected, after all, that some of the crumbs from the American superpower table would fall into the lap of its closest ally, as had been the case in the past. Moreover, Blair like Bush possessed a genuine missionary drive and believed that the transformation of Iraq into a democratic country would lead to the democratisation of the entire 'Greater Middle East'. Most other countries, however, dismissed this notion as illusory. For France and Germany the conflict, which had been brought about by Bush's Iraq policy, was about American dominance and whether or not the future global order would be entirely dominated by Washington or whether it would include a sizeable European dimension, including everything the egalitarian and somewhat socialistic 'European model' stood for.[23]

Once again it became clear that France and Britain were continuing to draw very different lessons from the Suez Crisis of 1956. The Suez Crisis was the event that changed Britain's and France's role in the world as no other crisis had done since the end of the Second World War. In November 1956 the Eisenhower administration's lack of support for Britain's and France's joint Suez adventure had led to a hasty and undignified withdrawal of both countries' forces from Egypt. In secret collusion with Israel, London and Paris had embarked on an air-borne invasion of the country in early November 1956 in order to reverse Nasser's nationalisation of the Suez Canal and teach him a lesson to be more attentive to the needs of Europe's major colonial powers.[24] The enforced and highly embarrassing hasty British and French withdrawal, shortly before Christmas 1956, however, made it perfectly clear that without American support or at least American tolerance, neither Britain nor France had any longer the resources to embark on any foreign adventures. In particular President Eisenhower's imposition of economic sanctions against Britain undermined London's economic ability to remain in Egypt. The president, for example, refused to provide Britain with oil deliveries when the Arab countries imposed an oil embargo on Britain and France. Moreover, when the pound sterling fell dramatically on the world currency markets after the beginning of the invasion, Washington refused to support the UK application for a dollar loan from the IMF.[25]

In the process of recovering from the humiliating Suez Crisis and after the resignation of Prime Minister Anthony Eden, British statesmen arrived at the conclusion that ignoring or even opposing the USA in any major foreign policy initiative made little sense and was indeed counterproductive. From now on Britain would move ever closer to the United States and do its utmost not to be divided from Washington in any major crisis. Close consultation with Washington became the *ne plus ultra* for any British prime minister. London had realised that without close co-operation and collaboration with the United States, Britain would no longer be able to punch above its weight and maintain an important voice in global affairs.

This was also one of the main reasons why Tony Blair joined George W. Bush in the invasion of Iraq. Blair believed that due to Britain's precarious international influence, the country was in no position to openly oppose US foreign policy or even to quietly abandon its support for an American foreign policy initiative as important and as long lasting as the war on terror and related activities. Blair also genuinely believed that with the toppling of Saddam Hussein a process of reform would begin in the Middle East and Britain had to be part of this from the beginning to insure its continuing influence with both Washington and the new democratic Middle East.[26] He even indicated in a recent interview with BBC talk show host Michael Parkinson that he was convinced that God guided him when he took the difficult decision to commit British troops to the invasion of Iraq.[27] Prior to the invasion Bush had indeed offered Blair a way out. The president told him that he would understand it if for domestic political reasons Blair was unable to contribute British forces for the invasion of Iraq. Yet, the British Prime did not use this 'escape clause' to avoid sending British troops into war.[28]

France, however, drew the opposite lesson from the Suez Crisis. In the French view Suez had demonstrated that the United States was an unreliable ally and that France needed to emphasise its independence and develop its own strength in order not to be dependent on American good will and support. Essentially all French governments from de Gaulle to Chirac have viewed the American preponderance of power with a great deal of suspicion and have attempted to develop their own independent standing in world affairs, propped up by France's role as a leading member of the EC/EU.[29]

While Franco-American and Franco-British relations remained poisoned and cool throughout 2003, by the end of the year both sides had begun a cautious charm offensive to improve relations. This was no doubt made easier for the French by the fact that they had been proved right in the Iraq crisis – though no one dared to explain this too openly to American officials. No WMD were ever found in Iraq. Moreover, in view of the chaos into which Iraq threatened to sink due to the lack of American post-war planning for Iraq, the commitment of an insufficiently large number of troops and wholesale incompetence on the part of America's Coalition Provisional Authority (CPA) led by Paul Bremer, there was increasing pressure on the European powers, in particular France and Germany, to get involved.[30] Soon they began contributing by means of humanitarian aid deliveries to alleviate the suffering of ordinary Iraqis and by training Iraqi police and army forces outside the country to help improving the security situation.

Still, it would take more than a year before even something approximating normal relations between France and the United States as well as between France and Britain had been established again. Mutual Franco-British interest in European defence co-operation and the attempt to develop ESDP further contributed decisively to this.[31]

Franco-British defence collaboration since St Malo and the EU leadership structure

While French politicians have been suspicious regarding Prime Minister Blair's belief that there is no inherent contradiction between Britain's continuing pursuit of the 'special relationship' with the United States and a deeper British commitment to the European Union, initially Blair's election in 1997 was regarded as a milestone on the road to a proper British commitment to the European project. And indeed both Britain and France agreed that in the wake of the humiliating European military performance in the Kosovo War of March 1999 and in view of past successes in integrating Europe economically and to some extent politically, it was high time that greater attention was paid to the integration of European defence. Already at the Franco-British conference at St Malo in December 1998 both countries had declared that the EU must develop the capacity for independent action which in turn must be backed by a sufficient number of military forces. In fact, St Malo inaugurated the ESDP and effectively ended the British opposition to militarising the EU by successfully integrating the WEU into the EU. In addition in the late 1990s there was still great concern as to whether or not NATO would be able to survive the demise of the Cold War; the development of a genuine European security dimension was seen as a decisive factor in reinvigorating the NATO alliance. Thus, in the aftermath of the St Malo declaration rapid progress towards an effective European Security and Defence Policy (ESDP) could be observed.[32] The Iraq crisis of 2002–03, however, put a halt to all this.

Franco-British collaboration in making progress with ESDP stalled and although the force had become partially operational in 2003, by early 2006 less progress than anticipated had been made with a genuine European defence policy. Yet, some progress could be noticed. For example, the EU relieved NATO of its peacekeeping functions in Macedonia in 2003 and in both Bosnia and Herzegovina in late 2004. Above all, this resulted from the impact of 9/11 and the decision at the NATO summit in Prague in November 2002 to establish a NATO

Response Force for close co-operation with the USA in the 'war on terror', including its deployment out-of-area. Britain's interest was in being in the forefront of the development towards both the envisaged central European enlargement of NATO and the transformation of the alliance into a global NATO. For Blair and the British defence establishment, a regional European security policy made increasingly less sense. This was not the French view. Chirac refused to accept that NATO would act as a global policeman while the EU and its military arm would be relegated to doing more lowly tasks and focus on post-conflict nation-building, which NATO and the US had no interest in. France insisted on a greater transatlantic balance and believed that both NATO and the EU should be able to fulfil 'hard' and 'soft' approaches to international security requirements.[33] Franco-British squabbles also extended to other areas, such as the EU's planned stabilising force in Macedonia and the reform of CAP. In November 2002 the envisaged Franco-British summit was suddenly cancelled as Britain was upset over a Franco-German agreement to postpone the planned reform of CAP.

Blair was not happy with the fraught relations with his European partners and behind the scenes he worked hard to overcome the potentially disastrous crisis. Essentially, however, the Iraq crisis and its aftermath forced Tony Blair to give up his project to make Euro membership palatable to the British public and forced him back into the traditional British policy of supporting the USA and NATO and paying less attention to Britain's role in Europe. Once again Britain found itself on the margins of the EU, while the EU continued to be dominated by France and Germany.

Blair's solution to overcome this unsatisfactory situation was twofold: first, by pacifying France with the help of a certain focus on the development of common European security institutions in which Britain as well as France could play important roles, and second by attempting to persuade France and Germany to develop a new leadership structure for the EU, a leadership consisting of the 'Big Three' rather than just France and Germany.[34] It is on this much overlooked attempt by Blair to include Britain in the EU's traditional 'Big Two' leadership club that the remainder of the article will focus.

Even in September 2003, when emotions over how to stabilise Iraq in the aftermath of the war were still running high and mutual distrust between above all France and Germany on the one hand and

Britain, Italy, Spain and Poland on the other hand still dominated the agenda in Europe, progress towards a European triumvirate was made. German Chancellor Schröder, Chirac and Blair managed to overcome their political difficulties and personal animosities when they met in Berlin for a trilateral get-together, the first time they had met since the Iraq War.[35] They happily agreed to disagree over Iraq and managed to make progress with a common outlook on a future European defence policy. Much to the consternation of the smaller EU countries they also achieved a consensus on simply ignoring the limits on the national debts as prescribed by the European Growth and Stability Pact. Furthermore they insisted on including new voting procedures within the Council of Ministers in the envisaged European constitution, thus again riding roughshod over the desires of the smaller nations.

Shortly afterwards the 'Big Three's foreign ministers travelled to Tehran to put pressure on the Iranians to abolish their nuclear weapons programme. In late November 2003 Paris, Berlin and London managed to work out a blueprint for a future European security and defence policy and agreed to downsize the initially envisaged establishment of a European military headquarters to a much smaller planning unit attached to the EU military staff in the secretariat of the Council of Ministers.[36]

Thus, by late 2003 it looked as if an informal directorate of Europe's 'Big Three' had more or less been established. British Foreign Secretary Jack Straw confirmed in mid-January 2004 that with regard to the 'tangible signs' of 'Big Three' co-operation 'for Britain to form a partnership with the Franco-German motor' of the EU 'would be logical once Europe moves from 15 to 25 members'.[37] Only a month later, in mid-February 2004, Schröder, Chirac and Blair once again met in Berlin. They discussed the way forward after the failure of the constitutional EU Rome summit in October 2003 and prepared the March 2004 conference which dealt with the rather ambitious aspiration as expressed in the Lisbon agenda of March 2000 and renewed and modified in 2005 to elevate the EU to one of the globe's most dynamic economic areas by the year 2010.[38]

What was behind the new though somewhat short-lived realignment of the EU's 'Big Three'? When stripping away the rhetoric about the triumvirate's intention of giving the EU a new boost of dynamism and working for the common good of Europe, essentially two main reasons remain: fear of the detrimental consequences of EU enlargement on the ability of France and Germany to continue deciding on the main directions of policy within the EU, not least in the area of a common European defence and foreign policy, and the insight that relations with the United States needed to be patched up and put on a much more stable and enduring basis.

Britain, it was believed, could play a helpful role with both objectives; in turn this was likely to result in strengthening London's influence within the EU. It was thus not the mystic hankering after the notion of a Europe guided by a small cosy number of states as in the early years of the Community but hardnosed realism and the clear pursuit of the national interest of the 'Big Three' which led to the emergence of a new 'ménage à trois' in Europe. Instead of reuniting the continent, however, this ran the danger that enlargement would lead to a new differentiation between first tier and second tier countries in the expanded EU.

It appears that both Germany and France feared that the enlargement of the EU to 25 members and the continuation of decision-making procedures under the Nice Treaty would undermine their traditional role as the decisive 'steering group' and change the balance of power within the EU decisively. Since the very foundation of the European Communities in the late 1950s, France and Germany had essentially been able to work out the guidelines for important EU policies before any formal summits. Subsequently they usually managed to convince the other member states to follow the wisdom of the strategy worked out by the two leading countries.

Yet, after enlargement it was assumed that it would be much more difficult for any two countries to dominate the EU. A looser Europe with much weaker common institutions and an increased role for the national governments of the enlarged EU's 21 medium-sized and small countries would rapidly change the very character of the entire European project. The German and French dream of overseeing and guiding an 'ever closer union' and succeeding in developing a more significant European voice on the global stage threatened to become a thing of the past.

This was particularly disconcerting with regard to foreign and defence policy; the big EU project for the coming years. It was the one hugely complicated and expensive area which the EU still needed to develop in a substantial way if it was to play a major role in world affairs. In this context, as seen from Paris and Berlin, the recent divisions between 'old' and 'new' Europe over the war in Iraq and Europe's inability to develop a common policy of how to deal with the Bush administration's global hegemonic aspirations and pre-emptive warfare designs were particularly disconcerting.[39] Moreover, the failure of the constitutional Rome summit in late 2003 saw largely the same alignment of forces as during the Iraq War. France and Germany were massively opposed by above all Poland and Aznar's Spain as well as by most other Eastern European governments, which preferred siding with the United States rather than with Paris and Berlin during the Iraq War.[40] It was here that Britain could play a crucial role.

Chirac had dirtied his copy book with the Eastern Europeans when shortly before the Iraq War he proclaimed in February 2003 that the new EU members 'missed a good chance to keep quiet' when they loudly proclaimed their support of the American position.[41] Schröder's relations with Poland were severely damaged by his row with Polish Prime Minister Leszek Miller when the latter refused to sign up to the new European constitution which included the envisaged voting procedures favouring the large countries.[42]

Britain, however, kept quiet during the row and maintained a fairly neutral position. Previously London had earned a lot of respect in Eastern Europe for refusing to be bullied by Paris and Berlin into changing its position within the UN on alleged Iraqi weapons of mass destruction; the UK stuck to the Bush administration's unpopular position. Thus, from the point of view of many Eastern European countries as well as naturally seen from London, Britain was an ideal mediator between 'old' and 'new' Europe. The same applied to Tony Blair's role as a confidant of President Bush. While both Chirac's and Schröder's relations with the American administration improved substantially in the course of 2004 and 2005, they would never enjoy the general admiration and influence which Blair possessed in Washington.

Moreover, the construction of a European defence policy was not feasible without the British. When in April 2003, in the middle of the Iraq crisis, Belgium invited Germany, France and Luxembourg to a defence summit to consider setting up an independent European force and pointedly excluded the UK, this met with worldwide anger, disbelief and indeed ridicule.[43] After all, the defence field was the only crucial and increasingly important area where Britain with its highly developed professional army and its global expertise in guerrilla warfare and weapons development was way ahead of its European partners. Grudgingly even the French and more admiringly the US armed forces respected British professionalism and expertise in the defence field. With the partial exception of France, such expertise still cannot be found in any other European country.

Thus, if it was the EU's intention to focus on the realisation of a common foreign and defence policy, it could hardly do without allocating a leading role to the UK. Together with Britain's aspiration and partial ability to assume a mediating role with both Eastern Europe and the United States, this contributed to motivating Berlin and Paris to open their hitherto fairly exclusive bilateral relationship to welcoming London with open arms. However, it soon proved that this was merely a temporary opening and that a certain caution in their dealings with London continued to this day.

After all, Britain still was not a member of the Euro area, had not signed up to the Schengen Agreement on passport-free travel within the EU and still insisted on its national veto in tax, defence and foreign policy matters. There were also other problems. Although they largely consisted of problems of perception, they still had a profound impact. Despite Blair's much more constructive policy towards European integration since he came to office compared with almost all of his predecessors, with the exception of Edward Heath, the country's traditionally lukewarm attitude to European integration had not been forgotten.

Not least the long-standing impression, once again confirmed during the Iraq War, that London valued the 'special relationship' with Washington much more than its relations with Europe, and would continue to act as America's Trojan horse within the EU, was regarded as a serious concern in Paris and to some extent also in Berlin. Yet, in the aftermath of the Iraq War neither the development of a substantial European defence policy nor a genuine rapprochement with the United States appeared to be feasible without British involvement. This explains the cautious welcome to the Franco-German leadership club which was reluctantly extended to Britain in the aftermath of the Iraq War. After all, in the wake of the Iraq War and under the impression of an ever increasing American unilateralism, Germany and France regarded both aims as a priority if a 'unipolar' world was to be prevented.

Similarly, the Blair government fully realised that the critical perception of Britain's influence in world affairs as 'Bush's poodle' would be improved if London was able to emancipate itself a little from American overlordship and if with the help of British guidance the EU became a more independent international player than hitherto.[44] It had not escaped Tony Blair's attention that despite his supposedly excellent relations with both Presidents Clinton and Bush, his real influence on American decision-making had remained severely limited. Moreover, the hoped-for economic benefits and the more elusive perceived advantages of increasing Britain's great power status by fighting side by side with America in Iraq had not materialised by 2005. Turning the Franco-German leadership club into a 'ménage à trois', however, promised to offer real tangible benefits, in particular if they were combined with rapid progress in the Franco-British driven ESDP. Yet, while some progress had undoubtedly been made, by early 2006 it was NATO which had been reinvigorated rather than ESDP. The impact of the 'war on terror' and the Iraq War had essentially led to a new emphasis on NATO as symbolised by NATO's central European enlargement in 2004. A truly effective European defence policy and military force were still a long way off, despite some tangible progress since St Malo and the war in Kosovo which, for instance had led to the deployment of EU forces in countries such as Macedonia, Bosnia and Herzegovina.

Brief conclusion

While Franco-British relations throughout the 1990s were not free from conflict, in many important crisis situations, such as the process of German unification, the first Gulf War and wars in the former Yugoslavia, London and Paris eventually – and after a prolonged initial period of intense tension – managed to work with each other. After the invasion of Iraq in early 2003 this proved to be much more difficult. Although transatlantic relations as well as Franco-British relations have been patched up again since then, mutual distrust and suspicion remain at a fairly high level. This applies to both the political as well as the defence fields. Only intelligence co-operation among the major western countries appears to have been largely unaffected by the distrust within the western alliance caused by Bush's war. Thus, it may well be that only a change of leaders in Britain and France will enable their successors to arrive once again at closer and more constructive relations overall. This, however, could happen fairly soon. Prime Minister Blair has announced that he will step down before the next general election in Britain and Chirac cannot stand for re-election when the next French president is elected in 2007. There is hope yet. After all, the change of government and chancellor in Germany from Schröder to Angela Merkel in late 2005 has contributed to a certain improvement in the transatlantic atmosphere.

Notes

1. For overviews of Franco-British relations during the Cold War and the post-Cold War world, see Joseph Ruane, Jennifer Todd and Anne Mandeville (eds), *Europe's Old States in the New World Order: The Politics of Transition in Britain, France and Spain* (Dublin: University College Dublin Press, 2003); Philippe Chassaigne and Michael Dockrill (eds), *Anglo-French Relations 1898–1998: From Fashoda to Jospin* (London: Palgrave, 2001); Alan Sharp and Glyn Stone (eds), *Anglo-French Relations in the 20th Century: Rivalry and Cooperation* (London: Routledge, 2003). For both countries' ethnic politics, see Joel S. Fetzer and J. Christopher Soper, *Muslims and the State in Britain, France and Germany* (Cambridge: University Press, 2005); Erik Bleich, *Race Politics in Britain and France: Ideas and Policymaking since the 1960s* (Cambridge: University Press, 2003).
2. See for example Alistair Cole, *Franco-German Relations* (Harlow: Longman, 2001); Julius W. Fried, *Unequal Partners: French-German Relations, 1989–2000* (Westport, CT: CSIS, 2001).
3. See for example John Dumbrell, *Anglo-American Relations in the Cold War and After* (Basingstoke: Macmillan, 2001).
4. See Stanley R. Sloan, *NATO, the European Union, and the Atlantic Community: The Transatlantic Bargain Reconsidered* (Lanham, MD: Rowman and Littlefield, 2001); also Beatrice Heuser, *NATO, Britain, France and the FRG: Nuclear Strategies and Forces for Europe, 1949–2000* (Basingstoke: Macmillan, 1997).
5. See Heuser, *ibid.*, and also for example Martin Butcher, 'Will the common foreign and security policy of the European Union lead to a Europbomb?' (1995): <http://www10.antenna.nl/wise/index.html?http://www10.antenna.nl/wise/beyondbomb/>.
6. All quotes from Nick Assinder, 'Blair and Chirac's explosive chemistry', BBC NEWS: <http://news.bbc.co.uk/1/hi/uk_politics/3818551.stm>. In particular Chirac had a chummy relationship with Chancellor Schröder; his relations with Schröder's successor Angela Merkel are somewhat cooler.
7. See Philip Zelikow and Condoleezza Rice, *Germany Unified and Europe Transformed: A Study in Statecraft* (Cambridge, MA: Harvard University Press, 1995).

8. See Margaret Thatcher, *The Downing Street Years* (London: HarperCollins, 1993); also James I. Walsh, *European Monetary Integration & Domestic Politics: Britain, France, and Italy* (Boulder, CO: Lynne Riener, 2000).
9. See Micah L. Sifry and Christopher Cerf (eds), *The Iraq War Reader: History, Documents, Opinions* (New York: Simon & Schuster, 2003).
10. See the highly critical book by Brendan Simms, *Unfinest Hour: Britain and the Destruction of Bosnia* (London: Allen Lane, 2001). See also James Gow, *Triumph of the Lack of Will: International Diplomacy and the Yugoslav War* (London: Hurst, 1997).
11. John O'Sullivan, 'The great game in Europe: How the U.S. can play', *National Review* (24 February 2003): <http://www.findarticles.com/p/articles/mi_m1282/is_3_55/ai_97347245>.
12. See for example Pierre Martin and Mark R. Brawley (eds), *Alliance Politics, Kosovo, and NATO's War: Allied Force or Forced Allies?* (New York: Palgrave, 2001); Anne-Marie Paquez, *La politique de la France au Kosovo: était-elle 'gaulliste'?* (Genève: Euryopa, 2003); Andrew J. Bacevich and Eliot A. Cohen (eds), *War Over Kosovo: Policy and Strategy in a Global Age* (New York: Columbia University Press, 2001).
13. For a good overview, see Anne Deighton, 'The European security and defence policy', *Journal of Common Market Studies*, 40, 4 (2002), 719–41.
14. See Heinz Gärtner and Ian M. Cuthbertson (eds), *European Security and Transatlantic Relations After 9/11* (Basingstoke: Palgrave, 2005).
15. See for example David Cole, 'Are we safer?', review article of Daniel Benjamin and Steven Simon, *The Next Attack: The Failure of the War on Terror and a Strategy for Getting it Right* (New York: Times Books, 2006), in *New York Review of Books*, 9 March 2006, pp. 15–18; James Risen, *State of War: The Secret History of the CIA and the Bush Administration* (New York: Free Press, 2005); Richard A. Clarke, *Against all Enemies: Inside America's War on Terror* (New York: Free Press, 2004).
16. See for example Phillip Gordon and Jeremy Shapiro, *Allies at War: America, Europe and the Crisis of Iraq* (New York: McGraw-Hill, 2004); William Shawcross, *Allies: The US, Britain, Europe and the War in Iraq* (London: Atlantic, 2003).
17. See the literature in note 15.
18. See Glen Frankel and Rajiv Chandrasekaran, '45 minutes: Behind the Blair claim', Washington Post, 29 February 2004, p. A16: <http://www.washingtonpost.com/ac2/wp-dyn/A15697-2004Feb28?language=printer>.
19. See President George W. Bush, 'Address to a joint session of Congress and the American people', 20 September 2001: <http://www.whitehouse.gov/news/releases/2001/09/20010920-8.html>.
20. See Klaus Larres, 'Mutual incomprehension: US-German value gaps beyond Iraq', *The Washington Quarterly*, 26, 2 (Spring 2003): <http://www.twq.com/03spring/index.cfm?id=40>.
21. See BBC News World Edition, 'Outrage at "old Europe" remarks', 23 January 2003: <http://news.bbc.co.uk/2/hi/europe/2687403.stm>.

22. For an excellent overview, see 'The United Nations and the Iraq War', in Wikipedia: The Free Encyclopedia: <http://en.wikipedia.org/wiki/The_UN_Security_Council_and_the_Iraq_war>.
23. See Klaus Larres, 'The Bush administration and Europe', in Iwan W. Morgan and Philip J. Davies (eds), *Right on? Political Change and Continuity in George W. Bush's America* (Washington, DC: Brookings Institution Press, 2006). For two somewhat optimistic books about Europe's long-term potential, see T.R. Reid, *The United States of Europe: The New Superpower and the End of American Supremacy* (New York: Penguin, 2004), pp. 75–91, Jeremy Rifkin, *The European Dream: How Europe's Vision of the Future is Quietly Eclipsing the American Dream* (New York: Penguin, 2004).
24. In fact, Britain, France and Israel had agreed on the cover plan that Israel would attack Egypt and then Britain and France would get involved and send their troops in to separate the two combatants and secure the Suez canal base in the process.
25. See Jonathan Pearson, *Sir Anthony Eden and the Suez Crisis: Reluctant Gamble* (Basingstoke: Palgrave, 2003); Diane B. Kunz, *The Economic Diplomacy of the Suez Crisis* (Chapel Hill: University of North Carolina Press, 1991); James M. Boughton, *Northwest of Suez: The 1956 Crisis and the IMF* (Washington, DC: IMF, 2000); Cole C. Kingseed, *Eisenhower and the Suez Crisis of 1956* (Baton Rouge: Louisiana State University Press, 1995); Keith Kyle, *Suez* (London: Weidenfeld and Nicolson, 1992). See also Peter G. Boyle, 'The Hungarian Revolution and the Suez Crisis', *History*, 90/300 (2005), pp. 556 ff.
26. For accounts of the thinking of Tony Blair with regard to the 'war on terror' and Iraq, see Anthony Seldon, *Blair* (London: Free Press, 2004); John Kampfner, *Blair's Wars* (London: Free Press, 2003); Philip Stevens, *Tony Blair: The Price of Leadership* (London: Politico, 2004).
27. For the transcript, see BBC News, 'PM on Iraq War judgement', 4 March 2006: <http://news.bbc.co.uk/1/hi/uk_politics/4773874.stm>.
28. See Bob Woodward, *Bush at War* (New York: Simon & Schuster, 2002).
29. See Helen Drake (ed.), *French Relations with the European Union* (London: Routledge, 2004); Steven P. Kramer, *Does France Still Count? The French Role in the New Europe* (Westport, CO: Praeger, 1994).
30. See Peter Galbraith, 'The Mess' [review article of L. Paul Bremmer, *My Year in Iraq: The Struggle to Build a Future of Hope* (New York: Simon & Schuster, 2006) and George Packer, *The Assassin's Gate: America in Iraq* (New York: Farrar, Strauss & Giroux, 2006)], in *New York Review of Books*, 9 March 2006, pp. 27–30.
31. Charles Grant, 'Stumbling towards unity', *Global Agenda Magazine*, 2004: <http://www.globalagendamagazine.com/2004/charlesgrant.asp>.
32. See the articles in Ester Brimmer (ed.), *The EU's Search for a Strategic Role: ESDP and its Implications for Transatlantic Relations* (Washington, DC: Center for Transatlantic Relations, 2002); Anne Deighton, 'The European security and defence policy', *Journal of Common Market Studies*, 40, 4 (2002), 719–41; also Lisa Watanabe, 'The ESDP: Between estrangement

and a new partnership in transatlantic security relations', *Journal of Contemporary European Studies*, 13, 1 (2005), 5–20.

33. For an excellent article on these issues, see Jolyon Howorth, 'France, Britain and the Euro-Atlantic crisis', *Survival*, 45, 4 (Winter 2003–04), 173–92; see also by the same author, 'Britain, France and the European defence initiative', *Survival*, 42, 2 (Summer 2000), pp. 33 ff.
34. See Klaus Larres, 'Leadership and America. Time for a threesome', *The World Today*, 60, 4 (2004), 7–9.
35. See Grant, 'Stumbling towards unity', *Global Agenda Magazine*, 2004: <http://www.globalagendamagazine.com/2004/charlesgrant.asp>.
36. *Ibid.*
37. See 'Britain backs role for EU "big three"', *Financial Times*, 15 January 2004: <http://www.vote-2004.com/mediacentre/display.asp?IDNO=1474>.
38. See Peter Schwartz, 'Berlin summit: Blair, Schröder, Chirac press for accelerated reforms', World Socialist Website, 21 February 2004: <http://www.wsws.org/articles/2004/feb2004/summ-f21.shtml>; 'Odd Man Out', Eurosoc, 19 February 2004: <http://www.eursoc.com/news/fullstory.php/aid/313/Odd_Man_Out.html>.
39. See Thomas S. Mowle, *Allies at Odds? The United States and the European Union* (New York: Palgrave, 2004).
40. See Peter Ludlow, 'Brussels breakdown: The failure to agree an EU constitution had many culprits', *Prospect Magazine* 95 (February, 2004): <http://www.prospect-magazine.co.uk/printarticle.php?id=5834&category=132&issue=0&author=&AuthKey=e55835c4c93997f2e00e0b739e70a477>. For an overview of the drafting and ratification of the European constitution, see 'European policy: Constitution', *The ALG European Service*: <http://www.alg-europe.gov.uk/webroot/Policy/constitution.htm>.
41. Quoted in 'Chirac tells Bush to keep his nose out', *Daily Telegraph Online*, 29 June 2004: <http://www.telegraph.co.uk/news/main.jhtml?xml=/news/2004/06/29/weu29.xml>.
42. See note 40 above.
43. See Paul Reynolds, 'Diplomatic warfare breaks out in NATO', BBC News, 30 April 2003: <http://news.bbc.co.uk/1/hi/world/europe/2989023.stm>.
44. See for example James K. Withers, 'British bulldog or Bush's poodle? Anglo-American relations and the Iraq War', *Parameters: US Army War College Quarterly* (Winter, 2003): <http://www.findarticles.com/p/articles/mi_m0IBR/is_4_33/ai_111852938>.

Index